Child Abuse and Human Rights

CHILD ABUSE AND HUMAN RIGHTS

(In 2 Volumes)

Child and Human Rights

(Volume-2)

Editor

Jyotsna Tiwari

ISHA BOOKS

DELHI-110 033

Child Abuse and Human Rights

Rs. 1600 (Set)
Rs. 800 (each volume)

ISBN: 81-8205-071-5 (Set)
ISBN: 81-8205-073-1 (Vol. 2)

Published in 2004 in India by
Isha Books, D-43, Prithviraj Road,
Adarsh Nagar, Delhi-110 033

Laser Typesetting at : Shree Vaishnavi Creations, Delhi
Printed at : Chawla Offset Press, Delhi

Contents

Preface

Human rights are the basic and absolute rights that every person has because he or she is a human being. They recognize the vulnerability of the human being in civil, political, economic, social and cultural processes and provide protection. All human rights apply to all boys and girls. While societies may vary in their ideas on childhood and child development, one thing that all can agree on is the importance of the well-being of children.

However, over the past few years, the stories of child abuse has grabbed the attention of the international community, provoking worldwide discussion of this issue. Child labour remains a major cause of child exploitation and abuse in the world, depriving millions of children worldwide of adequate education and good health. Many of these children are victims of the worst forms of child labour, which include slavery, bonded labour, drug trafficking, commercial sexual exploitation, domestic labour, armed conflict and all other physically and morally hazardous types of work.

Today, it is well recognized everywhere that children need special care and protection for healthy development because of their special needs and vulnerability. Numerous international organizations, governments in both developing and industrialized countries, and advocacy groups are creating and implementing strategies and initiatives to address the issues of child rights violations. Special instruments have been drawn up to safeguard and enforce child rights. The recognized standard is the UN Convention on the Rights of the Child (CRC), which was drawn up in 1989 and has been ratified by almost all countries in the world. The Convention gives guiding principles to protect child rights.

The present book is intended to make people aware of the importance of protecting human rights of children. It will be highly informative to teachers and researchers in sociology and child development studies, social welfare agencies, policy makers and other administrative bodies concerned with child development.

Editor

1

Introduction

Human rights are the basic and absolute rights that every person has because he or she is a human being. They recognize the vulnerability of the human being in civil, political, economic, social and cultural processes and provide protection.

Every human being has these rights although the extent to which they can be enforced in practice varies from country to country. Having rights comes with having duties and responsibilities. In preserving the freedom, rights and justice for all, everyone has a responsibility to abide by the law and everyone has duties in the community. In exercising freedoms and rights, everyone must also respect the rights and freedoms of others.

At the international level most of these basic human rights have been described in the United Nations (UN) Universal Declaration of Human Rights (1948)1. Some of the basic human rights include:

— the right to equal treatment and non-discrimination
— the right to nationality
— the right to own property
— the right to education
— the right to work and to just and favourable conditions of work
— the right to freedom from slavery and forced labour
— the right to equal access to public service in the country
— the right to freedom of movement
— the right to freedom of thought, opinion and expression
— the right to freedom of association.

The fundamental human rights are often described in each country's Constitution which guarantees the fundamental rights of its citizens, regardless of their sex, race, ethnicity, class or caste, religion, or other statuses. National legal rights are those rights which are defined by national laws in each country, usually consisting of constitutional rights, and specific rights laid down in national legislation such as the Penal Code, the Labour Code and the Civil Code and rules such as government regulations.

While there is considerable variation in national legislation between countries, most constitutions worldwide state that everyone is equal before the law, and that each person is entitled to equal protection under the law without any discrimination. If a person's legal right is violated, the person is entitled to seek justice and to a just and fair judicial process.

In 1998, ILO member States adopted the Declaration on Fundamental Principles and Rights at Work which sets out the core labour principles that are fundamental to the rights of human beings at work, irrespective of the level of development of countries. The core labour principles endorsed by the international community cover four main areas:

— the elimination of all forms of forced and compulsory labour

— the abolition of child labour

— the elimination of discrimination in respect of employment and occupation

— freedom of association and the recognition of the right to collective bargaining.

CHILD RIGHTS

All human rights apply to all boys and girls. While societies may vary in their ideas on childhood and child development, one thing that all can agree on is the importance of the well-being of children. It is well recognized everywhere that children need special care and protection for healthy development because of their special needs and vulnerability. Special instruments have been drawn up to safeguard and enforce child rights. The recognized standard is the UN Convention on the Rights of the Child (CRC), which was drawn up in 1989 and has been ratified by almost all countries in the world. It covers all persons under 18 years of age.

The Rights of the Child as defined by the CRC Convention include four core principles as follows:

— *Equality:* Like adults, children can be subject to discrimination which has a negative impact on a child's opportunities and conditions in life. Therefore, all children are entitled to equal rights and governments have an obligation to uphold these. For example:

  — right to birth registration

  — right to a name and nationality

  — right to protection from all forms of abuse, neglect, discrimination and exploitation.

— *Rights to survival and healthy development:* Every child has a right to develop to his or her fullest potential, and is entitled to:

  — right to basic needs, including food, shelter and access to healthcare

  — right to free primary education

  — right to childhood - to rest and play and to have friends

  — right to protection from economic exploitation or any work that interferes with education or that is hazardous and harmful to health, physical, mental, and social development

  — right to special assistance for children with special needs. For example: child refugees, displaced children, child victims of abuse and disabled children.

— *Participation*: All girls and boys, according their age and maturity, have the right to participate in making decisions that affect them. Boys and girls should be encouraged to take part in decision making at home, in school and in their own community. Key participation rights are:

— right to express views and opinions

— right to receive and give information in an accessible and understandable form

— right to be an active member of community - to enjoy own culture, to practice own religion and to use own language

— right to be a member of a group.

— *Best interest of the child:* The two notions of children as competent human beings on the one hand, and as children who are vulnerable and need protection on the other hand, may conflict when deciding what is best for the child. This principle provides the solution to this problem: all decisions that affect boys and girls must give primary consideration to them. In determining what is 'best' for them, it is important to seek the views of the affected girls and boys.

VIOLATIONS OF CHILD RIGHTS

CHILD LABOUR

Work is not always bad for children and can be healthy but it can also seriously hamper children's development. In order to decide whether children's economic activities are healthy or harmful, the international community has set the following yardsticks:

— *Child work*

  - light work (less than 14 hours/week) for 12-17 year olds
  - not harmful to a child's health and development
  - not obstructing schooling or vocational training
  - not hazardous in nature

- *Child labour*
  - regular work (14-43 hours/week)
  - causes physical or psychological damage
  - hinders education and mental and/or physical development
  - child under minimum age set by ILO Convention No.138
  - hazardous work as defined by provisions of ILO Convention No.182

- *The worst forms of child labour:*
  - all forms of slavery or practices similar to slavery, such as the sale and trafficking of children, debt bondage and serfdom and forced or compulsory labour, including forced or compulsory recruitment of children for use in armed conflict
  - the use, procuring or offering of a child for prostitution, for the production of pornography or for pornographic performances
  - the use, procuring or offering of a child for illicit activities, in particular for the production and trafficking of drugs

— work which, by its nature or the circumstances in which it is carried out, is likely to harm the health, safety or morals of children.

Table 1. Child Labour Statistics (number in 000,000s)

Age group & Sex	*Economically active children*	*Child Labour*	*Children in Hazardous Work*	*Definition of child labour based on ILO Conventions Nos. 138 & 182*
5-11	109.7	109.7	60.5	
boys	56.3	56.3	30.7	In ages 5-11 = all children in economically active activities
girls	53.4	53.4	29.8	
12-14	101.1	76.6	50.8	In ages 12-14 = all children in economically active activities except those in light work
boys	52.7	41.5	30.6	
girls	48.4	35.1	20.2	
15-17	140.9	59.2	59.2	In ages 15-17 = all children in hazardous work and other worst forms of child labour
boys	75.1	34.4	34.4	
girls	65.8	24.8	24.8	
Total (5-17)	351.7	245.5	170.5	Statistics does not include chi ldren engaged in work that is not considered"economic acti vities" such as domestic work, where girls are often found.
boys	184.1	132.2	95.7	
girls	167.6	113.3	74.8	

Source: ILO, Every Child Counts: New Global Estimates on Child Labour, ILO: Geneva (2002)

Table 2. Children in the worst forms of child labour

Worst form of child labour	*Global estimates*	*Estimates in Asia-Pacific*
Forced & bonded labour	5.7	5.5
Forced recruitment into armed conflict	0.3	0.12
Prostitution & pornography	1.8	0.59
Illicit activities	0.6	0.22
Trafficked children*	[1.2]	[0.25]
Subtotal	8.4	6.43
Children in hazardous work	170.5	104.
Total	178.9	110.5

What child workers do ?

According to ILO report *Every Child Counts: New Global Estimates on Child Labour,*

— 70% of child workers are in agriculture, fishing, hunting and forestry

— 9% child workers are in manufacturing

— 9% child workers are in wholesale, retail trade, restaurants and hotels

— 6% child workers are in community, social and personal service

— 4% child workers are in transport, storage and communication

— 4% child workers are in construction, mining and quarrying.

At the start of the new millenium, about 18 per cent of boys and girls up to the age of 14 were 'economically active,' in other words, were working for money or other compensation. In 2000, 211 million children aged 5-14 years were economically active. Sixty per cent (127 million) were found in Asia and the Pacific: one of every five children in this age group was working in this region.

In Sub-Saharan Africa, there were 48 million children working: one of every three children in this age group was working in this region. Just over 6 per cent (13.4 million) were found in North Africa and the Middle East, and 8 per cent (17.4 million) in Latin America and the Caribbean.

Following the ILO definitions of child labour, as many as 246 million children aged from 5 to 17 are in child labour. Of this group, 110 million are younger than 12. Of all child labour, as many as 170.5 million are found in hazardous work, and 60.5 million in this category are younger than 12.

Statistics should be considered critically because by nature child labour exploitation is hidden and getting accurate information is difficult. The number of working girls is often underestimated by statistical surveys, which do not generally account for unpaid economic activities such as domestic work or hidden activities such as prostitution – the type of work in which more girls are involved.

One of the most widespread forms of labour exploitation of children is domestic work. Traditionally, domestic work is seen as an easy and safe work for children, especially for girls. However, it has been proven recently that domestic work can be among the most dangerous work for children and has been recognized as a worst form of child labour. While domestic work with good employers can offer children in poverty a chance to develop, get education and earn a living, domestic work in most countries has a very low status and is among the lowest paid and many CDWs end up being exploited. Because most CDWs live in and have little freedom, their life and safety often depends on the mercy of the employers. An overwhelming majority of CDWs are girls, and many face physical, emotional or sexual abuses.

There are an estimated 1.2 million children being trafficking for labour and sexual exploitation worldwide, about 250,000 in Asia and Pacific. However, estimates of the number of children being trafficked often vary widely, depending on the source. For example, numbers of children trafficked for prostitution in India range between 25,000 and 500,000 respectively. Therefore, estimates should be considered with caution. Despite difficulties in determining the exact number of trafficked children, there is a clear trend that it is rising worldwide, particularly for sexual exploitation. In South and Southeast Asia, the overwhelming number of child victims of trafficking are girls with the exception of Sri Lanka and to a lesser extent Pakistan, where boys are also found to be trafficked for commercial sexual exploitation.

TRAFFICKING

Lack of economic opportunities at home, armed conflicts or natural disasters can encourage people to leave home – often from the rural to urban areas and sometimes across borders. While migration can be a positive experience, providing better opportunities for many, it can lead to serious violations of their human and labour rights.

There is increasing pressure on women to financially support their families and changing traditional roles have resulted in more women leaving their traditional place at home for work somewhere else – a process referred to as the feminization of migration. Often not aware of dangers, many who aspire for better opportunities elsewhere end up being trafficked for labour and sexual exploitation. Rights violations can occur from the recruitment stage to transit, and while living and working in the destination. At any of these stages, women and children can find themselves being exploited, abused, or trafficked.

Trafficking in persons is a particularly abusive form of migration. It is defined by the coercive, nonconsensual and exploitative or servile nature of the purpose of movement, and involves a number of serious human rights violations, including forced labour, sexual and labour exploitation, violence and abuse of the victims.

MIGRATION, TRAFFICKING AND LABOUR EXPLOITATION

Children most vulnerable to severe labour exploitation often come from disadvantaged, marginalized and socially excluded groups. They include orphans, children of single-parent or child-headed families, children of tribal or ethnic minorities, street children, migrant children, and refugees.

Younger children often migrate along with their parents, while adolescents may choose to take their own path. Although there is no clear linkage between migration and child labour, some studies suggest that foreign-born children are found in more exploitative and dangerous work than native children of similar economic status due to lack of legal status in the host country and discrimination of the local population against foreigners.

Children who migrate or are trafficked alone are separated from their familiar support networks which puts them in a new, often hostile, environment where they find themselves not able to speak the language, being excluded from the mainstream society, and not being able to attend school or have access to medical care because they do not have the necessary documents.

Many children born of migrant parents in a new city or country are not registered and do not have a birth certificate. This results in their being stateless and deprives them of social and economic opportunities and exposes them to many forms of discrimination.

In these conditions, often the only available options left to migrant and trafficked workers are to work in "3D" jobs – difficult, dirty and dangerous. Their jobs are often undocumented, unprotected, or illegal. Many lack immigration status, making them prime targets for police crackdowns, detentions and deportation. It is not uncommon for migrants to be asked by authorities to pay bribes and for women sex workers to be asked to provide free sex, to avoid penalties.

There are clear age and gender dimensions in trafficking of children into forced labour. That is, the younger the child, the less likely he or she is able to escape the forced labour situation. In addition, boys and girls tend to be involved in different activities, although there is considerable overlap.

Girls predominate in commercial sexual exploitation and domestic work, and boys in forced recruitment for armed conflict and for camel jockeying in the Middle East.

Gender is a determining factor in trafficking on both the supply and demand sides. In some areas the largest numbers of victims of trafficking are men, for example more than 80 per cent of migrants trafficked into Ukraine and Poland are men.

Generally, however, women and girls are more likely than men and boys to be the victims of trafficking. Women and girls are often trafficked into prostitution and sexual exploitation. However, trafficking should not be equated with prostitution and sexual exploitation because many other forms of labour exploitation also occur.

APPLICATION OF THE LAW

It is commonly accepted that basic human rights described in international declarations and conventions cannot be denied to any human being and governments cannot deny these rights to their citizens without justification. For example, everybody has the right to life. In case of war, soldiers from the enemy can be denied this right but not civilians. At the international level it has been agreed that no country can exclusively rely on the sovereignty principle to infringe on the basic human rights of its citizens.

This is still a politically sensitive issue but consensus on this agreement is growing worldwide, in an increasing number of countries, irrespective of their level of development. However application of basic human rights, laid down at the international level and in national laws and rules is often problematic as rights can only be enforced when there is a remedy i.e. a law, legal rule or procedure and a working judicial system (courts and application machinery). This is a problem in many countries. One of the more recent new mechanisms to provide vulnerable groups with a means to protect their basic human rights is the set up of National Human Rights Commissions in many countries.

Sometimes there is a conflict of interest in respecting rights. For example, the 'right to development' and 'absence from poverty' for all citizens cannot be met by many governments due to the different political stake holders within that government and lack of awareness and skills among the population and marginalized groups to express their rights.

Cultural norms and values also underlay the hierarchy of rights and often determine whether the rule of law is followed. Women's and children's human rights, laid down in international human rights instruments and national laws are often violated because cultural and social norms grant a lower status to them than men.

Protection of the rights of migrants and trafficked persons is difficult. For example, in the case of trafficking of young persons for labour exploitation rights protection usually involve trafficking laws, prostitution laws and child labour laws. However, these laws do not exist in some countries, and when they exist, weak enforcement, corruption, contradiction in the laws, and traditional biases against women and girls undercut the effectiveness of these laws. Moreover, the laws, in particular prostitution and trafficking or migrant labour laws tend to be more punitive rather than protective towards the victims.

Migrant workers and trafficked victims often end up being penalized and deported for illegal entry, while employers and traffickers rarely face punishment. In the case of trafficking for child prostitution, punishment for clients is rarely mentioned.

2

Child Labour

Child labour remains a major cause of child exploitation and abuse in the world, depriving millions of children worldwide of adequate education and good health. Many of these children are victims of the "worst forms" of child labour, which include slavery, bonded labour, drug trafficking, commercial sexual exploitation, domestic labour, armed conflict and all other physically and morally hazardous types of work.

The link between poverty and child labour is well established; thus, it is not surprising that children caught in the worst forms of child labour are commonly from the most vulnerable socio-economic groups. Children living in extreme poverty often work instead of attending school, sometimes because of social stigma, but more frequently because schools are either not available or their families cannot survive without the added income their children provide.

It is now widely known that a vicious circle is in operation: child labour hinders economic development and perpetuates poverty by keeping the children of the poor out of school and limiting their prospects for upward social mobility. This underlies the growing international recognition that targeting the worst forms of child labour and investing in the prevention of child labour is more than an issue of safeguarding children's rights; it is indeed an important strategy towards poverty alleviation.

INTERNATIONAL CHILD LABOUR

The dichotomy that exists between industrialized countries and developing countries is especially apparent when one looks at child labor. Child labour in industrialized countries almost exclusively means adolescents who are full-time students with part-time jobs. But child labour often wears a much different face in developing countries.

The International Labour Organization (ILO) estimates that more than 250 million children are working around the world, often in occupations that are "detrimental to their physical, mental and emotional well-being." An estimated 120 million children work full time, with no opportunities for education and the accompanying promise of a better future. These youths have been found working as miners; as laborers in rug, textile, glass, and brick manufacturing establishments; as domestic servants; and as prostitutes. But there is cause for hope.

Over the past few years, child labour has grabbed the attention of the international community, provoking worldwide discussion of this issue. Numerous international organizations, governments in both developing and industrialized countries, and advocacy groups are creating and implementing strategies and initiatives to address child labor.

CHILD LABOUR IN USA

Children have worked in America, contributing to the well-being of the family unit, since the arrival of the first colonists. European settlers, bringing social values with them that equated idleness with pauperism, were quick to pass laws that actually required children to work. Adopting "poor laws" similar to the English laws, the colonies required the apprenticeship of poor children—some at ages as young as 3 years. Children worked on family farms and in family cottage industries. The institution of slavery also encompassed the labour of children born or sold into servitude.

The industrial revolution ushered in the modern factory system and changed a predominately rural populace into an urban one. Factory towns grew up dependent on a labour supply of women and children, the children working not necessarily as apprentices but as factory labor. Children were seen as a cheap and manageable source of labor.

Child labour in USA was so widespread, and so much a part of economic reality in the early part of the 19th century, that no one looked toward or expected its abolition. But as the number of factories multiplied and the child workforce grew, the social conscience began to stir—not against child labour itself, but against some features of the factory system as they affected the children.

The earliest concerns were that factory children were growing up without receiving even a modest education. Long workdays and workweeks left little time for study. In 1813, Connecticut enacted a law encouraging manufacturers to provide young employees with lessons in reading, writing, and arithmetic, but the law was ineffective.

It was not until 1836 that Massachusetts passed US's first child labour law—legislation that required children under the age of 15 employed in manufacturing to spend at least 3 months each year in school. A few States soon adopted similar laws. After the Civil War, industry expanded and became increasingly mechanized. The textile industry flourished in the South and with it, oppressive child labor. Children as young as 6 or 7 years were recruited to work 13-hour days, for miniscule wages, in hot and dusty factories. Proposals to change these conditions met with stiff opposition. By the turn of the century, only a few southern States had passed laws limiting the number of hours that children could work.

The early 1900s saw a growing acceptance of the concept that States should provide for the general protection of children. In 1909, the Bureau of Labour Statistics issued a landmark report on working women and children. By 1913, all but nine States had fixed 14 years as the minimum age for factory work, and a majority of the States had extended this minimum to stores and other specified places of employment. Although Congress had made several attempts to restrict oppressive child labor, the attempts had failed, usually on constitutional grounds. It was not until 1938, with the passage of the Fair Labour Standards Act (upheld by the Supreme Court in 1941) that meaningful Federal child labour legislation was enacted.

The Fair Labour Standards Act (FLSA) remains the Federal law governing minimum wages, overtime, child labor, and recordkeeping. The child labour provisions of the FLSA establish a minimum age of 16 years for covered nonagricultural employment. However, they allow 14- and 15-yearolds to be employed in occupations other than in mining and manufacturing if the Secretary of Labour determines that the employment is confined to periods that will not interfere with their schooling and to conditions that will not interfere with their health and wellbeing.

The FLSA also prohibits minors under age 18 from working in occupations that the Secretary of Labour declares to be particularly hazardous for such youths or detrimental to their health or well-being.

The nature of child labour in the United States has changed over the last 50 years. Child labour now means, almost exclusively, teenagers—teenagers who are generally full-time students and part-time employees. But even with the increased emphasis on education and the improved economic conditions that this century has brought, the Nation's young people are still working today, and in large numbers.

The unique history of the United States, which both fostered and overcame some of the most oppressive types of child labor, still helps to create an environment conducive to youth employment that differs considerably from that of other industrialized nations. The most often cited difference is that the proportion of teens who work is relatively high in the United States compared with other developed countries.

Americans have always tenaciously believed in the value of work, for themselves and for their children.

They believe that positive work experiences during the teenage years can benefit a person's development, maturity, and sense of responsibility. Conversely, idleness is associated with delinquency.

Another difference lies in the reasons why teenagers, who have not yet completed their formal educations, seek employment. For the most part, the jobs held by U.S. teens are not conceived as stepping-stones on a life career path. Other developed countries, such as Germany, Denmark, and Switzerland, have long included adolescent employment as part of formal apprenticeship, School-to-Work, and Work Experience and Career Exploration Programs that are closely linked to the educational process and lead to specific adult jobs. Only in the last two decades has there been a concerted effort in the United States to link adolescent work experiences with school curricula to facilitate the transition from student to worker. The little research that has been done on why U.S. teens seek paying jobs suggests that the primary reason is money, not the value of the work experience.

E. Greenberger and G. Steinberg reported in 1986 that 74 percent of employed high school students in their sample said money was the primary reason for having a job. Most working teens spend their earnings as discretionary income, rather than helping to meet family expenses. And the size and impact of that discretionary income is enormous.

The United States began as a nation of farmers, and agriculture continues to enjoy a special place in the perceptions of its citizens. Growing up on the family farm, learning the value of hard work in the fresh air, is still viewed by many as the perfect childhood. Federal and State child labour laws governing agricultural employment reflect this belief—they are much less restrictive than those applied to other industries. Children working on farms owned or operated by a parent are completely exempt from Federal agricultural child labour provisions, and other teenage farmworkers are permitted to perform hazardous jobs at younger ages than are their counterparts who work in other industries.

Federal Child Labour Laws

The Fair Labour Standards Act of 1938 (FLSA) is the framework for Federal child labour provisions. The Wage and Hour Division of the U.S. Department of Labor's Employment Standards Administration is charged with the enforcement of the FLSA. To be subject to the provisions of the FLSA, an employee must be employed by a covered enterprise or individually engaged in interstate commerce or in the production of goods for interstate commerce, or in any closely related process or occupation directly essential to such production. Not all employment of young workers is covered under the FLSA. In addition, some jobs held by youths, such as delivering newspapers and performing in motion pictures and theatrical, radio, and television productions, are specifically exempted from the child labour provisions of the FLSA.

Nonagricultural employment. Under the FLSA, 16 is the minimum age for nonagricultural employment, but 14- and 15-year-olds may be employed for certain periods—which do not interfere with their schooling—in jobs that the Secretary of Labour has determined will not interfere with their health and well-being. Children under 14 years of age are generally too young for formal employment unless they meet a specific exemption. However, these youths may perform tasks where no covered employment relationship arises—such as babysitting on a parttime, irregular basis or performing minor chores around private homes.

The FLSA prohibits workers under 18 years of age from performing those nonagricultural occupations that the Secretary of Labour declares to be particularly hazardous for the employment of children under 18 years of age or detrimental to their health or well-being. There are currently 17 Hazardous Occupations Orders (HOs), which are contained in Subpart E of Regulations, 29 CFR Part 570 (Occupations Particularly Hazardous for the Employment of Minors Between 16 and 18 Years of Age or Detrimental to Their Health or Well-Being).

Agricultural employment. Unlike the rules governing nonagricultural employment, most of the child labour provisions applicable to agricultural employment are statutory. Under Federal law:

— A child working in agriculture on a farm owned or operated by his or her parent is exempted from Federal agricultural child labour provi- sions.

— Young farmworkers who are not the children of the farmer employing them are subject to Federal child labour provisions that differ by age:

— Youths are no longer subject to the Federal agricultural child labour provisions when they reach 16 years of age.

— Children aged 14 or 15 may perform any nonhazardous farm job outside of school hours, and, with proper training and certification, they also may perform certain hazardous duties.

— Children aged 12 or 13 may be employed outside of school hours in nonhazardous jobs, but only on the farm on which their parent works or with the written consent of a parent.

— Children under 12 may be employed outside of school hours in nonhazardous jobs on farms not subject to the Fair Labour Standards Act (FLSA) minimum wage if their parent also is employed on that farm, or with parental consent.

— Children aged 10 or 11 may be employed to hand-harvest shortseason crops outside of school hours under special waivers granted by the U.S. Department of Labor.

As directed by the FLSA the Secretary of Labour has found and declared certain agricultural tasks to be particularly hazardous for employees below the age of 16. Farmworkers as young as 14 years of age may perform some tasks otherwise prohibited by the Agricultural Hazardous Occupations Orders after completing, and in some cases participating in, certain vocational training programs. The FLSA prohibits hired farmworkers under 16 years of age from working during school hours, but does not give the Secretary of Labour authority to prohibit their employment during other times of the day or limit the number of daily or weekly hours they may be employed.

There are other labour standards laws, both State and Federal, that regulate the hours of work, types of jobs, and working conditions of children and adolescents.

State child labour laws. The adoption of compulsory school attendance laws by the States has done much to curb oppressive child labour in America. Every State also has a child labour law, usually enforced by a State labour department, that strives to preserve the health, education, and well-being of young workers. These laws, which often share extensive overlap in coverage with the FLSA, vary in the level of protection afforded young workers for both agricultural and nonagricultural employment. Within any State law, there may be some provisions that are more or less restrictive than provisions of the Federal law. If both the State and Federal law apply to the same employment situation, the more stringent standard of the two must be obeyed. The level of enforcement of State laws also varies widely.

While the laws differ from State to State in the standards prescribed, in the range of occupations covered, and in the age brackets to which they apply, Federal law is generally more stringent than the State laws with respect to prohibiting work in occupations involving physical hazards and assessing penalties for violations. This is true for both agricultural and nonagricultural employment. Federal law also is the same or more restrictive with respect to the minimum age for general employment. On the other hand, many State laws mandate standards that are absent from Federal law, such as maximum hours and night work restrictions for 16- and 17-yearolds, prohibitions on employment in occupations or in places detrimental to morals (hotel and liquor service), and mandatory work permits or age certificates.

Unlike the FLSA, more than half of the States regulate the daily or weekly number of hours that 16- and 17-year-olds may be employed, or restrict the evening hours during which 16- and 17-year-olds may work, or both. State hours and time-of-work regulations on the whole, however, tend to be less restrictive for minors under the age of 16 than are the Federal regulations.

Many States do not further limit the number of hours that youths under 16 years of age can work during a school day or week while school is in session. Of those that do limit work during the school year, many permit longer hours of work than allowed by the FLSA. Still other States allow teenagers to work later in the evening than permitted by Federal rules. Seventeen States (primarily in the South) either exempt agricultural employment entirely or do not identify it as a covered industry under the State's child labour laws. Eight States place restrictions on agricultural employment similar to Federal standards. Eight States have restricted daily or weekly hours of work, or both, for minors under the age of 18 employed in agriculture. Twelve States impose a higher age standard than do the Federal provisions and prohibit 16- and 17-yearolds from working in certain hazardous occupations; some restrictions may apply to agriculture. In some cases, States have specifically adopted standards for agriculture that are more stringent than those of the Federal government.

The Occupational Safety and Health Act, enacted in 1970, requires that employers provide work and places of employment that comply with specific safety and health standards and that are free from other recognized hazards that may cause serious physical harm. Working children and adolescents are entitled to the same protections as adults but, in most cases, receive no additional protection.

The Occupational Safety and Health Act, administered by the Occupational Safety and Health Administration (OSHA), requires that State regulations be as protective as the Federal rules. Some States have adopted rules that are more protective than the Federal rules. Most Federal and State occupational safety and health rules do not apply to agricultural employment.

State workers' compensation programs also affect the health and safety of working youths. Many programs provide, or have the potential to provide, incentives for employers to improve working conditions for all employees. State workers' compensation agencies also provide a range of services to help employers identify and correct real or potential workplace hazards.

Ensuring Compliance

Protecting the health and safety of young workers, while helping them enjoy positive work experiences, remains a high priority of the U.S. Department of Labor. Consistent with her goal of assuring every U.S. worker and especially young workers—a safe, healthful, and fair workplace, Secretary of Labour Alexis Herman launched the Department's Safe Work/ Safe Kids initiative.

Safe Work/Safe Kids is designed to focus public attention on the issues of child labour and both educate and mobilize all those who can positively affect youth employment. In order to help teens have safe and constructive early work experiences, Safe Work/Safe Kids employs a comprehensive strategy of enhanced, targeted enforcement; increased compliance education and outreach; construction of strong partnerships; and creation of heightened public awareness. These four components, employed simultaneously, greatly magnify the positive compliance effects that would be obtained if any were employed independent of the others.

Effective, credible, and targeted enforcement, which serves to detect, remedy, penalize, and deter violations, is a key component of the compliance strategy. Industries targeted for enforcement initiatives in 1999 included agriculture, through the "Salad Bowl" initiative; retail trade, especially restaurants; garment manufacturing; and health care. The use of the "hot goods" provisions of the FLSA,20 injunctions, and consent judgements are being emphasized for cases in which child labour violations are found. Civil money penalties—"fines" computed in proportion to the severity of the violations are assessed to affect the future compliance behavior of employers.

The child-labour civil money penalty system now provides for a fine of $10,000 for each violation contributing to the death or serious injury of a minor. The FLSA also contains criminal sanctions of up to 6 months imprisonment after a second conviction for violations of child labour regulations.

The second component of the compliance strategy is to educate all those who affect teen employment—employers, parents, teachers, other government agencies, and the working teens themselves—about the child labour provisions and the importance of compliance.

CHILD LABOUR IN INDIA

The 1981 Census of India divided child labour into nine industrial divisions:

— Cultivation,

— Agricultural Labour,

— Livestock, Forestry, Fishing, Plantation,

— Mining and Quarrying,

— Manufacturing, Processing, Servicing and Repairs,

— Construction,

— Trade and Commerce,

— Transport, Storage and Communication, and

— Other Services

A study conducted by the ILO Bureau of Statistics found that "Children's work was considered essential to maintaining the economic level of households, either in the form of work for wages, of help in household enterprises or of household chores in order to free adult household members for economic activity elsewhere".

Poverty has an obvious relationship with child labour, and studies have "revealed a positive correlation—in some instances a strong one - between child labour and such factors as poverty". Families need money to survive, and children are a source of additional income. Poverty itself has underlying determinants, one such determinant being caste.

The combination of poverty and the lack of a social security network form the basis of the even harsher type of child labour—bonded child labour. For the poor, there are few sources of bank loans, governmental loans or other credit sources, and even if there are sources available, few Indians living in poverty qualify. Here enters the local moneylender; for an average of two thousand rupees, parents exchange their child's labour to local moneylenders.

Since the earnings of bonded child labourers are less than the interest on the loans, these bonded children are forced to work, while interest on their loans accumulates. A bonded child can only be released after his/her parents makes a lump sum payment, which is extremely difficult for the poor. Even if bonded child labourers are released, "the same conditions of poverty that caused the initial debt can cause people to slip back into bondage".

Even though poverty is cited as the major cause of child labour, it is not the only determinant. Inadequate schools, a lack of schools, or even the expense of schooling leaves some children with little else to do but work. The attitudes of parents also contribute to child labour; some parents feel that children should work in order to develop skills useful in the job market, instead of taking advantage of a formal education.

From the time of its independence, India has committed itself to be against child labour. Article 24 of the Indian constitution clearly states that "No child below the age of fourteen years shall be employed to work in any factory or mine or employed in any hazardous employment". Article 39 (e) directs State policy such "that the health and strength of workers . . . and the tender age of children are not abused and that citizens are not forced by economic necessity to enter avocations unsuited to their age or strength". These two articles show that India has always had the goal of taking care of its children and ensuring the safety of workers.

The Bonded Labour System Act of 1976 fulfills the Indian Constitution's directive of ending forced labour. The Act "frees all bonded laborers, cancels any outstanding debts against them, prohibits the creation of new bondage agreements, and orders the economic rehabilitation of freed bonded laborers by the state". In regard to child labour, the Indian government implemented the Child Labour Act in 1986. The purpose of this act is to "prohibit the employment of children who have not completed their 14th year in specified hazardous occupations and processes".

ILO convention No. 138 suggests that the minimum age for employment should not be less than fifteen years, and thus the Child Labour Act of 1986 does not meet this target. A recent advance in government policy occurred in August of 1994, when then- Prime Minister Narasimha Rao announced his proposal of an Elimination of Child Labour Programme. This program pledges to end child labour for two million children in hazardous industries as defined in the Child Labour Act of 1986, by the year 2000. The program revolves around an incentive for children to quit their work and enter non-formal schooling: a one hundred rupee payment as well as one meal a day for attending school.

The government needs eight and a half billion dollars for the program over five years, and yet "about 4 percent of the five-year estimated cost was allocated for child labour elimination programs in 1995-1996". All of the policies that the Indian government has in place are in accordance with the Constitution of India, and all support the eradication of Child Labour. The problem of child labour still remains even though all of these policies are existent. Enforcement is the key aspect that is lacking in the government's efforts.

Poverty and the inadequacy of the school system play significant roles in causing child labour, but also affect each other. Poverty forces high dropout rates, and thus no matter how good schools are, school survival rates and literacy rates will still remain low. The concept of compulsory education, where all school aged children are required to attend school, combats the force of poverty that pulls children out of school. Policies relating to compulsory education not only force children to attend school, but also contribute appropriate funds to the primary education system, instead of higher education.

The Indian state of Kerala distinguishes itself from the rest of India with its educational system. The government of Kerala allocates more funds to education than any other state, with a per capita expenditure of 11.5 rupees compared to the Indian average of 7.8 rupees. It is not only the expenditure of more funds, but where the funds are used that make the difference. Kerala spends more money on "mass education than colleges and universities". No correlation exists between expenditure on education and literacy when comparing different countries because some countries, such as India, spend more funds on higher education than primary education.

Article 45 of the Constitution of India states that "The State shall endeavour to provide within a period of ten years from the commencement of this Constitution for free and compulsory education for all children until they complete the age of fourteen years". It is obvious that "the State" has not achieved this goal, shown by the literacy, dropout, and child work participation rates discussed previously.

A National Policy on Education was adopted in 1986, and it addresses the need to "expand and improve basic education". Recently, the central government implemented The District Primary Education Program (DPEP), in an attempt to act on the recommendations of the National Policy on Education. The program involves the subsidizing of approved investments, by the Government of India. The central government will provide a grant of 85% on expenditures by the states. Since these measures have been implemented very recently, results cannot be obtained and the effectiveness of the DPEP cannot be commented on at this time.

Child labour is a significant problem in India. The prevalence of it is shown by the child work participation rates which are higher in Indian than in other developing countries. The major determinant of child labour is poverty. Even though children are paid less than adults, whatever income they earn is of benefit to poor families. In addition to poverty, the lack of adequate and accessible souces of credit forces poor parents to engage their children in the harsher form of child labour—bonded child labour. Some parents also feel that a formal education is not beneficial, and that children learn work skills through labour at a young age.

These views are narrow and do not take the long term developmental benefits of education into account. Another determinant is access to education. In some areas, education is not affordable, or is found to be inadequate. With no other alternatives, children spend their time working.

The Constitution of India clearly states that child labour is wrong and that measures should be taken to end it. The government of India has implemented the Child Labour Act in 1986 that outlaws child labour in certain areas and sets the minimum age of employment at fourteen. This Act falls short of making all child labour illegal, and fails to meet the ILO guideline concerning the minimum age of employment set at fifteen years of age. Though policies are in place that could potentially reduce the incidence of child labour, enforcement is a problem.

If child labour is to be eradicated in India, the government and those responsible for enforcement need to start doing their jobs. Policies can and will be developed concerning child labour, but without enforcement they are all useless. The state of education in India also needs to be improved. High illiteracy and dropout rates are reflective of the inadequacy of the educational system.

Poverty plays a role in the ineffectiveness of the educational system. Dropout rates are high because children are forced to work in order to support their families. The attitudes of the people also contribute to the lack of enrollment—parents feel that work develops skills that can be used to earn an income, while education does not help in this matter. Compulsory education may help in regard to these attitudes.

Child labour cannot be eliminated by focusing on one determinant, for example education, or by brute enforcement of child labour laws. The government of India must ensure that the needs of the poor are filled before attacking child labour. If poverty is addressed, the need for child labour will automatically diminish. No matter how hard India tries, child labour always will exist until the need for it is removed.

The development of India as a nation is being hampered by child labour. Children are growing up illiterate because they have been working and not attending school. A cycle of poverty is formed and the need for child labour is reborn after every generation. India needs to address the situation by tackling the underlying causes of child labour through governmental policies and the enforcement of these policies. Only then will India succeed in the fight against child labour. India has the largest number of urban and rural child workers in the world.

The Government of India acknowledges at least 17.5 million working children. Estimates by various organizations range from 44 million 2 to over 100 million child workers. The exact number of child workers in India's export industry is not known. Major export industries which utilize child labour include hand-knotted carpets, gemstone polishing, brass and base metal articles, glass and glassware, footwear, textiles and silk, and fireworks.

Other industries in India alleged to use child labour are: locks; leather; pottery; granite, mica, slate mining and quarrying; auto parts and accessories; cashew processing; coir (coconut fiber) products; iron and steel products; wood, rattan, and walnut furniture; suitcases and trunks; sports goods; garments; tile; and shrimp and seafood processing. Further research is required to determine the nature and extent of child labour in these industries, as well as their link to export markets. Some of these industries, such as pottery and locks, probably produce solely for the domestic market. Hand-knotted carpets are exported in large quantity from India to the United States and Germany. Although there are weaving 5 centers scattered throughout India, the largest centers are located in the 'carpet belt' of Uttar Pradesh. Carpets are also produced in the Jammu-Kashmir region, as well as outside Jaipur in Rajasthan.

The South Asian Coalition on Child Servitude (SACCS) estimates that there are approximately 300,000 children working in the industry. In 1992, the American Embassy in New Delhi noted that estimates of children in the carpet industry range from 300,000 to 400,000.

Children work in almost every stage of carpet-making. In a comprehensive May 1994 report on child labour in India, the International Labour Rights Education and Research Fund (ILRERF) asserts that children's tasks include sorting, knotting, cutting, washing, and dyeing. They also rear sheep, roll yarn into balls, string the looms, and weave and bind carpets. Often children begin work at six or eight years old as unpaid 'apprentices.' Child carpet weavers typically fall into four categories: unpaid children working on family looms, unpaid children working with adult family wage earners, unpaid apprentices and wage earners.

A 1992 survey conducted for the Government of India by the National Council for Applied Economic Research (NCAER) estimated that 8 percent of the total work force in the hand-knotted carpet industry is child labor. A 1993, the International Labour Organization estimates that the ration of adult to child workers in the carpet industry of Mirzapur-Bhadohi is 1:2.254. Of the 500 carpet children surveyed by the NCAER, the average daily wage was 12.20 rupees; the survey found that wages were not promptly disbursed. Often both adults and children are paid per square yard, which makes the weavers work very long hours. Most looms are located in earthen shacks or sheds scattered throughout villages. These sheds are similar to a typical lodging for a family in a rural village. Only a small percentage of carpet production actually occurs in factories (housing multiple looms).

The NCAER study found that 91 percent of the children sampled lived and slept in weaving sheds, and basic amenities, such as light, ventilation, and toilets were deficient or unavailable. Anti-Slavery International described loom sheds as small, seldom more than twelve feet by nine feet, with very little light. Trenches about 3 feet deep and 21 feet wide are dug into the floor to accommodate the looms which are too high for the sheds. During the weaving process, three to six children and/or adults sit shoulder to shoulder. Usually there are one adult and two boys per loom, sitting in damp pits, which fill up with water during the monsoon season. Children are charged for meals, which include a few chapatis (bread), onions, and salt. They also suffer health- related problems.

The NCAER 1993 study found that cuts and injuries were common. Over 90 percent of the children complained of swelling of lower limbs and severe pain in the joints. Children also came into constant contact with woolen fluff causing skin troubles including scabies and respiratory ailments. Work in ill-lit sheds impacted the eyesight of 40 percent of the children. Similarly, SACCS reveals that bonded children rescued from the carpet looms say they were overworked and beaten. When children suffered cuts to the fingers during weaving, the loom owners scrape sulphur from matches heads into the wound and then set the wound on fire to stop the bleeding. In addition, children have also been known to suffer loss of eyesight due to poor lighting and deformed backs due to long hours of sitting in cramped conditions. Children suffer from psychological distress, and are beaten and even tortured if they attempt to escape from the looms.

A 1991 study by the Institute of Development Studies in Jaipur provides extensive documentation of child labour in the gem industry of Jaipur. For example, the study cites a 12 year old girl using a drilling machine, children stringing gems, a 14 year-old girl cutting tiger stone, turquoise, amethysts and garnet, and a 9 year-old boy polishing stones. According to noted academic Neera Burra there are two categories of children working in the gem industry in Jaipur: Children from 6 to 10 years old belonging to families of manual laborers and poorly paid people. These children work from 8 a.m. to 6 p.m. and are completely illiterate; and Children from 10 to 14 years old belonging to families with a fairly steady income. These children go to government schools and work about four hours a day after school.

According to Burra's 1991 study, children are involved in large numbers in the making of the 'ghats'(rough cut stones), faceting and polishing of semi-precious stones. In the precious stone industries, children use oxides in the final stages of gem-polishing. In fact, in the final polishing with oxides, the entire labour force consists of children below fourteen. Burra found that although children in the gem polishing industry are engaged as 'apprentices,' they are in fact a source of cheap labor. The learning process takes five to seven years-during the first two years children receive little or no remuneration. Children work for 10 hours a day. After the two years, a child worker is paid 50 rupees per month.

According to the Burra, local doctors revealed that more than 30 percent of the children get tuberculosis, presumably due to unhygienic conditions, overcrowding, and malnutrition. Children complain of body ache and finger tips grazed by the polishing disc. The most common complaint was eye strain and allergic dermatitis due to constant use of dirty water. Brass products, such as vases, figurines, planters, plates, dinner services, and tea sets are made in Moradabad in Uttar Pradesh, and exported all over the world, including to the United States. It is reported that more than 90 percent of the goods produced in Moradabad are intended for export. The brass industry is made up of numerous unregistered shops in the guise of household units, thereby skirting child labour regulations.

The Operations Research Group documented occupational hazards of children working in the brass industry in 1993 and found that the average income of a child was 174 rupees per month for eight to 10 hours of work six days per week. A dated, but detailed, study by Neera Burra in 1989 estimated that 40,000 to 45,000 children work in the brass industry in Moradabad. Children were recruited by middlemen called 'dalals,' who receive a commission from the employers for finding child workers. Contractors, or 'thekedars,' and workshop owners prefer children because they are easy to control. Burra notes that, except for the process of engraving and coloring, child workers in the brass industry do not work with their families. Almost all the children in Moradabad work as wage laborers and are unrelated to workshop owners.

Children work in almost all aspects of brassware production for long hours and low wages, and are exposed to health hazards. Children remove molten metal from molds near furnaces. Burra observed these children standing, without protective gear, on top of furnaces with a temperature of 1,100 degrees celsius. Burns were a constant danger. Children were also observed working in electroplating, polishing, and applying chemicals to the wares. The constant inhalation of fumes from the furnaces and metal dust leads to tuberculosis and respiratory problems. During acid washing of the brassware, Burra noted that green and blue vapors rising into the air cause irritation to the eyes.

Estimates of the number of children working in the glass industry range from 8,000 to 50,000. The glass and glassware industry in India is concentrated in Ferozabad. The glass factories of Ferozabad produce a number of glass items, such as bangles, chandeliers, wine glasses, beads, crockery, bulbs, and cut glass items. The factories also produce test tubes, beakers, and laboratory glass products. The ILRERF Report referred to a glass-factory floor as Dante's 'Inferno' due to the intense heat of the furnace, lack of ventilation, broken glass everywhere, dangling electric wires, and workers with no protective equipment. Both adult and child workers stand outside furnaces dipping iron rods into molten glass, bringing it out, and throwing it to glass molders or blowers. Boys as young as 11 or 12 sit on the floor for long hours in front of the pot furnaces, melting and fastening glass bangles and beads.

Often glass splinters injure the workers, and pieces of glass cut into the bare feet of the children. The children bump into each other as they have to run very fast before the molten glass can cool, and may scorch each other's bodies. An earlier study in 1987 by Cox newspaper reporters found boys under 14 running from the furnaces to the glass blower carrying molten glass. The glass blower would then throw the hot iron pole, javelin style, to a child several feet below him, who would put water on it.

The reporters observed children walking barefoot over glass littered floors, some with scarred eyes and burnt scalps. In addition, children of the glass factories in

Ferozabad suffer mental retardation, asthma, bronchitis, eye problems, liver ailments, skin burns, chronic anemia, and tuberculosis.

A recent study by Dr. Asha Singh of the Maulana Azad Medical College in New Delhi revealed genetic damage in the body cells of the laborers working close to furnace heat for three years or more. In 1993, India exported more than $107 million worth of footwear to the United States. The American Embassy-New Delhi advises that "child labour is known or widely believed to be used in the shoe export industry. The American embassy further states that children are employed in the manufacture of shoes in the Agra area and that Agra shoe manufacturers are beginning to find markets in the West, possibly including the United States. Some sources estimate that as many as 25,000 children may be involved in shoe making, both for the domestic and international markets. Children between 10 and 15 years old are assembling shoes. Some 80 percent of the children work for contractors at home.

The ILRERF report found children working in shoe factories throughout Agra, including road stalls, and in small factories. It is reported that children also work in larger factories. Children are allegedly found in sericulture, silk weaving, and in the silk handloom industry. The May 1994 ILRERF report states that children, mostly girls, work in the silk industries. Children work in sericulture and silk thread spinning in the villages of southern Karnataka, as well as in silk handlooms in Varanasi and Kanchipuram. There are approximately 5,000 children employed in the silk thread industry in southern Karnataka. ILRERF observed factories with children ranging in age from 5 to 16 who work from 7 a.m. to 9 p.m. spinning silk. Another factory was found to employ young bonded workers, mostly girls. In contrast to the sericulture and silk thread weaving industry, it is difficult to witness child labour in the silk handloom industry, as it is a household industry.

A 1994 study mentions that because of scant governmental attention paid to child labour in the silk industry, a growing number of children are working in the industry in Bhagalpur. The study was drawn from a sample of 250 child workers under 14 years of age in the silk industry in Bhagalpur. Most child workers were between 11 and 13 years old, the smallest children being 5 years old. The majority of the child workers received 5,000 to 10,000 rupees per year ($170-$340). The largest number of children belonged to a disadvantaged class or are Muslims. Moreover, data revealed that there were more boys than girls in this industry, and girls were generally below the age of 10.

Some of the health hazards include poor work conditions (lack of sanitation, water, and fresh air), diseases of the lungs and sight problems. The Central Tessar Research Training Institute in Ranchi stated that silk weavers suffer from heart and skin diseases, and various other lung diseases. Children are involved in virtually the entire process (about 14 phases) of silk manufacturing. Specifically, children dye the silk. This process involves boiling the skeins in water to remove the gum. The children then place the yarn on bamboo hangers for drying, after which, it is starched. Children about 14 years old commonly put prepared yarns on beams, weave the silk and then take it to the market.

An ICFTU/APRO study in 1992 estimated that 55 percent of the workers are below 14 years. Many begin working at age five to seven. According to findings by the ICFTU-APRO study in 1992, there are approximately 300 licensed fireworks factories and several hundred unlicensed units. These units account for 90 percent of India's fireworks production. Most of the items are used for Diwali. Estimates of the number of children working in Sivakasi's fireworks industry range from over 30,000 to 70,000, according to SACCS. Working in the fireworks industry at the age of 10 or 12. According to Manjari Dingwaney of the Rural Labour Cell (India), children are carried in buses from their villages to the work sites between 3 a.m. and 5 a.m. in the morning and return home between 6 p.m. and 9 p.m.

The ILRERF found that children were paid on a piece rate basis which varied between boys and girls. Hazardous work environments in match and firework factories, including highly inflammable chemicals spread on the unprotected floor have resulted in fatal accidents. Article 24 of the Constitution of India prohibits employment of children under 14 years in factories, mines, or other hazardous employment. India has numerous laws pertaining to child labour which span over 100 years.

The Children (Pledging of Labor) Act, 1933 prohibits any agreement to pledge the labour of a child. Pledging means the taking of advances by parents and guardians in return for bonds. In 1986, the Child Labour (Prohibition & Regulation) Act, was promulgated to consolidate the various other child labour laws. It provides penalties for employing child labor; a uniform definition of 'child' (14 years or under); machinery for proclaiming a list of prohibited occupations for children; and permission for any person to file a complaint against anyone employing children.

Proscribed occupations include: carpet weaving, cloth printing, dyeing, weaving, manufacture of matches, fireworks, and explosives. The 1986 Act also limits child work for six hours between 8 a.m. and 7 p.m. with one day of rest per week, and provides penalties of imprisonment and fine up to 10,000 rupees for violations.

For repeated offenses, imprisonment can be up to three years. Critics of the Child Labour Act of 1986 note that the determination of age is left to the Inspector, and that the Act lowers some higher standards established by earlier acts.

More specifically, the 1986 Act: lowers the age of entry for employment in motor transport, merchant shipping, and factories; puts child workers in agriculture or the unorganized sector outside the reach of the Act, and provides exemptions for family-based work. According to the Advocate Supreme Court of India, labour statistics for 1992-1993 show that there were 349 prosecutions and 162 convictions under the Child Labour (Prohibition and Regulation) Act of 1986.

The record shows that Uttar Pradesh was the only state with convictions under the Child Labour Act of 1986. The Government of India has reportedly approved draft legislation to tighten provisions of the Child Labour (Prohibition and Regulation) Act of 1986 and improve enforcement.

The amendments would make violations of the law subject to the provisions of India's 'Code of Criminal Procedure 1973,' increase penalties, and empower Magistrates to dispose of cases speedily. The enforcement of child labour laws, however, is weak in India. The Standing Committee on Labour and Welfare and the Ministry of Labour found inadequate enforcement of the

Child Labour Act of 1986 by the States. This Committee questioned the commitment of the Central Government to eliminating child labor. The 1993 Operations Research Group study was even more critical; it concluded, "[S]heer callousness, almost bordering on sadism, on the part of government officials is the main reason for the exacerbation of the sufferings of the child labor.

The implementation of child labour legislation in India is entrusted to labour inspectors, representatives of the Ministry of Labour at the district level. Labour inspectors are responsible for ensuring that no child below the stipulated age is employed. The judicial department inquires into complaints. Enforcement is divided; some labour inspectors enforce the Factories Act; others enforce the Child Labour Act of 1986. While conducting seminars for enforcement officials, the National Labour Institute's Child Labour Cell instructors found that many inspectors were uninformed about the laws. Moreover, credible sources maintain that rampant corruption further compromised enforcement of child labour laws.

Although the Constitution of India directs the States to provide free and compulsory education to all children up to 14 years of age, it is not implemented. India has one of the highest illiteracy rates in the world, in addition to a very high drop out rate from school. Myron Weiner, professor at Massachusetts Institute of Technology who has written extensively on education in India, attributes the prevalence of child labour in India largely to the failure of the educational system. Professor Weiner notes that, due to a lack of compulsory education, half the population of school age children between 6 and 14 years old is at home or in the labour force. Weiner argues that it is not poverty which prevents India from investing more in its children, but rather the caste prejudices and value systems of those who create and implement policy in India. Professor Weiner notes, however, that the central government is calling for a substantial increase in expenditures for elementary education, though responsibility for funding remains primarily in the hands of state governments.

A Child Labour Advisory Committee was set up to advise the Central Government on the addition of occupations and processes to the schedule contained in Child Labour (Prohibition & Regulation) Act of 1986. General development programs benefitting child labour are being undertaken by State Governments. Nine National Child Labour projects are being implemented in five states and special schools have been set up which provide non-formal education. Child workers in the many sectors were to receive priority attention because either the employment processes in which they work were prohibited under the Factories Act, or the Child Labour Act of 1986, or the work was such as it was likely to affect the child's well-being.

The International Labour Organization and the Government of India are working in cooperation under the International Programme on the Elimination of Child Labour (IPEC). The priorities for India in 1994-1995 will continue to be in the areas of bonded child labour and hazardous work, including the carpet industry, and the match and fireworks industries. The ILO, through its Child Labour Action and Support Program (CLASP), is concentrating on target groups which mirror the Indian Government's child labour policy. The ILO's programmes covered approximately 33,000 children between 1992 and 1993. Many of these programs are run by community-based non-governmental organizations which establish special schools for working children. No information on the curriculum, attendance rate, or effectiveness of these schools is available. Many of the schools are open only for a few hours per day so that the children are able to work and attend school.

The South Asian Coalition Against Child Servitude, by far the most well-known, initiated a 'Not Made by Children' campaign to effect India's carpet export earnings since carpets are frequently made by children. SACCS also has a program to release, and sometimes rehabilitate, bonded children. There have been several well-publicized raids conducted by SACCS targeting carpet factories. After the children are liberated, Satyarthi and SACCS attempt to provide them with social support, return them to their families, and pressure the local government to respect India's constitutional commitment to free and compulsory education.

The Indo-German Export Promotion Programme (IGEP), in cooperation with the Indian government, NGOs, international organizations such as UNICEF and the ILO, and leading carpet exporters was developing a system called 'rugmark' to certify and label carpets made without child labor. The negotiations for this project recently faltered, but the 'rugmark' project has reportedly moved forward, on a reduced scale, in cooperation with a number of smaller carpet exporters who belong to an association called the Carpet Manufacturers' Association Without Child Labor.

The Concerned for Working Children (CWC) has been working in the field of child labour since 1980. In its early years, CWC was involved in the unionisation of the informal sector where children below the age of 14 years comprised nearly 40 percent of the total work force.

These children, who in many ways were more militant than the adult members were deeply disappointed when they found that the agreements as a result of collective bargaining had not given them any benefits as laws did not recognise them. They wanted to change the law to one that recognised them as workers and protected them as children at the same time. The children and the members of the union embarked on an exercise to draft an alternative legislation for working children in 1985.

In 1985, the Central Labour Ministry agreed to convert the draft into an official Bill of the Ministry. In 1986 the official Bill was presented to the Central Cabinet for approval. A watered down version of this draft was presented to parliament and passed in October 1986. Though the Legislation was fraught with loopholes and definitional difficulties, it did generate a major debate on child work in independent India for the first time. The children also proved that they could engage in policy debates and make major contributions in this area. Objectives are following:

i) Solve the child labour problem and be able to declare areas 'child labour free'

ii) Facilitate protagonism of working children so that they may enrich their lives and contribute towards building a more just and equitable society

iii) Create the 'time and space' for children to be empowered by making an impact on National and State policy, legislation and programmes.

iv) Develop theoretical and practical models that effectively and efficiently deal with the problem and can be replicated both by the state and by NGOs.

v) Influence state and National Governments and International agencies and organisations to focus on child labour as a major part of their political agenda.

vi) Influence state and National Governments and International agencies and organisations to focus on child labour as a major part of their political agenda.

vii) Participate and influence in National, Regional and International forums in order to bring the issue of child labour into the political spotlight.

viii) Use all forms of media, including main stream, to sensitise the public to the issue and change perceptions in order to create a climate where child labour is not acceptable.

ix) Build relations with NGOs, institutions, trade unions, social and political movements and individuals in order to build a strong lobby in support of the rights of children.

x) Develop with others, an alternate agenda for India where there will be no exploitation of children.

INTERNATIONAL PROGRAMME ON THE ELIMINATION OF CHILD LABOUR

The core of IPEC's work involves the prevention of child labour — particularly the worst forms as defined under Convention No. 182 – the withdrawal and rehabilitation of those already in intolerable work situations, and the protection of children above the legal minimum working age from hazardous activities. To ensure impact and sustainability, the withdrawal of children from the workplace must be accompanied by measures to offer them and their families appropriate education, income and employment alternatives. Of equal importance are measures preventing other children from entering the labour market.

Targeting the elimination of child labour contributes to achieving all four of ILO's strategic objectives. While the elimination of child labour falls squarely within the first of these objectives — to promote and realize standards and fundamental principles and rights at work — it also cuts across the other three: creation of opportunities for decent employment and income; enhancement of coverage and effectiveness of social protection for all; and strengthening of tripartism and social dialogue. Enhanced in-house cooperation between IPEC and other ILO units and programmes during 2000-01 helped to reinforce this common mission. Collaboration with ILO's tripartite constituents – governments, and employers' and workers' organizations – continued to be a salient feature in the design and implementation of IPEC programmes.

The work of IPEC on the elimination of child labour goes hand in hand with the policy of promoting "decent work" – productive work with social protection, social dialogue and rights at work. By offering education and training alternatives for working children on the one hand, and employment and substitute income possibilities to their parents on the other, IPEC activities improve the capacity of national economies to enhance income security, consolidate equality of opportunity and generate productive jobs. IPEC's programmes thereby contribute directly to the reduction of the decent work deficit.

With the restructuring of the Office in 1999 and the implementation of the Programme and Budget 2000-01, IPEC became one of eight ILO InFocus Programmes. InFocus Programmes implement activities which are of high priority for achieving the ILO's strategic objectives and are founded on a symbiosis of three elements: knowledge, advocacy and service. This symbiosis is reflected in the evolution of the IPEC Programme, which now covers all aspects of work on child labour and provides member States with comprehensive support in the implementation of the ILO Conventions on the minimum age for employment and the worst forms of child labour. In the ILO organization, the InFocus Programme on the Elimination of Child Labour is part of the Standards and Fundamental Principles and Rights at Work Sector.

In the early years, IPEC supported its partner organizations in developing and implementing innovative and experimental activities. These included determining the nature and extent of the child labour problem; devising national policies and protective legislation; setting up mechanisms to provide in-country ownership and operation of national programmes of action; and creating awareness in communities and workplaces. This "country programme approach" was instrumental in mobilizing broad support against child labour and enhancing capacity in many national institutions. Since 1997, IPEC has gradually enlarged the scope of its operations, bringing experience to scale, including coverage of large geographical areas and specific economic sectors. In the meantime, IPEC programmes have also begun to address the issues of workplace monitoring monitoring and social protection. These programmes have helped withdraw several hundred thousand children from hazardous work, while endeavouring to *keep* workplaces child-labour free and ensuring that former child labourers and their families are provided with viable alternative livelihoods. Another significant development of IPEC's technical cooperation programme is the implementation of comprehensive projects aimed at combating child labour on a national or regional scale. These initiatives have generally yielded positive results. They often combine a multitude of activities, including specific projects to withdraw children from work, child labour surveys, and sensitization of political leaders and the general public. Moreover, in order to address the issues of vulnerable groups (children trafficked for labour or sexual exploitation, for example) and hazardous sectors more effectively, IPEC recently launched several major cross-border regional projects to address trafficking in children, child soldiers, and child labour in domestic work, mining and commercial agriculture.

The development and subsequent adoption of ILO Convention on the Elimination of the Worst Forms of Child Labour, 1999, (No. 182) was a significant step for IPEC. The clear commitment to eliminating the worst forms of child labour has helped place the issue on national development agendas. For example, the Time-Bound Programme (TBP), as a product designed to assist member States in implementing Convention No. 182, aims at the eradication of the worst forms of child labour within a determined period of time. TBPs are also expected to demonstrate that the elimination of the worst forms of child labour can have a significant impact on sustainable development.

IPEC's policy research, data collection and analysis, evaluation methodology, campaigning, communi- cations and legal advisory work are vital for the effectiveness of IPEC's technical cooperation programmes and the enhancement of national capacities to deal with child labour. These functions were enlarged considerably during 2000-01, reinforcing the ILO's role as a global centre for child labour information and legal expertise. The rapid expansion of the programme has raised IPEC's public profile worldwide and generated increased public interest in the programme. Simultaneously, the remarkable rate of ratification of Convention No. 182 is changing the nature of IPEC's communications work – from intense focus on the ratification campaign to wider advocacy related to the Convention's implementation.

IPEC's early programmes targeted children using underlying baseline data that were often not disaggregated by sex. The result of this was that it was difficult to ascertain to what extent girls, who are particularly vulnerable to abusive exploitation, had been provided with effective assistance. As Convention No. 182 requires that special attention be given to girls, IPEC stepped up its efforts to mainstream gender in its approach during 2000-01.

IPEC now operates in 75 countries across the world. Over its ten-year history, IPEC has built up a substantial network of key partners in member countries, including government agencies, employers' and workers' organizations, community leaders, non-governmental organizations (NGOs), the media, parliaments, religious institutions and private businesses. It has also established partnerships with many donors and international agencies.

During 2000-01, IPEC further consolidated its resource base. Three new donors provided funding support, namely Hungary, New Zealand, and the Spanish Municipality of Alcalá de Henares. New pledges by the United States have made it the single largest contributor to the Programme. Support from traditional large contributors to IPEC – the Governments of Canada, France, Germany, Italy, Netherlands, Spain, the United Kingdom, and the Nordic countries, among others – remained strong, thereby ensuring a broad and diversified funding base for the Programme. Because of decentralized decisionmaking by a growing number of donors and funding agencies, the potential for mobilizing resources at the country level remains high. There is also an increasing trend towards substantial cost-sharing for various projects with both public and private counterpart agencies.

The full commitment of the government, and in particular its Ministry of Labour, has always been a prerequisite of IPEC for undertaking large-scale work in any country. Traditionally, this commitment is expressed through a Memorandum of Understanding between the ILO and the government. With the development of Time-Bound Programmes, the principle of national ownership has been given even greater prominence. As Time-Bound Programmes aim at integrating child labour into national development efforts other government agencies (i.e. ministries of planning, social welfare, education, rural development, etc.) are taking on larger responsibilities in the programme. Employers' organizations also have an important part in the struggle against child labour, and IPEC maintains close contacts with the International Organisation of Employers (IOE) and such international organizations as the World Federation of Sporting Goods Industries.Many national employers' organizations do pioneering work by combining policy development, awareness raising among their membership and practical interventions.

In 2000-01, for instance, the Federation of Uganda Employers developed a training programme for managers on child labour and national legislation, which has contributed to the elimination of child labour in the sugar and rice sectors. The Employers' Confederation of Thailand is developing good practice guides for employers and child-friendly employers' networks, while at the same time promoting vocational training and apprenticeship schemes for older children. The Federation of Egyptian Employers is publishing its position paper, "Child Labour in Egyptian Industries", and the Indonesian employers association "APINDO" has developed a code of conduct for its members. Recently the Chocolate Manufacturers Association (CMA) and the World Cocoa Foundation have joined with IPEC to end child labour in cocoa production in West Africa.

Workers' organizations also play a key role in the programme, not only by mainstreaming child labour issues into their national agendas, but also by implementing concrete interventions on behalf of IPEC. Many programmes are implemented jointly by more than one organization. This is a trend in the trade union world: child labour is an issue that inspires trade union unity. In Nepal, all three national trade unions and two national teachers' unions have jointly adapted a policy on child labour (the *Dhulikel Declaration*).

IPEC currently works with two international workers' organizations, the International Confederation of Free Trade Unions (ICFTU) and the World Confederation of Labour (WCL). These contacts generally focus on issues of campaigning, campaigning, mobilization and policy development rather than implementation of technical cooperation activities. International trade secretariats also collaborate with IPEC in sectors where child labour is a problem, such as:

— *tobacco, cocoa* – the International Union of Food and Agricultural, Hotel, Restaurant, Catering, Tobacco and Allied Workers' Associations (IUF);

— *soccer and rugby balls* – the International Textile, Garment and Leather Workers' Federation (ITGLWF) and Union Network International (UNI);

— *surgical instruments* – Public Services International (PSI);

— *mining, diamonds and gemstones* – the International Federation of Chemical, Energy, Mine and General Workers' Unions (ICEM). IPEC has close contacts with Education International (EI) and the World Confederation of Teachers (WCT), and during 2000-01 there was a significant increase in the number of action programmes implemented by teachers' organizations.

Community groups are a rich source of motivation and action in the fight against child labour. Children and their parents must be part of the process, and community-based organizations are well placed to involve them. Community-based monitoring and strengthening of community ties are effective ways of preventing children from entering into the worst forms of child labour. Community-based organizations and NGOs are already focusing on the same problems and the same target groups that IPEC wants to focus on, so the partnership becomes natural.

Interventions designed to cover geographical areas with comprehensive programmes must be based on a careful mapping exercise of on-going, planned, and potential interventions by other actors.

As IPEC alone will not be able to mobilize the immense resources required for comprehensive technical support to member States, it is evident that collaboration with other UN agencies is vital for solving the vast and complex problem of child labour. To this end, IPEC has made, and will continue to make, a strong effort to ensure that the elimination of the worst forms of child labour is included in the children's rights agendas and poverty reduction and universal education programmes of other international organizations.

The preparation for the Time-Bound Programmes has broadened the scope for cooperation with other UN agencies at the national level. Partnerships have been strengthened with UNICEF, UNDP and the WFP. IPEC will also work closely with bilateral development agencies such as DFID (United Kingdom), NORAD (Norway), SDC (Switzerland), GTZ (Germany) and USAID (United States).

At the international level, IPEC is devoting considerable time and resources to ensure that child labour is properly reflected as the single most serious abuse of children in the world today in the outcome document of the UN General Assembly Special Session on Children (UNGASS).

IPEC also coordinated an Office report as a contribution to the Secretary- General's end-decade review of follow-up to the World Summit for Children. It participated actively at each of the preparatory meetings of UNGASS, and presented a paper on "Child Labour in

Africa" at the preparatory Pan-African Forum on the Future of Children.

The Office has been actively engaged in the development and the promotion of the Global Compact, an initiative of the UN Secretary-General to engage world business leaders in building the social and environmental pillars required to sustain the global economy by disseminating good practices based on nine universal principles.

One of these principles is the effective abolition of child labour, and in the ongoing institutional learning process under the Global Compact, IPEC has reviewed a primer on child labour for one of the Compact's corporate members, provided inputs for a training manual for business managers being developed by the Boston College Centre for Corporate Citizenship and an explanation of the fundamental principle of the "effective abolition of child labour" for the Global Compact's web site.

Currently, IPEC and the Inter-Parliamentary Union (IPU) are finalizing a handbook addressed to parliamentarians on child labour, and particularly its worst forms. The handbook is to be launched shortly.

The poverty reduction strategies of the World Bank and the International Monetary Fund are increasingly recognized as the framework for providing development aid in the developing world. Notwithstanding their importance and overriding concern with poverty, these strategies, as spelled out in Poverty Reduction Strategy Papers (PRSPs), so far have generally neglected the elimination of child labour as an explicit target for attaining the development objective.

PRSPs are crucial in shaping the policy environment in which IPEC programmes are planned and implemented. Their strategies and policies in regard to poverty alleviation, employment creation, investment and primary education are of great importance for child labour. Some headway in this direction has already been made. In both Nepal and the United Republic of Tanzania, the master monitoring plans of the PRSPs contain references to combating the worst forms of child labour, and it has been possible to use PRSPs as part of the strategic framework for the development of the Time-Bound Programmes.

With regard to direct cooperation, the World Bank, UNICEF and IPEC have joined forces through the Understanding Children's Work (UCW) Project to improve the knowledge base on child labour. IPEC is also working with the Asian Development Bank on child labour issues with a view to strengthening child labour considerations and the observance of all core labour standards in the Bank's project development and lending activities.

The IPEC InFocus Programme aims at the progressive elimination of child labour through implementation of measures for prevention, protection, withdrawal and rehabilitation. To this end, IPEC's work encompasses social mobilization, focusing on gaining support of civil society and its organizations to enhance the capacity of social and labour market institutions, for IPEC also recognizes the need to ensure greater impact and sustainability of its programmes.

Moreover, the issue of child labour, especially its worst forms, is a convenient strategic entry point to promote the decent work agenda. Political and social commitments to eliminate the worst forms of child labour are not difficult to secure, but these commitments imply legislation reform, promotion of gender equality, removal of hazardous working conditions and introduction of programmes for education, skills training, income generation and job creation. IPEC's work is particularly relevant to ILO's mainstream programmes on promoting decent youth employment and enhancing employability and productivity of adult workers.

IPEC's collaboration with other technical programmes at headquarters and in the field has been further intensified since 1999 following the establishment of the eight InFocus Programmes.

In the Standards and Fundamental Principles and Rights at Work Sector, cooperation was stepped up with the International Labour Standards Department on issues regarding Conventions Nos. 138 and 182.

IPEC is also collaborating with the InFocus Programme on Promoting the Declaration on the preparation of the Global Report on Child Labour for the next International Labour Conference and various technical assistance projects. For example, joint action has been undertaken against bonded labour in Nepal where both adults and children are involved because they belong to a family of bonded labourers. The two InFocus Programmes have cooperated in Bangladesh on the transformation of the ILO/UNICEF/BGMEA garment industry project on child labour workplace monitoring and social protection into a broader project which, in addition to child labour, is now also covering health, safety and working conditions for adults.

An ILO-ADB project has joined IPEC with the Equality and Employment Department (EGALITE) and the InFocus Programme on Safety and Health at Work and the Environment (SAFEWORK) to explore the socio-economic benefits of the implementation of core labour standards in selected Asian countries in the areas of gender, occupational safety and health, and child labour. IPEC works very closely with the Employment Sector, especially in its operational programme.

It is collaborating with the InFocus Programme on Skills, Knowledge and Employability in the preparation of an education and training manual targeting 14 to 17-year-old children and on self-employment activities for their parents. Both of these efforts will apply ILO's modified Modules of Employable Skills (MES) and Community-based Training (CBT) approach.

IPEC and the Department of Gender Promotion (GENPROM) jointly implement the project "Combating Trafficking in the Greater Mekong Sub-Region" and promote the linkages between decent employment for women and the reduction of child labour in Bangladesh and the United Republic of Tanzania. In the latter countries the project builds upon research and practical work already being done by IPEC.

IPEC also worked with the Enterprise Department on programme development in Pakistan and India, with the Social Finance Unit on its thematic evaluation of the impact of micro-finance on child labour and measures for preventing child labour as collateral; and with the Employment Department on the design of anti-poverty strategy and country employment policy reviews and the inclusion of child labour data in the "Key Indicators of the Labour Market (KILM)".Work has also begun with the InFocus Programme on Crisis Response and Reconstruction in the area of child soldiers in Central Africa.

Another good example of interdepartmental collaboration is IPEC's work with the Social Protection Sector in the field of occupational safety and health. In addition to the publication of a new edition of a manual on children and hazardous work and joint advice on labour inspection, IPEC works closely with SAFEWORK for the development of the network of national institutions to undertake research, training and advisory services concerning children working under hazardous conditions. The collaboration with this sector also covers the fields of HIV/AIDS and migration. With respect to the Social Dialogue Sector, the following initiatives are especially worth mention.

The cooperation between IPEC and the Bureau of Employers' Activities and the Bureau of Workers' Activities aims at strengthening the role of employers' and workers' organizations in combating child labour. Coordinated activities are being undertaken under the "Integrated Programme for Building Partnerships and Capacity Against Child Labour".

IPEC has also been working with this sector on the policy linking child labour and education within the framework of "Education for All". Through participation in selected sectoral meetings, IPEC benefits from the extensive research carried out by the Department of Sectoral Activities on specific industrial sectors. In turn, IPEC also contributes to the follow-up of these meetings with regard to the implementation of the resolutions concerning the elimination of child labour in the particular industry in question.

3

Child Trafficking

Trafficking in children is a common concern for many Asian countries. Children and are trafficked for the sex industry, for begging and soliciting, for manual labour, and as domestic workers. Around the world, a large number are trafficked to be sold for forced marriage or, in the case of infant boys, for adoption. Trafficked children often end up in virtual slavery, with little or no say over their lives and fates. And increasingly, with localized economic development, growing economic disparities, tourism, and improved communications, trafficking in children is becoming a transnational problem.

Trafficking in children threatens the social stability and development of many rural families and communities, and damages the lives of many people who are its direct or indirect victims. Globally, human trafficking has become the third-largest source of revenue for international criminal gangs, after trafficking of drugs and arms. The annual turnover of the illegal human trafficking industry reaches billions of US dollars.

A range of factors make some children particularly vulnerable to traffickers. Among these are poverty and debt, low levels of education, limited job opportunities, lack of information, dysfunctional families, the desire to repay the debt of gratitude towards parents (common in many Asian cultures), lax law enforcement and the promise of a more modern consumer lifestyle offered by the cities. Research indicates that more and more people are consenting to be trafficked, perhaps because they feel they have no other way to earn a living.

The fact remains that victims of trafficking, in particular children, still find themselves extremely vulnerable to continued exploitation, as they lack livelihood choices and access to services, have illegal status, and are often unable to speak the local language. Many children who have fallen victim to traffickers have been sold and resold several times. In many cases, the victims have never been heard from again.

In recent years, traffickers have gradually moved from only trafficking to abducting and trafficking children. Trafficking has become increasingly dominated by organized criminal networks. Public security agencies at all levels have established training teams for the handling of major cases, publicity teams, Internet consultation groups, and rescue teams, and have distributed various questionnaires as well as vital equipment for collecting blood samples.

A working system for suppression of human trafficking has been developed that utilizes advanced scientific and technological resources. It enables more rapid exchange of information and more timely identification of, and action against, human traffickers and rescue of trafficked children. The modern technologies used include optical data storage and DNA testing to trace and identify trafficking victims, particularly children. This working system has overcome many of the difficulties involved in the suppression of trafficking and rescue of its victims.

Today, children are being trafficked from almost every prefecture, district and municipality. However, there remain areas of concentration, particularly along the national border. Inter-provincial and cross-border trafficking are becoming increasingly common.

Human trafficking requires careful planning and coordination. From identifying to finally selling a victim, perhaps thousands of kilometres away, is a complex process involving many stages. The victim may be passed on from person to person, group to group, several times. These stages include abduction, transportation, transfer, any amount of selling and reselling between human traders, and even "training" for sexual exploitation, begging etc.

While in the past trafficking networks have usually been made up of independent operators, organized crime gangs that can oversee the entire process are increasingly dominating the trade. Often these gangs are members of the same family or clan.

Trafficking of children can involve a great deal of violence and cruelty. Many victims are virtual prisoners for several years, are raped, beaten and tortured, sometimes driving them to suicide. In many cases, children trafficked are sold into sexual exploitation.

As more and more rural women migrate for work, traffickers are moving from villages to labour markets, often luring victims with offers of legitimate work.

Traffickers are responding to a growing demand for young children. Whereas in the past traffickers generally found enough parents willing to sell their own infants, now they are resorting to kidnapping. In some cases, they have even been known to kill children's parents when they have resisted. However, in some very poor areas, parents still sell their children to traffickers.

Once almost exclusively dominated by men, the human trafficking industry now sees girls playing major roles, for example in luring other girls – even their own friends and classmates –by inviting them on seemingly innocent day-trips or offering them non-existent jobs. The potential victims are much more likely to trust a children, especially a familiar one. Children are also becoming involved in the other end of the trafficking process, aiding in the adoption of trafficked infants by pretending they are their own illegitimate children who they cannot keep.

FACTORS AFFECTING TRAFFICKING

Despite considerable successes and strict legislation against traffickers and their customers, however, the problem continues to grow. This section looks at some of the pull factors that drive the trade in children and allow it to continue, and at some of the push factors that make rural children and communities especially vulnerable.

PULL FACTORS

HIGH PROFITABILITY

The profits from trafficking a single person are several times what the average farmer can earn in a year. The huge potential earnings for relatively little input are enough to persuade people to flout the law and risk severe punishment.

THE MARKET

In many parts of rural areas, human rights awareness is low and few people perceive purchasing a woman or child as criminal or immoral. With the shortage of potential wives and the high cost of marriage ceremonies, there is a large internal market for trafficked children in rural areas. At the same time, there is a growing demand for trafficked children in the sex industry.

WEAK RESPONSE BY LOCAL-LEVEL AUTHORITIES

In areas severely affected by trafficking in children, grassroots authorities have generally failed to take effective action or to establish adequate prevention mechanisms. There have even been reported cases of village leaders aiding and abetting the traffickers, passing them valuable information, warning them of impending police raids, and even encouraging villagers to hinder rescue efforts.

Insufficient Punishment of Buyers

Chinese criminal law provides for up to three years imprisonment for people who purchase trafficking victims. However, to date, very few people have been prosecuted for this crime.

Weaknesses in the Legal Framework

Two loopholes exist in current legislation that complicate cases of trafficking for forced marriage and adoption. Firstly, even if a marriage is forced, the husband and his family can claim paternity of any child of the marriage. Secondly, if a child victim purchased for adoption stays with the adopting family for a certain length of time, the family can claim formal adoption rights. Aspects of law also make it difficult for the victims of trafficking or their families to take legal action against traffickers or to claim adequate compensation. While the legal guardians of trafficking victims can sue the traffickers for economic loss, the compensation they can claim is limited to direct economic losses caused by criminal activities, and no claim can be made for emotional distress or indirect losses. Trafficking victims and their families face a long, difficult and potentially expensive ordeal in seeking redress from traffickers. And the reality is that many such cases fail for lack of evidence.

Lack of Funds, Facilities and Human Resources

The efforts of the departments of public security and other agencies to suppress human trafficking have long been hampered by a lack of special funds and qualified, specialist staff. The public security departments also lacks necessary equipment and mechanisms to collect, analyze and exchange information on trafficking. Not enough specialist agencies are involved in providing transport, repatriation and housing services to rescued victims, with the result that these services are currently done on an ad hoc basis, with the local Public Security Bureaus and even the police sometimes having to contribute, taking away time and resources from their efforts to crack down on trafficking.

Push Factors

Poverty, Lack of Opportunity and Low Education

There is a well-established link between trafficking and underdevelopment. Those areas worst affected by trafficking tend to be poor, rural districts, where a growing number of young people, particularly children, are eager to escape the tough subsistence living of the farmer. They are drawn to the promise of a better life and better work opportunities in more developed, wealthier areas, particularly towns and cities. Losing young people in this way further exacerbates poverty in the villages.

Levels of education tend to be low in these areas. Only a few child victims of trafficking have attended even junior middle school, and the overwhelming majority are semi-literate or even illiterate, meaning that they cannot read about the changing realities of the world beyond their village. The older generations, among whom illiteracy is much more widespread, have little awareness of the dangers that their children might face. Optimistic, naive and unskilled, young girls continue to walk into the traps laid by the traffickers, despite frequent reports in the news media.

LOW AWARENESS OF RISK AND PERSONAL SECURITY

The burning desire to get out and seek a better life, coupled with low education and naivety, mean that most young girls and children migrating from their rural villages underestimate the risks they face. The participation of of friends and classmates in laying traps for potential victims only increases their tendency to misplace their trust.

FAMILY DISHARMONY

In rural areas, particularly among minority groups, underage marriage, or at least engagement, of girls continues to be common. Many such marriages are arranged by the parents, and even when they are not, the girls may not have the emotional maturity to make a wise choice.

RECOMMENDATIONS FOR ACTION

A programme that sets out to reduce trafficking in children must address all of the factors mentioned above. It should include measures in the fields of education, poverty alleviation and lawmaking. It must also build inter-regional and inter-country co-operation.

In recent years, the main response to the human trafficking has taken the form of legislation and regulations. Worl countries now has a comprehensive legal framework against trafficking, and yet rather than being brought under control, the problem continues its rapid growth. A new mechanism is needed to deal more effectively with the problem of trafficking of children. Central to this new mechanism should be a new Public Security Department trafficking-suppression system capable of mounting quick and effective responses, with clear definition of roles and duties and appropriate rewards and punishments.

A second key measure should be intensified monitoring and management of migrant workers, particularly in labour markets, main traffic arteries and railway or bus stations, where abduction for trafficking is most likely to occur.

The public should also be encouraged to participate actively in efforts to suppress trafficking, by remaining vigilant, passing on information about trafficking and traffickers to the relevant authorities, and assisting in the rescue of trafficking victims.

Legislation and Law Enforcement

In part, the failure of current responses to trafficking can be blamed on the inherent weaknesses in the existing legislation. Far more important is the failure to enforce laws and regulations in a rigorous and even-handed way.

Public security agencies need to put new energy into cracking down on trafficking networks, and punish convicted traffickers severely. Once again, the co-operation of the public should be encouraged. At the same time, the relevant legislation needs to be improved. In particular, authorities should prioritize punishment of people who purchase trafficking victims.

LOCAL AND MASS ORGANIZATIONS

Local administrative and mass organizations in rural areas have generally not been as active as they could be in the elimination of human trafficking. Government organisations at all levels need to pay close attention to maximizing the potential of these organizations in implementing trafficking-related national policies.

MOBILIZING THE RELEVANT AGENCIES

A comprehensive response to trafficking in children requires the co-operation and coordination of a wide range of public sector agencies. The roles and responsibilities of these various agencies should be as follows:

— Government at different levels should play an important role in overall administration and coordination of measures to against trafficking;

— The Politics and Law Committee and the Public Security Comprehensive Control Office should examine and evaluate the achievements of local authorities in cracking down on trafficking, and discipline those who are found to have been lax in their duties;

— The Child Development Authorities should assist local police in rescuing and supporting victims of trafficking;

— The courts and Procurators' offices should cooperate with local Public Security Bureaus in taking action against those who hold or transport trafficking victims. Also, they should not allow registration of marriages where the bride is a trafficking victim and is unwilling;

— The Finance Department should provide adequate funds for action against trafficking;

— The Justice Department should promulgate laws and regulations relating to trafficking and publicize the severe impacts of trafficking on the victims and on social stability, in order to promote public vigilance and alert children and young their families to the legal protection available;

— The Family Planning Department should monitor children who may be trafficking victims, and pass on their information to the local police;

— Public Security Bureaus should be responsible for action against traffickers and for rescuing victims of trafficking.

In addition, working groups should be set up at county level comprising the Child Development Authorties, the Education Department, the Health , the Labour and Employment Department, the Justice Department, the Public Security Department, the Court, the Procurator, the Civil Affairs Department, the Finance Department, the Agricultural Department, the Industrial Department, the Travel Department and the Statistics Department, and others. Concrete interagency action plans should be drawn up and implemented in the target counties.

Raising Public Awareness

Within nationwide promulgation activities, special attention should be given to raising awareness of trafficking-related laws among local people, particularly children. A short pamphlet should be published containing information on legal issues relating to human trafficking, which could be used as study material for both teachers and students. Students should also be encouraged to act as "home teachers", passing on what they have learned to their families. Law popularization and girls' education activities should prioritize areas where there is a lot of trafficking, and very poor areas.

Health Education

Most children trafficking victims end up being sold into sexual exploitation and the psoobilities of HIV infection is even more prevalent. Without adequate education about HIV/AIDS and its prevention, trafficked girls will be at even greater risk of infection. In addition, if they are able to return to their home villages, they may inadvertently pass on the disease. This makes it even more important to conduct public health education campaigns, dealing with prevention and treatment of disease, particularly HIV/AIDS.

Children Development Programmes

The legal protection section of the Programme incorporates issues relating to prevention of human. It includes, alongside general rules and regulations, detailed guidelines for implementation to be supervised by local governments. This will help trafficking prevention to become a routine concern of government agencies and catalyze inter-sectoral co-operation.

CROSS-BORDER CO-OPERATION

Countries around the world should be urged to strengthen their co-operation and adopt a range of measures in the areas of education, economic development and law enforcement to eliminate gradually the fundamental causes of vulnerability to trafficking of children. At the same time, countries should co-operate in the pursuit, capture and prosecution of traffickers and their clients.

4

Discrimination Against Girl Child

Worldwide there is a growing consensus that all human beings are born free and equal in dignity and rights and that the human rights of all individuals, including children and women need to be respected. This is reflected in many United Nations (UN) and ILO conventions that have been developed by the world community, and have been ratified in the majority of countries. However, giving equal chances to boys and girls, and men and women is not only a matter of human rights and social justice. It is also a matter of sound economic judgement, because a healthy, educated workforce is a pre-condition for the sustainable social and economic development of countries and societies do not reach their economic potential when their human resources are not fully utilized. It is, therefore, crucial to educate and train both boys and girls, and emphasize the joint responsibility of men and women to look after the future generations.

Experience has learned that development efforts, which do not explicitly address gender equality issues, tend to make life harder rather than easier for girls and women. Worldwide, more women than men belong to the poor, women's poverty is more severe and the incidence of poverty among women is increasing, a process referred to as the feminization of poverty.

Poor women can not look after their children properly and many of them find themselves in a vicious circle transferring poverty from one generation into the next one. This cycle needs to be broken because of both social justice and pragmatic considerations.

Strong arguments exist for investments in women, in particular, because they are known to spend resources and benefits that they receive on improving the welfare of their families rather than on themselves only. Promoting the elimination of child labour and equality between the sexes is not only the right but also the smart thing to do.

The United Nations Convention on the Elimination of All Forms of Discrimination Against Women (CEDAW) is the key overall UN instrument for gender equality promotion. It was adopted in 1979 with a view to combat the continuing discrimination against women because earlier human rights instruments reflected mostly male concerns and perspectives.

It identifies many areas where there has been notorious discrimination against women, for example in regard to political rights, marriage and the family, and employment. The Convention spells out specific goals and measures that are to be taken to facilitate the creation of a global society in which women enjoy full equality with men and, thus, full realization of their guaranteed human rights.

DISCRIMINATION IN CHILD LABOUR

In analyzing child labour, it is important to understand that boys and girls have different experiences. First of all, many parents tend to have different expectations of daughters and sons. Children are socialized from an early age to copy the gender roles of their parents, for example boys are expected to take after their father and girls after their mother. In most societies this means that boys and girls engage in different activities and are channeled into men's jobs and women's jobs respectively. For example, while both boys and girls are found working for the family in the field and at home, in small restaurants, in factories or on the street, boys are often found to work in male-dominated sectors such as mining and fishery, and girls in typically female-dominated sectors, including garment production and services such as domestic work and work in the entertainment industry.

Secondly, boys and girls may also have different motivations and reasons to be engaged in child labour or to leave home. Usually poverty and lack of opportunity are among the driving forces in child labour and migration of children seeking work. However, some underlying causes such as parents' expectations, children's own curiosity and sense of obligation, and more pervasive consumerism often determine the ways in which boys and girls work, migrate or are trafficked.

Other reasons including family fights, a broken home, physical or emotional abuse, political situations, and natural disasters also contribute to children's motivation to leave home. Research findings also suggest that boys tend to be more prone to peer pressure, while girls are driven by family and peer pressure.

All societies aspire the best for the younger generation and it is widely agreed that all children have a right to healthy development. However, in many families and societies boys are still favoured over girls. In fact, different treatment starts at – or even before – birth. Evidence of this can be found in the killing of female fetuses and infanticide of baby girls, circumcision of boys, other different birth rituals for girls and boys, and variations in nutritional status between them.

Poor parents often invest more in their sons and tend to put their daughters to work to help looking after the basic family needs. Even in cases where girls are given the opportunity to study, they often learn that being a boy is better and worth more than being a girl. In many cultures, girls internalize this attitude which often makes them shy and less assertive than boys.

This results in their growing up to be women with greater constraints and fewer opportunities. In turn, they are less able to positively influence the life of their daughters, thereby perpetuating the cycle of poverty and exploitation from one generation of women to another. The low status of women and girls is ingrained in cultural values and customs as can be seen in proverbs from many countries. For example:

— If you have 10 daughters, you do not have children. If you have a son, you have a child.

— Having a daughter is like having a toilet installed in front of the house.

— Men are the front legs and women are the hind legs of elephants.

TRAINING FOR LABOUR

Norms, values and practices related to favouring boys over girls, especially regarding access to education, are changing and impressive improvements are being made, especially in providing equal access of girls and boys to basic education, but enormous hurdles remain. Girls continue to have less access to education and training, especially at the secondary and tertiary levels. This is particularly true in societies in which the status of women is subordinate to that of men, and girls and women are confined to unpaid household duties and family care within the home and the community. Among children who are not going to primary school worldwide, 60 per cent are girls. Even among working children studies found that girls have less education than boys.

Cultural traditions may prevent girls from going to school, for example in some cultures girls are not allowed to attend classes with boys. Sometimes parents keep their daughters at home because school may be too far and unsafe. Other times parents keep their daughters at home simply because they need help with domestic chores. In addition to lack of equal access to basic education, girls are often channeled into a narrower range of occupations and lower levels in the job hierarchy than boys from families with similar income levels. As a result, worldwide women have had less education than men when they were young and the majority of people who are not functionally literate are women. They continue to have fewer chances for education and training compared to adult men from the same income categories. This means that many women in poverty do not have the opportunity to earn a decent income for themselves and their children.

Education and training systems often reinforce existing inequalities in societies. For example: Curricula and training materials portray girls and women in dependent or subordinate positions and as sole caretakers of household duties in the family. Men are often portrayed as sole decision makers and travelers. Trainers tend to reinforce sex and gender stereotypes when providing career guidance, as it is more difficult for both women and men to find a job and earn an income in an occupation that is considered to be a men's or a women's job respectively.

Sex segregation in the labour market is a serious problem. Across the world there are around seven times as many 'male' as 'female' non-agricultural occupations and women's share in top positions in the largest companies worldwide is limited to 2-3 percent – processes known as horizontal and vertical occupational segregation by sex.

Jobs in which many women are found often have a lower status than 'men's' jobs. For example: In many societies doctors are usually men and nurses are predominantly women. In Eastern Europe and the former USSR the profession of doctor has been femaledominated, and has been accorded lower status and pay than the male-dominated job of engineer.

UNPAID AND LOW QUALITY WORK FOR GIRLS

Women and girls continue to have primary responsibility for unpaid work in the household, such as cooking, cleaning and caring for young and old dependent family members. This type of work is not rewarded and considered to be of a non-economic nature. It is, therefore, usually not measured in labour statistics, and thereby becomes invisible. However, when counting the total hours of work spent on economic activities and family and household care, women and girls worldwide work often considerably longer hours than men and boys. In contrast, both boys and men have more access to leisure time.

Millions of people particularly women and children work as unpaid family workers on the land or in a family enterprise, often in the informal sector. This type of work is officially recognized as an economic activity, but undercounting continues to take place, because women and children and the enumerators who interview them do not consider these activities as work.

Girls often start working at an earlier age than boys, particularly in rural areas where the majority of child workers are found. They also do household work in both rural and urban areas. Many of them are excluded from education or suffer the triple burden of house work, school work and economic work.

The last three decades have witnessed an increase in paid work for women globally – a process known as the feminization of employment but much of this work has been of relatively low quality. In many developing countries employment patterns have changed in the following ways:

— Rapid urbanization and development of cities in many countries are attracting more and more men to cities. This has led to the feminization of agricultural work in many rural areas, for example, in China and India.

— Young women also migrate from the rural areas and many have found work in factories or workplaces manufacturing labour intensive goods in export processing or industrial zones or in services.

— Economic need has forced many women from poor households to become own account workers in the informal economy and generate income through self-employment in whatever way they can to prevent the family from starving. For example: in street trade in cities or craft producers in rural areas.

— An increasing number of women also work at home, performing piece rate work for manufacturing enterprises at the end of the subcontracting chain.

— More women work in the service sector as compared to men. In most countries, more women and girls are found in jobs that tend to extend traditional female reproductive roles such as domestic work, cleaning, provision of entertainment and commercial sex work.

Children, particularly girls, often work alongside their mothers in the informal sector and in homework and sometimes girls are also employed in manufacturing industries. In the majority of cases the income earned and the working and employment conditions are quite low. Women workers in the informal sector operate at the subsistence level.

Many women have limited literacy and numeracy skills and start the same type of small businesses. This leads to overcrowding and competition. Homeworkers in the subcontracting chain can only work when orders are available and they generally have little bargaining power with subcontractors.

Women in manufacturing industries, for example those in industrial zones, are often employed as unskilled workers and are easily fired in case of marriage or pregnancy. Working hours in all three cases tend to be long, and labour protection, social security and safety and health regulations are often not in force or inadequately applied.

Illegal Work

Among the most invisible child labourers are child domestic workers. There are clear links between children in domestic work and trafficking in children for labour exploitation both within and across countries. An obvious example of illegal (and invisible) child labour is commercial sex. Although trafficking for prostitution has received much attention from authorities, society and media, trafficking of young children for domestic work has only recently been recognized, although both are global phenomena. Girls (and women) predominate in these types of work which are not covered by labour legislation and protection.

In some countries, such as Nepal, more boys work as child domestics and increasingly more boys are found in sex work worldwide. Because these types of work are usually hidden from view in private households or in difficult-to-reach workplaces, working children in these sectors are often isolated from society. For instance, child domestic workers are often separated from their families, making them vulnerable to emotional, physical and sexual abuse. In addition, due to the low status and the illegal nature of the work, child sex workers are often victimized, held captive, and exposed to extremely abusive and even life-threatening conditions.

Increasingly girls and women, but also boys and young men, are trafficked for labour exploitation. Ending up in prostitution, domestic service, small factories or workplaces, they are the most vulnerable of all, particularly if they do not speak the language. Without a legal status that allows them to live, go to school or do light work legally, foreign migrant children –as well as native children without appropriate legal documents – tend to be exploited in debt bondage, in forced labour and in sexual exploitation. Their rights are not recognized nor protected. Moreover, they can be prosecuted as illegal aliens, when caught, causing them to hide from the authorities, which in turn makes it even harder to reach them.

EARNINGS AND EXPENDITURES

On average women typically earn two-thirds of what men earn in economies of all types and women still earn less than men at every level of education. Only a part of this gap in earnings can be explained by differences in educational attainment and job experience which means that gender discrimination in receiving equal pay for work of equal value is still widespread.

The same seems to be valid for girls. On average, they are paid less than boys for the same type of work. For instance, half of the girls working as domestics in Dhaka, Bangladesh are paid less than Rs. 4,000 (US$51) a year, as compared to only 28 per cent of boy domestics. 6 It is also more common for girls to receive no pay at all for the work they do.

Girls often do not have control over the income they earn, because they are obliged to hand it over to their fathers, mothers or husbands. In East Asia, many women keep the household purse and they must ensure there is income to fulfil the family's basic needs. In such cases, women have control over the day-to-day expenses but are often also mainly responsible for earning the income needed for survival purposes. In addition, research continues to confirm that, in cases where girls and women have control over their income, they spend it on meeting the basic needs of their families to a larger extent than boys and men.

Women and girls are preferred workers, because they are often willing to work hard under poor conditions. They have been socialized to be obedient workers who work hard, do not protest or make demands. Girls are, of course, particularly vulnerable because of their age. Women often work in sectors which are not unionized. Even in unionized sectors women often find it difficult to become actively involved in trade unions, because of their household duties and family obligations.

If girls and women are given a choice, many of them would prefer not to work under the conditions in which they are actually working. However, generally, they consider that they have to work to contribute to meeting the basic family needs, even if the work is dirty, dangerous, demeaning and not well paid.

Indications are that women and girls prefer paid employment to unpaid work and are willing to accept low salaries and abuses such as sexual harassment or other types of violence. While girls and women do not always have control over the earned income, the fact that they contribute to the family income usually means an increase in bargaining power within the family.

RELATIONS BETWEEN WOMEN'S WORK AND CHILD LABOUR

Little information is available on the relations between women's work and child labour. However, it is clear that parents who are struggling to make ends meet for family survival purposes will resort to child labour if they have no other alternative. Many mothers are in this position. Their situation needs to be addressed to ensure that child labour problems are not perpetuated from one generation to another. An overview of family survival strategies involving child labour follows below.

— *No family planning and reproductive rights*. Families with many children often find themselves unable to provide adequately for all of them. Although family planning has become widespread in most countries, there remain many families in rural areas and in marginalized social group such as migrant populations, which lack access to family planning. As a result, the children end up having to work to help their parents.

— *Single female-headed households*. Adults who are in charge of a single-headed household usually lack labour, as they have to look after children, take care of household duties and earn an income to meet the families' basic needs. Most households with only one adult are female-headed households, and, when they are poor, their only option often is to resort to child labour for survival purposes.

— *Working alongside their mothers*. Many women work in agriculture or produce for the market at home, on the streets or in other workplaces. When child care for younger children and schooling for older children are not available or affordable, mothers will often take their children to work. Gradually, these children will start helping their mother with her work.

— *Specific risk for the older daughters in the family.* When mothers go out to work in addition to fathers, and other adult family members are not available to look after dependent family members, older girls are often kept at home to look after the household and the family.

— *Greater chances of children becoming involved in the worst forms of child labour exploitation.* Children, often girls but also boys are sold to intermediaries with false promises to both the children and their parents of safe, paid work for the children elsewhere. Many children end up as child slaves in prostitution, sweatshops or domestic services in an environment where they have no other option than to stay and do what they are ordered to do. A similar scenario exists for children, again often girls who are being 'given away' by poor parents to intermediaries who promise to give them a better life than they had at home. These children often end up in the same exploitative situations as children who are sold.

— *Teenage pregnancies.* In rural areas girls continued to be married off at a young age and need to take up the duties of wives and mothers without the benefits of further education and training. Girls who have become pregnant outside wedlock are often taken out of school. Often they have to fend for themselves and their children on their own as they are no longer accepted in their family or community. Thus, they become child workers themselves and will involve their own children when these grow up due to lack of other alternatives.

Studies worldwide confirm time and again that women spend family income on meeting family needs such as food, shelter, children's education and family healthcare, while men tend to allocate resources elsewhere. Generally men have more control over the overall family budget than women, even in societies were women keep the household purse. It is, therefore, increasingly becoming realized that fathers need to learn to share decision-making power with their wives on how to spend the family income.

The majority of unpaid household work, including cleaning, cooking and family care is carried out by women and girls although boys and men slowly start to carry out more household duties than in the past, particularly if they are educated. Worldwide, however, women and girls continue to have longer working hours than men. Sometimes this means that they jeopardize their health because they do not get enough rest. Almost always it means that girls and women have less time for socializing and training. More equal sharing of family responsibilities between men and women is, therefore, an essential condition for achieving equality between men and women at work and in life.

Women are usually seriously under-represented at the decision-making levels in communities, organizations and political bodies, and are often excluded from formal and informal decision-making processes. This limits women's capacity to have a say in community and public affairs on issues which directly concern them and their children. For example, decisions on whether to use a local community fund for the building of a school, a health clinic, a road, clean water facilities, or a power supply for electricity or communication, are often taken without women's involvement.

At the local level, women are often organized in women's committees or village women's groups. While these groups tended to have a welfare orientation only, recent years have witnessed a change towards a more comprehensive role for these organizations in many countries. However, giving women a more equal voice in more formal decision-making bodies continues to be a challenge in many parts of the world. For example, their representation in village councils is rarely higher than around a quarter, and most often it is considerably less.

Within schools also, women form the majority of teachers, but they are seldom found to be head 'masters' of schools or chiefs of local government administrations. This situation is mirrored at the national level where women form the minority at the higher levels in government administration and in the political structure. Women's constraints in playing an equal role in decision-making is known to be often harmful to them and their children, and for this reason, many development and women's organizations advocate for change in this field.

PRINCIPLES AND FOR PROMOTING GENDER EQUALITY AND PROGRAMMES AGAINST CHILD LABOUR

1. *Achieving gender equality is not a 'women's concern' but the responsibility of all in society.* In the past most advocates for the promotion of gender equality were women. It is, therefore, sometimes thought that this subject only concerns women and not men.

However, this idea is now fast disappearing. There is increasing consensus that gender equality is as much men's as well as women's business, is the responsibility of all in society and requires contributions and inputs from both women and men.

2. *Promoting gender equality will benefit all in society.* Empowering women and girls towards greater participation in development means working towards more balanced and equal power relations between the sexes. Sometimes a fear exists that advancing the position of women means that something is taken away from men. However, the promotion of gender equality does not imply giving more power to women and taking away power from men. The promotion of equality between women and men is empowering for all. It allows both men and women to take part fully in social and economic life and leads to a win-win situation for both.

   'Power-over' which refers to a situation of subordination on the one hand and domination on the other, is unjust and detrimental to development because of the unequal exchange it entails. A win-win situation is created by advocating:

   — Power-to: creative and enabling type of power, people's empowerment

   — Power-with: group power, the whole is greater than the sum of its parts

   — Power-within: spiritual strength, self-confidence.

3. *Gender equality needs to be addressed in all development programmes and at all stages of the programming cycle.* It is sometimes thought that the promotion of equality

between men and women is only relevant in the 'soft sectors' such as education, health, welfare and other care- and servicebased jobs, and not in 'hard sectors' such as macro-economic policies, engineering, construction and other infrastructural development, or in decision making in politics. In other instances, it is considered that gender equality will be achieved if something small and extra is done especially for women and girls. These ideas do not lead to progress in practice, because gender inequalities are deeply ingrained in the social, economic, cultural and political fabric of societies. Gender equality is an issue which needs to be addressed in all development fields and at all stages of the programming cycle, in other words, at the planning and design, implementation, monitoring and evaluation stages.

4. *Gender-specific measures are needed in case of pronounced inequalities.* The relation between the promotion of gender equality and the advancement of women is not always well understood and sometimes it is thought that these are two different issues. This is not the case. The advancement of women and girls is a necessary strategy whenever they are in a disadvantaged position as compared to men and boys. As current inequalities are often quite large, equal treatment of men and women from now on is often not sufficient because existing inequalities could remain or might even become larger. Gender-specific measures are usually needed to redress existing imbalances between the position of men and women until women can participate in, and benefit from, development on an equal footing with men.

Of course, if boys and men are disadvantaged in comparison to girls and women, genderspecific measures may be needed to improve their position. In addition, note that genderspecific measures may involve activities for women, men or both. For example: Male leaders often need gender awareness raising to become committed to improving the position of disadvantaged girls and women.

5. *Address practical and strategic gender needs.* The roles of men and women in families, workplaces and institutions are generally different. Therefore, their needs may also vary. Two types of needs are usually identified to develop strategies which promote gender equality:

    — Practical needs arise from the actual conditions which people experience because of the gender roles assigned to them in society. They are often related to girls and women as homemakers and providers of basic needs, and concern inadequacies in living and working conditions, such as food, water, shelter, income, health care and employment. For poor families, these needs are often linked to survival strategies. However, addressing practical needs only can perpetuate the disadvantaged position of women and girls in their societies. Practical needs must be addressed but gender equality can not be achieved without addressing strategic needs.

    — Strategic needs refer to the subordinate position of women to men in society, and relate to the empowerment of women. They vary according to the particular social, economic and political context in which they are formulated. Usually they concern equality issues such as enabling women to have equal access to job opportunities and training, sharing of family responsibilities, equal pay for work of equal value, rights to land and other assets, prevention of sexual harassment at work and domestic violence, and freedom of choice over childbearing. Addressing them involves a slow and gradual process of changing attitudes and practices in societies.

5

Human Rights Violations of Indigenous and Tribal Children

According to recent global estimates, 211 million children between five and 14 are economically active. Of these, approximately 186 million are engaged in child labour. If we include children and youth between 15 and 17, the number of child labourers reaches 246 million. The number of indigenous peoples is similarly estimated to be between 250 million and 350 million globally.

Indigenous, tribal or ethnic minority children are more likely to end up in certain types of child labour than their peers. In South Asia, indigenous peoples predominate among certain forms of debt-bondage. In Thailand, hill tribe children, including refugees from Burma, are highly vulnerable to trafficking, particularly for commercial sexual exploitation. In Ecuador, nine out of ten indigenous children work, compared to one out of three non-indigenous children.

Child labour is often recognized as a major issue among ethnic minorities. A recent IPEC study from Romania, for example, showed that 49 percent of working street children interviewed were of Roma origin. While we know that many indigenous and tribal children work, we know little about the conditions and types of work in which they are engaged. Few governments make the effort to gather data on child labour in general, and even less consider gathering data in indigenous areas or follow through in this regard. Furthermore, because many indigenous peoples are victims of continuous discrimination, it is difficult to retrieve relevant information.

With the historical experience of being criticized as "backwards", acknowledging the existence of child labour can indeed be a difficult one. The fact is that approximately half of the world's child labourers are estimated to work full-time, many in hazardous forms of work. In certain countries, indigenous and tribal children comprise a large portion of such children and require immediate international attention.

EDUCATION AND CHILD LABOUR

In the 1953 landmark study "Indigenous peoples, living and working conditions of aboriginal populations in independent countries" the ILO listed a number of education challenges linked to child labour as they were perceived around 50 years ago. Under "Factors contributing to illiteracy," the working child was emphasized:

It has been calculated that more than 10 million children in Latin America, both indigenous and nonindigenous are performing work, which should be done by adults. With regard to Guatemala, one investigator has stated that Indian parents cannot afford the "luxury" of sending their children to school. A survey carried out in 1934 by the American International Institute for the Protection of Childhood showed that the age at which the Indian child begins to work varies between nine and ten, and cases are known in which it has begun at four or five years. In 1943 children under 14 years of age were observed by the Joint Bolivian-United States Labour Commission working in certain mines in Bolivia.

The understanding of child labour as a practice harmful to child development that should be replaced with universal primary education is a well-established social goal that has its origins in the mid-nineteenth century. This has put indigenous peoples in somewhat of an awkward position.

Traditional forms of education include engagement in customary livelihoods in fields and forests or on the sea with parents and communities. The basic skills transmitted allow children to grow up and survive in often harsh environments. Practical competencies related to these livelihoods are viewed as a necessity for proper socialization. Indeed, prohibiting these by forcing children to participate in non-adapted schooling may risk removing access to traditional forms of education, ultimately threatening children's future ability to survive and make a living later on as adults. It may also provoke intergenerational conflict, particularly as educational services often include built-in discriminatory practices.

Examples of indigenous and tribal children "forgetting", neglecting or hiding their identity are numerous. One Mexican psychologist speaks of work as one of the most important pathways to enculturation among indigenous peoples, securing socio-cultural integration and collective identity. This is not new, nor is the co-existence of child labour and education a distinctive phenomenon of indigenous and tribal children. Still, traditional livelihoods as forms of knowledge transmission are often indirectly or directly dismissed by national projects promoting uniform notions of education and knowledge.

Notions such as customs, traditions and apprenticeship relationships are easily abused for exploitative purposes and are also frequently relied on to justify and legitimize child exploitation. Still, the importance of traditional livelihoods as an indigenous education strategy cannot and should not be neglected.

Literacy among indigenous peoples involves being proficient in their own languages, being able to read and navigate in local environments, and being able to communicate with and re-write the surrounding landscape to serve their own well-being and future. Literacy in the national language alone rarely provides this.

Traditional livelihoods can indeed be considered as "light work", particularly if the formal education system is adapted to the particular needs and visions of indigenous peoples. At the same time, notions such as traditional livelihoods or customary practices should not be looked at uncritically. In some instances, it is indeed the case that through their engagement in traditional occupations, indigenous and tribal children, particularly the poorer among them, are denied the right to learn to read and write by their parents and communities.

Child labour at home or in the fields is not necessarily beneficial nor necessarily a learning experience. When this is the case, the voices of the children and their communities are critical in setting indigenous criteria as to what is beneficial and in finding solutions for what is not. There is a need for more research and dialogue to address the differences between light work and exploitative forms of child labour.

CHILD LABOUR AMONG INDIGENOUS PEOPLES

Child labour among indigenous peoples takes many forms, from harvest work to prostitution. Data remains extremely scarce and sporadic, but nevertheless reveals several pockets of child labour, including some of the worst forms, defined by ILO Convention 182 as follows:

(a)all forms of slavery or practices similar to slavery, such as the sale and trafficking of children, debt bondage and serfdom and forced or compulsory labour, including forced or compulsory recruitment of children for use in armed conflict;

(b) the use, procuring or offering of a child for prostitution, for the production of pornography or for pornographic performances;

(c) the use, procuring or offering of a child for illicit activities, in particular for the production and trafficking of drugs as defined in the relevant international treaties;

(d) work which, by its nature or the circumstances in which it is carried out, is likely to harm the health, safety or morals of children.

While indigenous children are very often a vulnerable group, this is not always the case. We cannot assume a simple correlation between the presence of indigenous peoples and high rates of child labour. For example, an IPEC rapid assessment of the flower industry in Ecuador made it clear that indigenous children were only involved to a limited extent and that there was a far greater impact among white and mestizo communities. Such forms of child labour were perceived as "bad" by indigenous communities and highlighted the role of traditions and worldview in strengthening the ability of indigenous communities to resist socio-cultural changes. In Bolivia, statistical analysis undertaken by Cartwright and Patrinos showed that speaking an indigenous language was negatively associated with full-time work and that indigenous children were less likely to be working full-time. In Nepal, high-caste children may be more vulnerable than indigenous children for some forms of child labour.

It is likely that indigenous children face more difficulties when searching for formal employment, leaving the actual number of working children uncounted for in the informal sector. Indigenous peoples may not dominate national statistics in absolute figures, but they are over-represented in certain cases of the worst forms of child labour. Existing documentation only sporadically provides us with more details in terms of differences within and among different communities.

Gender differences are typically left unaccounted for as well. In Guatemala, for example, certain occupations such as manufacturing and the service sector were found to involve mainly indigenous girls, while indigenous boys were found to be more engaged in agriculture.

Specific data is crucial if we are to move beyond simply asserting indigenous children as a particularly vulnerable group.

The vast majority of indigenous peoples live in rural areas dominated by the informal sector and subsistence-based or mixed economies highly dependent on natural resources. It is also in rural areas that the vast majority of working children are believed to be found. Still, the issue of indigenous children working as rural labourers is not well-documented. With certain exceptions, as in debt-bonded labour in South Asia and in other specific cases in Southeast Asia and Latin America, no substantial documentation has yet been produced.

For a number of reasons, researchers and organizations have had difficulties in grasping the issues and complexities at work. Remote locations and language barriers have made it logistically difficult to include indigenous areas in major surveys. Moreover, because child labour in rural areas among indigenous peoples typically covers a range of forms, both exploitative and non-exploitative, it may be difficult to collect accurate information. Finally, even when indigenous peoples are included in surveys, disaggregated data is rarely used to reflect their particular conditions.

The predomination of child labour in rural Latin America is often emphasized, although there are rarely specific references to indigenous children. The documentation of child labour in rural sectors has from time to time shed light on indigenous child labour in different countries. Thus, for example, a study of child labour in tea estates of two districts in Nepal documented the indigenous Santhals as the most-represented ethnic group in the overall workforce (18,9%), without, however, exploring the issue in further detail.

In a statement made to the UN Working Group in 2000, a tribal representative from Assam, India highlighted the presence of child labour in tea estates, noting that children are becoming an economic "asset". In terms of rural child labour on a global scale, two major scenarios are emerging. In the first, increasingly dispossessed and marginalized households are forced to send their children into child labour. In the second, households engage in cyclical or permanent migration for wage labour elsewhere.

In both cases, traditional livelihoods and occupations may no longer respond to basic needs, increasing the risk of child labour. In Latin America, rural agricultural child labour is mainly found among the indigenous peoples of Mexico, Central America and the Andean Region, where most indigenous peoples are peasant farmers or wage labourers.

For example, it is estimated that more than 50 percent of the indigenous agricultural community in Guatemala, Mexico and Peru survive only as wage labourers. In Panama, it has been estimated that the child labour situation is most critical in rural and indigenous areas, particularly among the Ngobe-Bugle community in the west, with more than half of all children in indigenous areas suffering from malnutrition.

Rural child labourers are involved in sugar cane plantations and rice and coffee harvesting, with studies showing more than 40-hour work weeks for indigenous children. In rural areas in Mexico, it is estimated that around 170,000 indigenous children ages six to 14 work for little, if any, wages for their parents, family or neighbours.

Within the broader trend of members of indigenous households increasingly engaged as migrant agricultural workers in Mexico, the situation of indigenous child labourers in the northeast has been described as extremely critical. It is reckoned that between 35 to 40 percent of these agricultural labourers (jornaleras) are of indigenous origin from the south of the country. These include Mixtecos (Triquis) from Oaxaca, Tarahumaras from Chihuahua, Purépechas from Michoacan, Amuzgos from Guerrero and Mayos from Sinaloa and Zacatecas. It has further been estimated that 32 percent of the indigenous labour force in the agricultural regions in Northern Mexico are children:

Of the children from southern Mexico, 63 percent are hired by intermediaries in their place of origin and the rest in the state of Sinaloa. Forty-four percent of these child labourers are female and 56 percent are male. At the conclusion of the agricultural season, 72 percent return with their families to their respective states, 20 percent remain in Sinaloa and 9 percent continue the route of workers to other destinations. Fifty-five percent of the child farm workers have been working in the fields for one to five years and 14 percent for over five years.

Research has shown that migrant child labour is substantially higher among indigenous children (54.42%) than mestizo children (38.5%). In the Mexicali valley, 62 percent of migrant child workers surveyed were of indigenous origin. Among both indigenous and mestizo families, children form part of the contract signed by parents and are frequently given adult work from the age of nine. The impact of this is alarming. While both groups suffer from a range of diseases, malnutrition and illiteracy, research shows that indigenous children are:

— generally sicker. Within the last three months prior to research, 57.7 percent had been sick, compared to 50.1 percent among mestizo migrants.

— more malnourished. In research undertaken in Sinaloa, the highest malnutrition rates were found among indigenous Mixtecos, Tlapanecos and Triquis from Oaxaca and Guerrero.

— more illiterate. On an average, one out of three agricultural workers are illiterate. For indigenous workers, the figure reaches 46 percent.

The educational gap between indigenous and non-indigenous populations reflects both the situation in the sending area and the impact of the migration process. A survey by the Instituto Nacional Indigenista (INI) showed that 42,000 indigenous children have dropped out of school, mainly because they lacked the financial means to continue studying. In Oaxaca, only 5.2 percent of the indigenous population enrols in middle or higher education, compared to the national average of 26.0 percent. No more than 2.0 percent of the indigenous population undertake occupational studies, compared to the national average of 10.8 percent. Migration has been found to interrupt children's school attendance, with one survey indicating that 69.0 percent of indigenous migrant children do not attend school.

There is comparatively less information from lowland South America, although various forms of slavery have been documented among indigenous groups in rural areas in Brazil. Among the Guarani inhabiting the Gran Chaco plains in the south of Bolivia, indigenous child labour has been observed among debt-bonded, landless families living on large haciendas. The few schools available provide only primary courses, tending to reinforce high rates of illiteracy and the bondage system.

The phenomena of indigenous children working with their parents as agricultural migrant labourers highlights the need to view and respond to their situation in light of the broader family, social and cultural context. In other words, such forms of child labour are intimately linked to the working conditions of indigenous agricultural workers and indigenous communities as such.

The presence of hazardous forms of child labour among migrant agricultural workers needs to be investigated, given such facts as the increasing use of chemicals in agriculture. Other forms of child labour among indigenous peoples in rural areas also need to be further explored and documented. For example, indigenous children, particularly girls, are often pulled out of school to work as domestic workers for richer households. While their conditions are rarely described in detail, such practices may be part of a vicious circle based on debt-bondage.

In the case of tribal children in India involved in Beedi leave collection. The children of landless tribals are also very vulnerable as far as child labour is concerned, particularly as opportunities for cheap manual labour develop. Sometimes the children are bonded, while sometimes they are simply exploited as cheap labour.

An example is the bidi (local cigarette) rolling industry in Angul district in Orissa where an estimated 25,000 children and adults work in deplorable conditions: poor lighting, crowding of 30 to 40 children in one room and continuous exposure to nicotine. There are reports of high incidence of tuberculosis, gastric infections and bad eyesight in the area. Given the difficulties faced by the

Beedi producers today due to lowering demands, there is even more reason to closely monitor the child labour situation.

FORCED LABOUR AND DEBT-BONDAGE

A 1953 ILO study described the recruitment of indigenous children in Latin America as follows:

> [Recruitment] often involves an obligation on the part of labourer's children to perform certain services on the farms or in the owner's houses. In some districts the Indian family is so poor that it is compelled to take the children away from school to place them as servants in the house of some local landowner or official, in exchange for food and clothing. Elsewhere unpaid labour by his children is one of the tenant-labourer's conditions of contract in return for the use of a small plot of land granted by the hacienda owner In South Asia, debt-bondage is a common issue among indigenous peoples. According to Anti-Slavery, the vast majority of the approximately 3 million mine and quarry workers of the Indian state of Rajasthan belong to "low" castes and tribal peoples (Adivasis). Many of these are caught in debt-bondage. The presence of debtbondage among the Advisasis of India is well-recognized in several other states, including Madya Pradesh, Andra Pradesh, Orissa, Jharkand and Bihar. Not surprisingly, certain poor or marginal segments of the indigenous and tribal populations are particularly vulnerable to debt-bondage. As marginalized tribal households may be caught for generations in the debt spiral, the impact on children in terms of labour and education are dramatic.

Recent ILO INDISCO research among the Bondo of Orissa has shown that the social safety net was particularly weak for children who had lost their fathers and who were thus required to pay back old family debts, often ending up working as labourers in other peoples houses.

Despite legal prohibition, debt-bondage continues to be a serious problem among Adivasis in India. The laws abolishing the practice of bondage are yet to be implemented. The laws and other regulations pertaining to the control of incidence of bonded labour are honoured more in the breach than in the observance. The bureaucracy responsible for their implementation are rarely interested in this. Thus, exploitation begins with indebtedness and also ends with it. Attempts by Adivasis to clear their debts from other sources earning have been frustrated in spite of 40 years of state intervention in the spheres of cooperation, credit and economic development. The monitoring systems have failed and seldom have needy Adivasis been the real beneficiaries.

The recently banned kamaiya system of debt-bondage found mainly among the indigenous Tharu in the Terai region of Nepal. It is estimated to have affected around 13,000 children. Many of them initially suffered even worse conditions being thrown off the lands of their former landlords without immediate rehabilitation opportunities. The ILO Project for the Sustainable Rehabilitation of Bonded Labourers has implemented a range of activities to assist these particularly vulnerable children, but also identified the continuous needs of two other major groups. These are, on the one hand, children continuing to live with their families on the land of the landlords. On the other hand, children in other forms of debt-bondage have yet to be reached.

In many cases, indigenous and tribal children in debt-bondage are exploiting resources belonging to land from which their communities have been dispossessed. Although little documented, this has been observed in countries such as Laos, Vietnam (personal communication) and the Philippines, where merchant-intermediaries advance food, hunting equipment or basic commodities to labourers, who are often cheated in payment for forest products.

As Legaspi et al note regarding the Philippines, because of their indebtedness, indigenous communities are often powerless. A key characteristic of rural child labour in general and debt-bondage in particular is the high dependence on a landlord, trader or other person for food, clothing and housing. The provision of these "services" on a regular basis is often what secures the continuation of the relationship, as the child or household often believe there are few other options for obtaining these regularly.

While children in particular may become victims, many forms of forced labour represent structural situations of exploitation faced by whole communities or particularly vulnerable households. The Global Report on Forced Labour identified indigenous peoples as a particularly vulnerable group, while simultaneously noting the need for more systematic documentation.

URBAN SETTING

There are clear indications that a growing number of indigenous children are migrating alone or with parents to cities in search of employment or better opportunities. The types of work found are most often in the informal sector and are rarely safe. The situation of indigenous domestic workers in Latin America remains extremely under-documented, with a few exceptions. The old practice of "criadito" service still persists in some parts of the Bolivia. Criaditos are indigenous children of both sexes, usually 10 to 12 years old, whom their parents indenture to middle- and upper-class families to perform household work in exchange for education, clothing, room, and board. There are no controls over the benefits to, or treatment of, such children, who may become virtual slaves for the years of their indenture.

In India, there has been some documentation of tribal girls migrating to urban areas to work as domestic workers through both religious and non-religious bureaus. Particularly in Latin America, South and Southeast Asia, indigenous peoples constitute a growing proportion of the new urban migrants, the urban poor. IPEC has supported some education activities with indigenous communities in urban settings in Peru and Guatemala through the "Fe y Alegria" education project network.

In Asia, a recent ILO study of socio-economic vulnerability of tribal migrants in the cities of Chiang Mai and Chiang Rai in Thailand showed that the majority of street children under the age of 15 were from hill areas in Thailand and Burma. Most were boys who earned a living from selling flowers, begging, or offering sex services. Similar evidence is emerging from other Asian cities within or neighbouring on indigenous areas.

In Africa, urban migration of indigenous children and youth is also raising growing concern among indigenous organizations, which have highlighted the spiral of unemploymentdelinquency, alcohol and drug addiction, prostitution and AIDS. There are indications that tourism has led to increases in child labour in certain areas, with children lured into commercial sexual exploitation, involvement in producing and selling handicrafts/ goods and begging. So-called communitybased "ethno-tourism" and "eco-tourism" initiatives need to be critically assessed in this regard.

TRAFFICKING AND PROSTITUTION

Human trafficking affects a considerable number of indigenous peoples. This has been particularly documented in South and Southeast Asia. In Nepal, an IPEC Rapid Assessment of trafficking in girls, with specific reference to prostitution, shows the presence of several different ethnic groups. Trafficking of indigenous girls is also being documented in Thailand, Burma, Indonesia and Cambodia.

In India, abduction, trafficking of Adivasi girls linked to brothels, forced concubinage and the overall inadequacy of legal protection available to Adivasi women at risk of rape or trafficking requires urgent action. B. Janardhan, quoting M. Devi from 1984, notes that traffickers still continue to purchase Adivasi children and women openly, often at a price cheaper than that paid to "purchase animals". A whole network of slaves exists, stretching from the Adivasi villages to centres as far away as Ludhiana, Jalandhar, Amritsar and Hoshiarpur districts in Punjab. A large proportion of Adivasi migrant workers are women, and face sexual exploitation at all stops in that belt. A group of contractors recruit these Adivasi women through older women who themselves have been victims of these practices. After receiving the recruits, the contractors transport the "human cargo" to states such as Punjab. The recipients of the "human cargo" auction the Adivasi girls in the open market. These slaves are paid roughly Rs. 15 a day or Rs. 1000 on an average.

Similar processes have been described in Taiwan, China where high numbers of indigenous girls have been trafficked to work in the sex industry. While indigenous peoples account for only 1,6 percent of the Taiwanese population, estimates of the percentage of indigenous women involved in the sex industry range from 20 to 60 percent. Moreover, the presence of minors and debt-bondage is considerable.

Known as sold daughter prostitution girls are contracted for a period of years or even for life against an initial payment to her parents, with or without her informed consent. The girls are usually minors and find themselves in the low-price brothels, where conditions are worst.

There is little information regarding trafficking and prostitution among indigenous peoples in Africa. However, abduction raids taking place in Sudan during the last 15 years of civil war are known to have particularly focused on one conflict zone, Bahr El Ghazal, and have mainly affected Dinka children. Often put to work to look after cattle for Arab Baggara pastoralist groups from North Sudan, the total number of children involved ranges from 5.000 to 14.000. In many cases, children who have been forced into labour have also been forced to forget their own language and identity.

As noted in a recent IPEC rapid assessment on trafficking in children in the Thailand, Laos and Myanmar border areas, surveys may not necessarily succeed in identifying trafficking among indigenous communities. It may exist, but be hidden away by already stigmatised communities.

MINING

Mining areas are often found in traditional indigenous and tribal areas across Latin America, Asia and Africa. While the issue of indigenous involvement in mining operations is rarely the focus of documentation, some studies offer indications of ethnic diversity or places of origin of workers, as in the ILO country studies on child labour in small-scale mining, for example. Other studies look in detail into either traditional mining activities of indigenous communities or the particular involvement of certain groups in large-scale mining operations.

In Latin America, indigenous children have been found to work in mines in Colombia, Peru and Bolivia. There is growing evidence of bonded labour among indigenous peoples, including children, in mines in India, although the issue definitely deserves a more comprehensive survey.

While it has been observed that the children involved in mining activities in many indigenous areas are migrants, these migrant children may in fact be indigenous children from other areas, as has been somewhat documented in Latin America. Finally, it should be noted that the impact of outsiders involved in mining on indigenous areas can be severe. It is clear, for example, that outside miners have brought with them previously unknown diseases, food habits and pollution, considerably disrupting the situation of indigenous and tribal children.

IMPACTS OF MILITARIZATION ON CHILDREN

Because indigenous and tribal areas are often border areas or home to insurgency movements, militarization is a frequently encountered phenomenon. Despite the limited documentation on the issue, there are indications from some countries that indigenous and tribal children are recruited as child soldiers or helpers in government operations and counter-insurgency movements. In Latin America, indigenous children in Peru were targeted by Sendero Luminoso and underwent prolonged indoctrination. In Colombia, the militarized and violent situation has had serious impact on children in indigenous communities.

In the North-East of India, the consequences of armed conflict have been dramatic for the indigenous children. Children's involvement in insurgency movements in Bangladesh and the Philippines has also been noted. In Myanmar, according to UNICEF, there have been cases of parents volunteering children for the Karen army, which offers them clothing and two meals a day. In 1990, the 5,000-strong army was estimated to comprise around 900 children under the age of 15.

In Central Africa and the Great Lakes area, there have been cases of Batwa children and youth enrolled by force into armed groups. The general impact of militarization is being documented and appears to stem mainly from the overall disruption of everyday lives caused by militarization in terms of lack of schooling, mental health problems and extreme working conditions. Despite extremely scarce and sporadic information on children involved in armed conflict, there is sufficient evidence to show the high vulnerability of indigenous and tribal children caught in the crossfire. It is therefore highly recommended that close monitoring and targeted assessments in conflict-ridden areas include the living and working conditions of indigenous and tribal children.

The following eight broad recommendations came out of a Minority Rights Group workshop report on indigenous and minority child soldiers in Africa:

1. Actors at all levels should prioritize sensitization on minority and indigenous rights and the rights of the minority and indigenous child.

2. Locally appropriate forms of multicultural and intercultural education and education for peace should be promoted, drawing on the best existing models.

3. International standards should be effectively incorporated into domestic law, with state-level actors and others undertaking monitoring and reporting, promoting best practice and seeking just punishment for perpetrators of abuses.

4. Traditional approaches to conflict-prevention and peace-building in Africa should be far more widely recognized and supported.

5. The marginalization of ethnic minorities should be addressed at all levels, including their empowerment at state and local levels through political power-sharing and more inclusive politics.

6. The international community, states, opposition movements and civil society should sharpen their concern for the rights and best interests of the child, with special attention to the girl child.

7. Donors, relief organizations, state agencies and others should urgently address the exclusion of ethnic minority children and their communities from aid programmes and humanitarian relief

8. Links and cooperation between local, regional and international bodies, especially NGOs, require strengthening to help build the impetus for constructive change.

EDUCATION CHALLENGES

Discrimination against indigenous children continues to exist in educational systems and practices. These children constitute a relatively over-represented group among those still to be reached by the Education for All process. Some of the challenges remaining in education are discussed below.

At a virtually global scale, indigenous and tribal children have literacy rates lower than the national average. In India, according to 1991 figures, literacy rates among tribal peoples were only 29.6 percent compared to a national rate of 52.0 percent. In China, education problems have been noted among the so-called national minorities.

In Central Africa, enrolment rates among Batwa children in Rwanda were markedly lower (around 15%) than the national average of 89 percent. It is estimated that less than 0.5 percent of Batwa have completed secondary education. In Latin America, several studies have documented the difficulties of indigenous children in completing their education, their high dropout rates and the frustrations they encounter. In Bolivia, indigenous children receive about three years less schooling than non-indigenous children.

Education statistics are often used to provide important indicative data on the presence of child labour, particularly in cases where labour surveys and other statistical data are either absent or do not segregate data according to ethnicity. Low educational performance among indigenous peoples is on its own an insufficient indicator of a high presence of child labour; rather, it is an indicator of inadequate education facilities. When this co-exists with increasing socio-economic vulnerability and high poverty rates, the presence of child labour is is very likely.

Lack of access to basic education is an issue frequently raised in both country studies and programme statements. The quality of existing educational services is often very bad, as in the case of the Shankargarh mining area. Here, the main reason for children dropping out is the quality of education in the government schools.

Frequently, one teacher is responsible for 250-300 children. Many villages do not have a school, and where schools exist, teacher absenteeism is high. Children belonging to lower castes face discrimination in school. Almost all upper-caste children go to school. Invariably, teachers also belong to upper castes and their tendency is to discourage lower-caste children from attending school.

Compulsory education laws are often not enforced in indigenous areas. Schools rarely function properly, and there are extremely high levels of teacher absenteeism and turnover rates in most areas. Teachers are rarely sensitized or properly trained to the particular needs of indigenous children.

The growing movement of bilingual and multicultural education, which is often highlighted as a solution, is itself giving rise to new types of challenges. The teaching community rarely receives sufficient training, and actual resources typically lag considerably behind policy statements on multicultural education. Communities, their representatives and organizations may be unaccustomed to developing pedagogical materials. The presence of several, often small, linguistic communities in the same area presents further complications, both logistically and in terms of course development and programming.

When measured in non-Indigenous terms, the educational outcomes of Indigenous peoples are still far below that of non-Indigenous peoples. This fact exists not because Indigenous peoples are less intelligent, but because educational theories and practices are developed by and controlled by non-Indigenous peoples this failure is that of the system, not of Indigenous peoples.

Indigenous peoples are conceptualising their education vision in terms broader and different than those of existing education services. The Coolangatta statement on indigenous peoples' rights in education, adopted as a core policy outcome of the World Indigenous Peoples Conference on Education (WIPCE) held in Hawaii in 1999, highlights that "'dropout rates and failures'... must be viewed as what they really are – 'rejection rates'." The six-page-long Statement situates indigenous rights to education in its historical context of social exclusion and marginalization. Through a human rights approach, the statement reclaims the right to be indigenous as well as the right to selfdetermination in general and in the area of education in particular.

Education International has recently taken the Coolangatta Statement on board, inviting affiliates to endorse it as well as promoting the view "that United Nations' bodies, governments and education trade unions must review, transform and improve policies and practices in this matter, in order to implement the Education For All objectives.

SOCIAL EXCLUSION

Issues surrounding child labour and education among indigenous children cannot be viewed in isolation from the wider context of structural challenges faced by indigenous peoples as a whole. These involve a number of socio-economic and cultural aspects that distinguish them from the average non-indigenous adult, household or community. Awareness of these particular forms of social exclusion needs to remain in the forefront of problem analysis and solution building.

The major driving forces behind many social problems encountered by indigenous and tribal children go beyond their immediate needs and are rarely identified by conventional income-based poverty analysis. These include profound changes in terms of selfperception, well-being, cultural identity and social interaction. It is well-acknowledged that assimilation policies and marginalization have had serious impact on levels of social and cultural disruption. An indigenous girl may no longer be spoken to in the indigenous language by siblings and friends, she may not be taught it at school, and she may find life easier rejecting its existence.

Socio-cultural disruption and identity conflicts are often linked to a range of internal as well as external processes and may result in the breakdown of family ties, non-formal social protection measures and mutual self-help. The disappearance of these bonds can be considered as explanatory factors in several cases of child labour – not least when children are removed from families to work for others in their fields or homes or when they are trafficked to brothels. In many countries, indigenous children and youth are steering away from traditional livelihoods. Beyond purely economic reasons, such changes are led by changes in identity, value-systems and future aspirations.

New ideals of social status through material consumption influence indigenous peoples just as much as other groups in society, creating new "needs" for cash, social status and recognition. While there is limited data in this area, it should not be ignored as a factor contributing to the increasing numbers of indigenous and tribal children involved in migration and urban labour markets.

FORMAL EDUCATION

Formal education has been, and in some cases continues to be, a double-edged sword for indigenous peoples. On the one hand, it is a fundamental tool used to empower themselves and their communities and to raise awareness of their rights. On the other hand, education has been one of the major tools used to further marginalize communities through policies designed to educate, proselytize and promulgate foreign values and "modern" knowledge.

Indigenous values linked to child development and growing up may involve work. IPEC and INDISCO Philippines research has shown that parents in one indigenous community did not necessarily consider child labour to be a problem. The same research team noted, however, that "as much as possible, they want their children to be educated." While statements disregarding the danger of child labour may represent pride, it is also possible that working may not be seen as detrimental to the personal development of the child. Such notions often co-exist with the valuing of education

In the Cordillera region of the Philippines, another research team found that while over 80 percent of the children surveyed were involved in some form of child labour, this was rarely considered hazardous or disadvantageous. The attitude among parents was that "children must learn how to work, earn money, contribute to the family's needs, be responsible for one's upkeep and the like."

A considerable number of indigenous and tribal intellectuals have resisted schools and promoted the ideas of decolonizing knowledge and educational institutions and reappropriating languages through various forms of indigenous-controlled experimental learning. Such scholars interpret the high dropout rates, poor educational performance and absenteeism among indigenous and tribal children as forms of resistance to inappropriate education. Still, for indigenous and tribal households such choices are rarely based on a political agenda.

On the contrary, while it may be normal to find indigenous peoples resisting schools or simply regarding them as irrelevant, it is probably even more common to find strong values attached to schooling. As García-Moreno notes for Ecuador, schools have enormous symbolic significance and are often requested by indigenous communities, even though children may still be kept working.

Indigenous parents often consider the language and practices of the dominant culture to be valuable assets, representing the opportunity for social mobility. It should not be forgotten that a majority of indigenous peoples are continuously barred from educational institutions, workplaces and other opportunities due to lack of proficiency in national or metropolitan languages.

Parental resistance is therefore more likely to emerge as the consequence of practical choices and priorities, where households and children judge other forms of knowledge transmission and work more relevant for their future projects. The task is therefore not so much, as one often gets the impression, to convince parents about the relevance of formal education, but to make formal education relevant.

Continuous extension of non-adapted primary education services, despite perhaps an immediate interest on the part of indigenous and tribal communities, may have very limited impact on alleviating child labour. It may, in fact, even perpetuate cycles of poverty and marginalization, if it interferes with indigenous forms of education that prepare children to survive socially, economically and environmentally in their adult lives.

Recognizing indigenous rights to design and manage formal education services is therefore a fundamental ingredient in the reformof formal education systems. Building a broader consensus between parents, community leaders and children on the character and forms of education is essential. International organizations and policymakers must go beyond taken-for-granted notions of education and child labour to address the particular challenges faced by indigenous and tribal children. Innovative approaches are needed to assess and refine traditional forms of knowledge transmission, and formal education that works.

Poverty and Traditional Livelihoods

The gradually accumulating data documenting the socio-economic exclusion of indigenous peoples paints a grim picture of poverty, malnutrition and a corresponding lower access to basic services for health, social protection and education. In other words, an indigenous or tribal child is very likely to grow up poor, undernourished and illiterate – and involved in child labour.

Poverty as a driving factor behind child labour is a well-established fact, although there is considerable disagreement as to how important it is in comparison to other factors. In relation to indigenous peoples, this is highly dependant on how poverty is defined.

As Amarty Sen has underlined our understanding of poverty needs to go beyond income disparities and include the deprivation of basic capabilities and rights. For indigenous peoples, such a context of deprivation would also involve addressing the increasing pressures on traditional resources and areas leading to threatened livelihoods and environmental degradation. The resulting dispossession and marginalization has led many communities from independent subsistence or cash-based livelihoods to a wage- or labour-dependent economy. Ill-designed formal education may hinder indigenous education and knowledge transfer perceived as inappropriate or "backwards". Traditional livelihoods and non-formal customary education needs to be perceived as localized ways of fighting poverty, rather than simply a result of poverty. Formal education introduced to replace customary practices may thus risk provoking higher degrees of child labour by weakening indigenous education and survival strategies.

While projects may highlight in "objective" terms how education facilitates further education and off-farm employment, this may actually be interpreted as an effort to turn communities away from traditional occupations, lands and resources. Whether due to diminishing resource bases, hardships related to traditional livelihoods or changing aspirations, the increasing trend towards migration among indigenous peoples can be considered as a major root cause behind the increasing presence of child labour.

In Mexico, income from indigenous migrant child labourers may constitute a third of the household income, acting as a prohibitive barrier for education. Costs of schoolbooks and clothing and loss of income are frequently presented as reasons for keeping children out of school, leaving little doubt that economic need is a key force leading to child labour. The predominance of debt-bondage among certain indigenous peoples also confirms the wide presence of economic marginalization.

While rural child labour has sometimes been viewed as an exceptional survival strategy in times of hardship, it is possible that such "exceptional" measures have become the norm, considering the tremendous stress indigenous economies are facing. The kamaiya system in Western Nepal, for example, has indeed involved families in situations working for a neighbour for an agricultural year as a coping strategy; however, the same exchange practice has been abused to exploit labourers with permanent or semi-permanent status over several generations.

Despite the overall relevance of poverty to child labour, an overemphasis on economic arguments tends to neutralize the broader context of societal acceptance of the working fate of indigenous children. The traditional focus on poverty also risks ignoring the broader socioeconomic processes through which poverty was created in the first place. For indigenous peoples and their organizations, the question of ancestral lands is unavoidably part of the answer to the problem of poverty.

Ancestral Lands and Dispossession

Indigenous peoples have a special attachment to their ancestral lands and territories. On the one hand, they play a fundamental role for indigenous and tribal cultural identities, cosmologies and spiritual beliefs. On the other hand, indigenous peoples are deeply dependent on the land and resources through highly adapted livelihood systems and practices. This has been recognized in ILO Convention 169, which recognizes the right of ownership and possession of indigenous and tribal peoples over the lands they traditionally occupy. However, many communities can be found today working as cheap or even bonded, landless labourers on their own ancestral lands.

Whether dealing with education, child labour or processes of social exclusion among indigenous peoples, there is considerable emphasis on land exclusion as a major problem and on recognition of land rights as the required way forward. This is one of the key issues in which it is also apparent how child labour and other forms of indecent work among indigenous peoples are linked to global economic processes of marginalization and exploitation. Indigenous and tribal ancestral lands continue to function as unexploited frontiers for commercial agriculture, large-scale development, mining and land-settlement schemes.

While there has been some progress, land rights remain a highly contested field. Even in countries with progressive legislation, indigenous communities face considerable challenges in terms of protecting their traditional territories against encroachment, industrial exploitation and dispossession. Crawhall has identified land and resource loss as one of the major threats to language and cultural diversity. While they may not be obvious, there are clear-cut links between livelihood loss and reduced knowledge of surrounding environments. Both socio-cultural disintegration and livelihood loss are intimately linked with high levels of child labour. The case of the Manobo in the Philippines illustrates this point.

Displacement of tribal communities in India by large development projects, mining operations, denial of traditional forest rights and land encroachment by commercial agriculture has intensified within the last few decades. This has been reported as a direct factor in increasing debt-bonded labour in several areas compared to the "pre-relocation" period.

There is also increasing documentation from India that many migrants working in bonded-type situations in both cities and rural areas are from tribal communities dispossessed from their traditional lands and livelihoods. While Adivasis account for eight percent of the total population, it is estimated that they account for between 40 and 50 percent of displaced people. According to information from Andra Pradesh, 90 percent of children being sold for adoption come from hamlets relocated from traditional lands as a result of the construction of the Nagarjunsagar Dam.

In a study entitled "Exploitation of child labour in tribal India" that focuses on the state of Orissa, the author underlines the role of British rule leading to processes of exploitation and land alienation through land settlement schemes for non-tribal people and revenue schemes. Subsequent laws passed to prohibit land transfer came too late. Another example is that of the Tharu in the Terai region of Nepal, who, due to their high resistance to malaria, were used as labourers to clear traditional forest areas for agricultural and further outside settlement – thus becoming the "instruments of their own marginalization" and leading the way towards debt-bondage. Not surprisingly, the most exploitative cases have been found among kamaiyas who were both landless and indebted.

The result has been a growing indigenous and tribal peasantry in Latin America and Asia, landless or with very small plots, working as agricultural labourers, migrant workers or trying their luck in cities. With market fluctuations and the lack of viability of more diversified livelihood strategies, vulnerability has escalated considerably. Whether speaking of tribal children in India seeking low-income seasonal employment or urban migrant children in Central America, the lack of basic food security and long-term perspectives for their lives is a common problem. Statements from indigenous peoples continuously raise the disastrous results of displacement and dispossession. There is a clear need for innovative approaches seeking to integrate ancestral land concerns into child labour elimination efforts.

LACK OF DEMOCRATIC PARTICIPATION

Lack of democratic participation continues as a major root cause leading to social exclusion. Democratic participation, respect for customary institutions and the right of indigenous and tribal peoples to decide on their own priorities, as underlined in Convention No. 169, are fundamental rights and ingredients of healthy governance practices and decision-making processes. Nevertheless, they are continuously ignored and violated in many fora and institutions. Whether one speaks of destructive dam projects, land grabbing, imposed education or development solutions, the disregard for customary institutions and other representative organizations is a common experience.

A number of indigenous peoples, including those in areas such as Thailand and Central Africa, lack citizenship, national identity cards, or basic civil rights. It is calculated that around 70 percent of the almost 800.000 hill tribe people in Thailand do not have citizenship. From Central Africa to South and Southeast Asia, the lack of citizenship poses serious obstacles to accessing government services such as education and health facilities, property rights and minimum wages. For example, in the Nepalese Government's rehabilitation efforts, land distribution required individuals to have identity cards; however, well into the distribution process, many had still not received them, thus hampering their rehabilitation considerably.

The link between these and child labour issues was highlighted by an IPEC trafficking project in Southeast Asia. In Northern Thailand, in particular, ethnic minority girls and women were identified as a target group for trafficking aimed at commercial sexual exploitation and housework. Lack of citizenship was accentuated as a clear push factor.

A major issue in terms of democratic participation and citizenship rights – and one that links closely to education and language issues – is the extent to which indigenous languages are used in administrative and day-to-day matters. In some countries, such as Norway and Finland, indigenous languages are recognized as official languages in certain municipalities, providing people with the right to obtain public services in their own language. In other countries, this may informally be the case in areas where indigenous peoples form the majority. In most cases, high rates of illiteracy in national languages prevent effective use of public services.

Practical ways of working with indigenous peoples involve safeguard mechanisms and consultation practices to address their specific concerns in policy initiatives, capacity building and direct support activities. The elaboration of national strategies, action plans and targeted initiatives on child labour involves research, stakeholder consultations and rapid assessments, which may benefit considerably from the effective participation of customary institutions and other representative organizations. These are fundamental steps if the excluded are to be included.

DISCRIMINATION

Discrimination against indigenous peoples was widely recognized in the declaration and programme of action adopted in Durban in 200110 and represents a fundamental root cause when discussing child labour. Negligence and ignorance render indigenous and tribal children and their conditions invisible in public debates, policy and project approaches.

Beyond the often urban or semi-urban focus of researchers, there is an even more common tendency to "forget" indigenous areas or simply consider them too far away for the researchers to easily access. Such negligence may in some cases be linked to official policies arguing against the use of "indigenous" and "tribal" terminology, viewing its use as a post-colonial effort to undermine national unity through "divide and rule" tactics.

In many African countries, the use of ethnic criteria is seen as contradictory to broader efforts at healing and reconciliation. In both Asia and Africa, the "we are all indigenous" argument is frequently raised by governments. Such statements, however, do not change the fact that indigenous peoples suffer from discrimination and similar processes of historical marginalization and dispossession, confirming the relevance of the principles and rights at stake.

Those Batwa who manage to find the money and are admitted to school frequently suffer discrimination, teasing and bullying. Their lunch boxes may be examined by other pupils to see if they are eating taboo foods. In many cases other children will not play with Batwa, nor eat or sit with them at lunchtime. Once in the classroom pupils from other ethnic groups will refuse to share a school bench with them. Many schools have special benches exclusively for Batwa students, where they often sit three or four instead of two to a bench as other children do.

It is not uncommon to find arguments referring to socio-cultural practices of child labour to justify the failure to provide these children with any education whatsoever. According to this kind of thinking, indigenous and tribal children are not children with rights, but different – not children with the right to be different, but children who are stigmatized as inferior and therefore not in need of education.

Stereotypical images may portray indigenous and tribal children as culturally more inclined towards work than education. In India, it has been suggested that the institutionalized discrimination against children of lower social strata through government education policies is a major factor leading to high levels of child labour.

Girl victims of trafficking in Nepal, meanwhile, may pretend they are low-caste in order to avoid being beaten by police officers. Society may tolerate prostitution and trafficking among low-caste girls, but others are judged as acting "immorally". Such forms of discrimination are part of the "natural order" of differences. As Bindman notes in relation to the high levels of prostitution of Taiwanese indigenous peoples, there is a perception that "indigenous peoples are culturally inferior and have physical rather than intellectual natures." While it is true that many indigenous children do in fact work as part of growing up and learning in their communities, one must be extremely careful in taking such "cultural" explanations at face value. The frequent citation of customs and traditional attitudes as explanatory causes behind child labour is often contradicted by documentation of communities undergoing profound changes and disruption. On the contrary, discriminatory practices may be firmly rooted in legal institutions and practices.

A common example of discrimination concerns the non-recognition of indigenous peoples' right to self-definition. In many cases, national definitions tend to exclude or not sufficiently accommodate indigenous criteria. One example of this is the use of blood criteria, as with the Bureau of Indian Affairs in the US, which requires individuals to prove 50 percent of a federally recognized tribal bloodline in order to be eligible to benefit from certain schemes as "indigenous". In some cases in Africa or Asia, indigenous peoples are simply not recognized at all. In terms of addressing child labour and education, this has profound implications on the creation of a policy foundation for bilingual education and on funding priorities as well as for reaching consensus on grassroots needs. Moreover, even where constitutional measures are in place, this is no guarantee that appropriate laws will be enacted or that legal regimes will actually lead to increasing tolerance.

In 1987, the Sub-Commission on Prevention of Discrimination and Protection of Minorities came out with a comprehensive report on discrimination against indigenous peoples. In terms of education, the conclusions were clear:

— The right of indigenous populations to education has not been duly guaranteed and is not really observed.

— States frequently do not recognize traditional indigenous education based on autochthonous educational processes and often deliberately aim at doing away with it and replacing it by formal, alienating processes.

— Although there has been a significant improvement in the effective access of indigenous persons to public education of all kinds and at all levels, such education continues to be characterized to a greater or larger extent by a marked tendency to deprive indigenous pupils of everything indigenous.

— This unmitigated aggression against indigenous culture and life-style can in no circumstances be justified, particularly in contexts and environments of cultural and linguistical pluralism, which States nowadays espouse, or to which they at least pay lip service.

The need to address discrimination as a root cause behind child labour and poor education performances among indigenous peoples cannot be overemphasized. Similarly, the recognition of their distinct identities, concerns and rights represents a crucial step in eliminating and preventing child labour.

The principle of non-discrimination in the CRC is clearly relevant here. It should be noted that as part of state-party reporting procedures for the CRC, there has been continuous discussion of indigenous children, particularly in the Latin American context.

The Committee on the Rights of the Child has on several occasions noted the presence of widespread discrimination against indigenous children and their lack of access to information and economic, social and cultural rights as principal subjects of concern. The general lack of disaggregated data on indigenous children has also been noted on several occasions. As global efforts focus on child labour and push for the development of legal regimes addressing the rights of the child, the likelihood of exploitative child labour increasingly moving into the grey zone is unavoidable.

CHILDREN AND YOUTH SUPPORT INTERVENTIONS

An education initiative can both enhance cultural revitalization and social empowerment, as it can lead to cultural disintegration and alienation.

As is repeatedly noted by the Committee on the Rights of the Child, national authorities rarely maintain sufficient data on indigenous children. International organizations typically have a number of flagship programmes specifically targeting indigenous children, but mainstreaming continues to be a challenge.

As part of the IPEC programming cycle, a considerable number of rapid assessments and studies identify ethnic composition. For example, a study on trafficking in girls in Nepal identified "hill ethnic groups", particularly the Tamang, as the major high-risk group. Conversely, a study of child domestic workers in Panama that took into account ethnicity found indigenous children comprised only a relatively small percent compared to mestizo children (8% and 80%, respectively). Employers reportedly found indigenous children "too backwards" and often preferred not to contract them.

Ethnic composition is not a static factor, but one that typically evolves. In many urban areas indigenous youth and children are increasingly part of the urban child labour picture. Issues that previously concerned only one group are increasingly touching broader segments of the population. In the case of girls trafficked in Nepal, for example, the phenomenon has spread beyond the Tamang in Nuwakot and Sindhupalchowk and is now found increasingly among broader sections of Nepalese society.

Disaggregating data according to ethnicity is increasingly acknowledged as a fundamental step in analyzing child labour. Baseline studies and rapid assessments from Latin America, for example, have provided a more detailed picture of ethnicity of child labourers. However, to what extent this identification actually leads to the elaboration of adapted strategies and initiatives is questionable. While it is clear that participatory methods are often applied, the extent to which specific approaches and mechanisms are included to directly ensure the integration of indigenous concerns is less evident. In other words, projects may identify distinctive communities, but may not necessarily elaborate specific approaches.

There is a need to strengthen capacity building of relevant government agencies in dealing with indigenous and tribal peoples' concerns. This could involve raising awareness on the principles of Convention 169 and its application in this context as well as developing workshops for more specific problem identification and solution.

EXPLORING APPROPRIATE EDUCATION MODALITIES

The elimination of child labour in part depends on the quality and relevance of educational services. In removing children from work, there is always a risk that they will return to other, more hazardous forms. As an alternative to the frequently failing formal school system, the provision of non-formal education (NFE) has been a common feature in indigenous areas.

A number of NFE initiatives have had considerable success in terms of attendance as well as in building literacy and numeracy skills. In such cases, success factors include the necessary flexibility in terms of curriculum design and school attendance modalities.

Formal education is inherently too stiff and rigid to respond to the needs of indigenous and tribal children. Others argue that formal education should not be pursued blindly as the only solution, but should be considered as a key option along with other, more specifically focused, education and training options that offer the flexibility needed.

NFE allows too much laxity and results in the provision of lowquality education, particularly when it replaces formal efforts. A major problem remains that NFE may not qualify the child to take up other education or vocational training opportunities afterwards. Such dangers are not least present under the umbrella of decentralization efforts in the education sector, which risk reinforcing disinterested local bureaucracies and result in lack of uniformity in terms of teaching quality.

Although NFE is often considered to be a transitional phenomenon, the flexible approaches developed under NFE may very well be institutionalized and adapted as part of a less rigid model of formal education. A recent analysis undertaken by an IPEC initiative against trafficking in the Mekong region in Southeast Asia highlights the vast pool of NFE experiences in that area in targeting particular sub-groups such as ethnic minorities. It includes a number of good practices in adapting NFE to the specific needs of child labourers.

More important than whether the provision of education is strictly formal or non-formal are a number of key elements such as community ownership, locally-adapted curriculum, use of local languages and teacher incentives and training. The goal is to reach unified government-funded education systems, which recognize indigenous rights to quality education through a number of key elements such as community ownership and locally-adapted curriculum.

MULTICULTURAL EDUCATION

In the wake of the broader recognition of indigenous rights, "bilingual," "multicultural" and "inter-cultural" education have become frequently evoked terms. Many education policies now speak of multiculturalism, although the actual implications on the ground are not always as evident as the overall political message. Actual programmes may be transitional, maintenance-oriented, enriching or restorative. While the former aims at assimilating minority languages, the latter three, respectively, describe efforts to maintain language skills, affirm cultural identities and revitalize languages.

Opponents to the new tendency see bi-lingual education as further burdening the already constrained situation of ITP education rather than in fact seeing it as part of the solution. This despite that research shows the importance of initial Mother Tongue education, indeed as the language of instruction, in fact enhances the capability of children to proceed with a second language.

Bi-lingual education is not a question of establishing a different parallel system to the national mainstream education system. Rather it provides a key resource for empowering ITP children to reaffirm their cultural identity and language in order to take on board the national language and engage in the national education system if they so wish.

"Bilingual education" was initiated in 1937 in Mexico and in the 1950s in some other Latin American countries, mainly by missionaries from the Summer Institute of Linguistics. Early bilingual efforts were often seen as transitory efforts to overcome "the problem of unilingualism" among communities that had not yet mastered the national language.

The bilingual strategy centred mainly on teaching Spanish and translating key religious texts into indigenous languages to facilitate proselytization. In contrast, there is now broad understanding that language learning should not take place to the detriment of the mother tongue and their cultural heritage as such Most indigenous peoples go even further and seek to promote education on their own terms.

In 1970, for example, the American Indian Movement (AIM) organized a parallel system of education to that of the Bureau of Indian Affairs, which it considered too Eurocentric in terms of the historical vision, culture and values being promoted. Similarly, bilingual education initiatives are key activities of newly formed indigenous organizations in Asia and Africa.

In Guatemala, bilingual education dates back to 1965, and following constitutional recognition in 1985 an administrative structure was established for the provision of bilingual education. USAID-funded research showed that girls in one bilingual education programme had a higher sixth-grade completion rate than girls in rural schools without a bilingual curriculum.

According to anthropologists who visited bilingual primary school areas in the 1970s, most parents expected children to leave school after three or four years (less for girls). When the same communities were re-visited in the

1990s, interviews revealed that parents believed children should remain in school longer due to the improvements in the educational services provided.

Decreasing drop-out rates, increased proficiency in Spanish and academic performance were among the noteworthy results. Positive attitudes from parents have particularly been linked to improved performance in Spanish. This confirms the relevance of a pedagogie convergente, which recommends the introduction of a second language only once a child is literate in the first.

In 1994, the Bolivian Education Reform Law recognized the importance of interculturalism and bilingualism for the national education model. Several international institutions have been involved in training of trainer activities and in producing materials in Quechua, Aymara and Guarani.

The Brazilian Education Act affirms the indigenous right to bilingual and multicultural education. Actual implementation has been undertaken mainly by indigenous organizations, NGOs, progressive missions and universities, together with some state departments.

In Thailand, INDISCO collaborated with IMPECT, a hill tribe organization, in strengthening approaches to indigenous-driven curricula among three selected groups: the Lahu, Mien and Hmong. The process was followed up at the policy level to explore ways of further integrating indigenous-driven curriculum development into the formal school system. This created a unique opportunity for dialogue between government agencies and indigenous representatives. The goal is now to ensure that an appropriate policy environment is combined with adequate institutional and budgetary means to mainstream the approach in hill tribe areas.

The use of new technologies has also met with some degree of success. In particular, the use of radio and, more recently, video and Internet school programmes has facilitated indigenous-driven education in countries like Bolivia, Ecuador and Mongolia.

Practical experiences with bilingual education processes show that:

— they are time-intensive, but not prohibitive.

— they require pragmatic, linguistically founded choices between different dialects.

— investment in local language leads to greater student participation, improved learning, greater school achievement, cultural preservation and self-confidence.

Costs involved in bilingual education vary according to a number of factors:

— costs to produce language materials,

— development, standardization and universalization of local language orthography,

— development of curriculum,

— availability of experts in the local language,

— time taken to build consensus on materials to be published,

— programme development costs,

— development and reform of national education and language policies,

— specialized teacher training and development of pedagogical material and

— testing, validation, monitoring and revision costs.

One study from Guatemala showed that bilingual education resulted in an increased cost of nine percent over the Spanish-only system. In fact, although bilingual education is initially somewhat more costly, there are considerable gains in terms of school performance, and, in the long run, the comparative cost drops as materials are reproduced. Still, cost estimates will vary considerably, depending on the scope of the education programme. In Norway, Sámi receive education in the indigenous language throughout the first 10 years, while in Sweden and Finland it is only offered as a medium of instruction for the first six years.

Despite considerable education reform and dozens of bilingual multicultural projects in Latin America, full coverage is a long way off. Inter-cultural bilingual education takes time to flesh out in practice, with the process of consulting, drafting and validating teaching material often taking several years. Ensuring a pool of trained (and certified) indigenous teachers goes even further into the future.

Many initiatives remain in a pilot stage, and others receive only lip service. In Guatemala, critical voices note that there is an overemphasis on bilingual education, and that intercultural programmes reach only a limited number of schools and are not fully integrated. Training of bilingual teachers still lags behind in many countries, and actual government commitment to multicultural education policies remains piece-meal in several countries.

There is also fear that decentralization efforts will result in budget constraints and secondrate education services in indigenous areas. Furthermore, there is a clear danger of limiting multicultural education to a question of promoting bilingualism or simplifying cultural or livelihood curricula to only a subsection of "typical" traditional livelihoods. The risk of indigenous knowledge ending as a static, folkloric picture is in that case probably even more dangerous than had it been left out of the school system in the first place.

There is no blueprint for such efforts. Some groups prefer education only in the lingua franca of their country, while others seek various forms of bilingual or even trilingual education. There is now a broad consensus in the education community that using mother tongue is the primary language of instruction significantly enhances the learning capacity of the child. Emphasis may be on formal types of education, national curriculum or informal knowledge transmission.

Opportunities may exist for strengthening traditional forms of education and knowledge transmission that are linked closely with traditional livelihoods and indigenous knowledge systems and practices. These should be considered on an equal basis with access to formal education when discussing priorities with indigenous communities and organizations.

The link between livelihoods and education is not new. Indeed, most child labour initiatives seek to integrate economic rehabilitation measures and skills training with education. The case of indigenous peoples is unique in terms of the linkages between traditional forms of education, indigenous territories and livelihoods.

Still, even adapted education efforts do not provide a panacea to the problems leading to child labour or poor educational performance among indigenous children. The processes of marginalization leading to the vulnerability of indigenous children are manifold. Therefore, it is all the more important that bilingual or multicultural efforts are firmly anchored in a rights-based approach.

Although technical language issues are of paramount importance, there is also a need to emphasize the significance of cultural identity issues that are not easily captured by a "technical, grammar-oriented vision of education." This involves not only what is taught, but a number of "who, when, where and how" questions that relate to whether the socializing character of education forms or deforms cultural identity.

Traditional knowledge and oral means of knowledge transmission have often been marginalized or simply ridiculed as folklore. Attempts to simplify this knowledge in a "comprehensive" local curriculum rarely succeed. Indigenous peoples have continuously highlighted the fact that books and formal education cannot replace other forms of - knowledge transmission. What is needed is a more inclusive learning environment and teaching structure rather than a simple addition to existing curricula.

Some indigenous peoples show no interest in the formal integration of indigenous languages into the school curriculum. Rather, learning the indigenous language is seen as a home affair, whereas the national language is what they aim to learn in school. Reversing the segregationist policies of the colonial experience remains a priority. Still, there may be differences in opinion between parents seeking "the best" for their children and children preferring the easier learning environment provided by education in their mother tongue. Evaluations highlighting such differences continue to remain scarce.

Experiences point to the fundamental importance of vernaculars as the language of instruction, particularly at the primary school level. Furthermore, there is a fear that traditional forms of knowledge transmission and livelihoods are manipulated to justify the continuous lack of primary and secondary education services in indigenous or tribal areas. At the policy and budgetary levels, such notions may have considerable impact on the allocation of resources.

Although there are indeed other ways of sensing, experiencing and learning about the world, multicultural education is very much about bridging the gap between indigenous concerns, rights and resources and the national education agenda. Multicultural education involves more than just bilingual education and has practical implications for content, teaching practice and even classroom design. In Mongolia, a recent attempt to establish mobile pre-school units has been successful in using the traditional gers as training centres during the summer. Teachers are nomads as well, moving with their families and stock together with a group of households involved in the pre-school education programme.

In India, the Rural Litigation & Entitlement Kendra (RLEK), together with the Van Gujjars (indigenous forest nomads) in Uttaranchal, has devised an innovative approach whereby local teachers migrate with the community and implement a culturally adapted curriculum.

There is a critical need for a more holistic approach that takes multicultural education beyond the language agenda. This will involve multicultural education breaking the cultural domination of national education authorities and empowering communities to strengthen, implement and control their own visions of educational programmes and practices. However, while innovative teaching methods such as bilingual and multicultural education seem to be dramatically changing the education landscape, new education modalities are not miracle solutions to the massive challenges faced in terms of land and resource loss and degradation. An indigenous child may improve his or her educational performance through bilingual education, only to be considered a more interesting candidate on the child labour market.

While new approaches to education may avoid old problems, they cannot alone change the broader socio-economic processes leading to increased migration, language loss or livelihood disintegration. Such processes require a scope of activities extending beyond the realm of education. At the same time, if education is considered to be an empowerment strategy, it would seem that raising awareness of basic rights and social exclusion processes would form core elements of education efforts.

Teacher Incentives and Training

In most indigenous areas, a lack of teacher availability remains a chronic problem. In Greenland, for example, the Teacher College in Nuuk has yet to graduate sufficient numbers of teachers to cover the need for teaching in the mother tongue. Many Danish teachers have thus been hired over the years, with accompanying problems in terms of language and cultural barriers. Other solutions have involved hiring part-time teachers without sufficient training. However, experience shows that being an indigenous or tribal person does not make one a bilingual teacher.

The picture is similar in many other countries, where the best alternatives are sought through non-formal education, teacher certification schemes and incentive measures. Training material and programmes are critical for ensuring that the needed skills are present in the community. For outsiders, a teaching position in an indigenous area is often considered to be a temporary "hardship" post. In the worst cases, teachers are poorly motivated, poorly qualified and have few incentives to stay in the area. Moulton sums up three major challenges for rural schools: producing qualified teachers, deploying them to rural schools and giving them professional and sometimes moral support.

For indigenous peoples looking among their educated youth for teachers, the critical challenges usually involve securing appropriate qualifications. For others, the challenge is one of identifying appropriate pre-service training and sensitization arrangements to guide the teacher into the area. The resource issue is again important in terms of actual incentives provided to youth to continue teaching in rural areas.

Given the challenges faced by indigenous as well as non-indigenous teachers, a number of countries have initiated training and incentive measures to improve teacher capacity and conditions. A number of countries in Latin America run certification and diploma programmes on intercultural bilingual education.

Unfortunately, in most countries, the demand for indigenous teachers well exceeds the numbers available. While some countries are seeking to increase the pool of available teachers through teachers colleges, affirmative action policies and other incentive measures, it is also clear that there is a consistent need and potential to mobilize the broader teaching community in assessing the situation and developing appropriate responses. In this respect, a 1998 resolution from Education International included activities for establishing indigenous education committees, promoting indigenous rights and determining the quality needs of indigenous education.

Poverty Alleviation and Community Development

Poverty alleviation has been and remains a crucial weapon against child labour. However, experience shows that poverty alleviation measures may actually perpetuate child labour through failed income-generation initiatives that indebt households and increase dependency on the meagre income of children. Poverty alleviation measures may even lead to increased workloads of children in small-scale enterprises, home-based industries and similar schemes.

An analysis that emphasizes poverty levels alone may easily replace one linking land encroachment and disintegrating traditional livelihoods with increases in child labour. The tendency to focus on an individual child or household may lead to the neglect of collective concerns at the community level. Because resulting interventions often fail to address the real root causes, the presence of child labour persists.

It is assumed that social and economic mechanisms such as the introduction of high-yield cash crops, the provision of loans or financing of road construction that have been successful elsewhere will function similarly among indigenous communities. While the first two schemes, in some cases, have indebted people considerably, the latter has often opened up indigenous areas for further land encroachment and settlement.

There is good reason to believe that projects to combat child labour run the same risk, unless proper voice is given to indigenous peoples and their children. In contrast, encouraging trends are emerging that involve indigenous organizations and integrate their issues and concerns into national programmes. Terms such as "ethnodevelopment" and "indigenous-driven development" have been applied to describe indigenouscontrolled and -managed development based on the visions of indigenous peoples and their representative institutions. While they do not offer quick-fix, miracle solutions, they do present an alternative agenda.

Initial rehabilitation efforts for ex-bonded labourers and their children in India have involved the provision of stand-alone grants or loans to individuals. In many cases, these have proven insufficient for people to gain independence, and in some cases they have left children even worse off than before. In Taiwan, China "social workers continue to comment on the difficulty of keeping girls in rehabilitation projects: in fact most leave to return to the sex industry." Indeed, the extent to which individual or household-based strategies alone can be effective in combating child labour is questionable.

In contrast, efforts to support self-help and cooperative organizations have shown some level of success. An illustrative case is that of the Paraja in the Indian state of Orissa. At one time shifting cultivators, these tribal groups were dispossessed of their lands and forced into bonded labour.

In the mid-1980s, with the help of AGRAGAMEE, a local NGO, one bonded labourer was freed and provided with two buffaloes under a government rehabilitation scheme. This led other bonded labourers to come forward, and, with the help of AGRAGAMEE, form a milk cooperative that both secured higher benefits and provided a collective stronghold against threats from the previous landlords.

In comparison to stand-alone individual-based schemes, self-help organization offers the means to empower poorer segments of indigenous communities to collectively build alternative and more independent livelihoods. Another interesting case, from Uttar Pradesh in India, involves Sankalp, an NGO that supported self-help organization of tribal mine workers in forming worker cooperatives and applying for mine leases as a tool against child and bonded labour.

Based on the observation that families were bonded to mining contractors, the NGO facilitated economic empowerment of parents in order to end child labour. By March 2001, 40 self-help organizations had been supported, three of which had obtained mining leases, and all children affected by the project were reportedly attending school. Other groups without leases have squatted on mining areas, claiming the existing leases were illegal. The social mobilization efforts in these areas have resulted in children being sent to school and adults starting up their own literacy classes. Self-help organization has also led to increased village control of schools in efforts to counter absenteeism.

In both Orissa and Uttar Pradesh, a major success criterion was the ability of indigenous and tribal communities to act collectively to solve what essentially constituted collective problems, or at least those issues that exceeded the capacity of empowered individuals or households acting on a more individual basis. The issue of land is indeed such an issue. Furthermore, eroding land, resource and food security may be identified as fundamental root causes of child labour among indigenous peoples.

Recognition of indigenous and tribal land rights remains a complicated field in terms of its technical, economic and political dimensions. It is therefore important to ensure that these rights and concerns are safeguarded and that best practices are promoted to the greatest extent possible. With certain schemes as the frequently employed cash compensation, however, rights are often neglected, with alarming social impacts as a result. Further harmful examples include resettlement initiatives that focus on the allocation of small, privately owned plots, thus eliminating important collective resources and potentially putting further pressure on children as incomegenerators.

The most encouraging results come from integrated "ancestral domain" initiatives, where collective rights over ancestral lands and resources are recognized by government agencies. Importantly, this model is generally accompanied by the strengthening of traditional decision-making bodies and organizations. The ILO INDISCO experience in the Philippines showed that this approach considerably enhanced the potential and, gradually, the capacity of indigenous communities to respond and solve collective problems.

This is of crucial importance to child labour initiatives, as the tendency has indeed been to focus on household needs and strategies rather than broader community needs and potential for action. It cannot, however, be assumed that securing customary rights will enhance the protection of child rights. As elsewhere, indigenous communities are made up of diverse opinions, and particular attention must be paid to the voices of the children. It is important to ensure that the rights of children, who may very well have different priorities than those expressed by male elders or women's groups, are highlighted in general policy and project approaches.

One emerging model for successful indigenous-driven development processes involves the integration of ancestral domain management into initiatives for empowerment through education, capacity building and skills training. Convention No. 169 provides an overall procedural framework by which to integrate these disparate issues. Using this framework for targeted child labour-related activities presents several advantages:

It provides an international consensus-based model for recognizing indigenous peoples as rights-holders.

— It underlines indigenous peoples as the main actors in their own affairs.

— It delivers an integral model covering the key issues at stake.

A Rights-based Approach

Indigenous peoples have continuously stressed the need for a rights-based framework that recognizes their rights as outlined in Convention No. 169 as well as in a range of other rights instruments and statements. The advantage of a constitutionally recognized rights-based approach is clear. In Honduras, for example, it was only after the ratification of Convention No. 169 in 1994 that an agreement was signed between the indigenous confederation and the government, a technical unit established and general guidelines issued on intercultural education.

Various international instruments provide legal provisions for the protection of children of indigenous peoples. Articles 17, 29 and 30 of the CRC refer specifically to the individual rights of indigenous and tribal children. Article 17 promotes access to media and information in indigenous and tribal languages. Article 29 emphasizes the need for education to respect cultural identity, language and values in a tolerant environment.

Furthermore, Article 30 specifically notes that:

In those States in which ethnic, religious or linguistic minorities or persons of indigenous origin exist, a child belonging to such a minority or who is indigenous shall not be denied the right, in community with other members of his or her group, to enjoy his or her own culture, to profess and practise his or her own religion, or to use his or her own language.

For indigenous children, the relevance of the broader principles and articles of the CRC goes beyond specific references.

A number of ILO instruments complement the CRC in promoting a rights-based approach to indigenous children. The ILO Declaration, containing eight fundamental ILO Conventions, cements the elimination of child labour as a fundamental right. Conventions No. 138 and 182 provide strong instruments in the fight against the worst forms of child labour based on a broad international consensus. Article 7 of Convention No. 182 specifically requires member states to "identify and reach out to children at special risk" when ensuring "effective implementation and enforcement of the provisions."

Conventions No. 107 and 169 are the only internationally recognized binding instruments to deal specifically with the rights of indigenous and tribal peoples. Convention No. 169 contains core principles for respecting indigenous and tribal peoples' cultures, their distinct ways of life and their traditions and customs within a rights-based framework.

ILO Convention No. 169 includes a number of general principles and specific articles with relevance for child labour and education. First of all, the Convention provides appropriate processes for governments to work with and respect the rights of indigenous and tribal peoples. Part VI of Convention No. 169 (articles 26 to 31) deals with education in far greater detail than the CRC. It emphasizes equal access, the right to establish educational institutions and the right to participate in the formulation and participation of educational programmes. Being taught to read and write in indigenous languages as well as national language(s) is also emphasized, together with broader awareness raising activities within the surrounding society.

General principles on consultation and participation substantially complement the individual-based CRC in recognizing the need for free participation and consultation with representative institutions (article 6). Article 7 underlines indigenous and tribal peoples' right to set their own priorities for the development process.

Additionally, Convention No. 169 provides normative directions for addressing some of the root causes behind child labour. For example, it delineates appropriate practices related to land rights, employment and social security, the application of which provide key benchmarks in challenging the institutionalized discrimination of indigenous and tribal peoples.

It may be argued that there is a danger of the individual-oriented CRC clashing with the group-oriented ILO Convention No. 169 (Cohen 1999). On the contrary, the respect for cultural diversity and customary institutions, which are central tenets of the Convention, should not be conflated with arguments justifying worst forms of child labour as culturally acceptable.

First of all, the Convention clearly notes that customs to be respected may not be incompatible "with fundamental rights defined by the national legal system and with internationally recognized human rights" (article 8). Secondly, most cases in which "culture" or "customs" are used to explain worst forms of child labour involve outsiders attempting to justify discriminatory practices such as child labour as being culturally more appropriate for tribal children than education. Thirdly, informal training and education in traditional occupations should not a priori be looked upon as child labour.

While some traditional occupations may, in fact, overlap with the worst forms identified by the ILO and prevent children from receiving proper education, the vast majority of traditional occupations are of fundamental educative importance and do not as such exclude further education. This puts them in line with the definition of "light work" that does not hinder the child from accessing appropriate education.

Beyond offering broad support to state ratification, promoting a rights-based approach to indigenous and tribal children involves putting this bundle of rights into concrete practice. A rights-based approach supports child labour and education initiatives in the wider context of indigenous-determined and -managed development planning. It can, for example, lead to the mainstreaming of appropriate consultation measures into sectorspecific decision-making processes.

Although many countries with indigenous peoples have enacted constitutional or legislative measures related to their collective concerns, there remains considerable potential for improving relevant educational policies as well as their implementation. This may involve facilitating the recognition of indigenous institutions in planning educational services to establish specific guidelines for curriculum development. It may involve communities assessing teacher-training facilities, promoting favourable conditions for teachers in remote areas and strengthening certification schemes for indigenous teachers. The critical question is how to integrate the rights-based approach at several levels, ranging from everyday management and consultation issues to broader programming and policy-level exercises.

Promoting rights at the national level remains a complex issue. Legal or constitutional measures have in very few cases been sufficient to fully protect indigenous rights or prevent child labour. Securing actual rule of law, effective judiciary mechanisms, state accountability and broader awareness are typically beyond the scope of individual initiatives. Public policies may not last longer than one governmental administration. Furthermore, intercultural education may at times be considered an "expensive" solution. This confirms the need for a high degree of vigilance when international organizations promote the rights-based approach. The nuts-and-bolts of the processes as well as a clear picture of the consequences need to be worked on.

In connection with legal provisions prohibiting child labour, the immediate dangers have been particularly clear. While prohibition of various forms of child labour have marked important milestones in combating child labour overall, they have also raised the danger of failing to ensure child protection and food security in the aftermath of such prohibition. The results have sometimes been contrary to the protective intentions, criminalizing or punishing children who work(ed) without providing alternative education and training opportunities.

ILO technical cooperation has played a pivotal role in moving the agenda. From a narrow legal perspective, the ban marked a key benchmark; however, a rights-based approach involves moving beyond policy action and supporting states in putting rights into practice.

Article 12 of the CRC guarantees children a say in deliberations on issues that affect them. ILO Convention No. 169 recognizes the right of indigenous peoples to determine their own future. Still, there is a long way to go in terms of securing indigenous participation in the control and management of education institutions and programmes in most countries. While there are examples of "First Nations control", indigenous education councils and other forms of participation, they remain for most countries relatively compartmentalized experiences influencing only a small number of communities.

A key challenge involves mainstreaming such practices beyond the lifetime of international projects or programme support interventions. In Bolivia, for example, indigenous peoples' councils have an influence on educational authorities through their rural municipalities. In other cases involving decentralization efforts or regional autonomy decisions, there is considerable potential to support "home grown" and sustainable processes of participation and consultation. One issue would be to critically assess the growing number of NGOs that have been handed over responsibility for implementing educational programmes in indigenous and tribal areas.

Indigenous peoples are emerging as important actors in the civil society arena. It is noteworthy that the number of indigenous organizations in Brazil increased from four in the mid-1980s to 290 as of April 1999. Obviously, non-registered, "informal" organizations were not listed, but the number is still significant: Indigenous organizations are here to stay. However, the majority of projects underway in Brazil still depend on strong external assistance from professionals, university researchers, missionaries and non-Indian indigenous specialists, whose motivations and training vary greatly.

The question of ownership is thus critical. In terms of government commitment, the presence of specialized agencies or technical units on issues of multicultural education, for example, may indeed facilitate the recognition and implementation of indigenous peoples' rights. Since April 2001, the Government of Peru has reopened the Dirección Nacional de Educación Bilingüe

Intercultural, conceived as the normative institution for integrating bilingual and multicultural education at all levels in the Peruvian education system. While such institutions are important partners in terms of strengthening policy approaches and government capacity, they cannot replace consultation with indigenous and tribal communities and their representatives. Furthermore, it is important to recognize the limits to the resources and activities of such institutions.

Involving indigenous children, particularly child labourers, in these consultation processes is of paramount importance. However, this may pose considerable problems that are not necessarily encountered in mainstream society. In many cases, public dialogue and discussion will be the domain of elders. While the voices of women may be heard, children may not be permitted to speak, or their voices may not be considered relevant. Alternatively, a broader tolerance and "ear" to children's voices may also be encountered.

Iindigenous organizations should not necessarily be considered representative of their communities, and in particular, not of the working children. As elsewhere, there may be powerful groupings or individuals who dominate the public debate and representative institutions through networks and contacts. Parents and children may even perceive child labour and education in very different manners. The need for a critical consultation phase is evident. There is a need to better understand what kinds of light work are acceptable and what is to be considered as harmful forms of child labour. A high degree of cultural sensitivity is needed to ensure constructive dialogues on education and child labour aspects of customary livelihoods.

Discussing issues such as child labour, education-related problems and human trafficking in public may not be considered appropriate. The difficulty may be compounded by the perception that this is yet another "critique" or stigmatization of indigenous communities. Furthermore, the tendency of government agencies, international organizations and researchers to look at the "problems" and ignore indigenous resources can generate resistance. Indeed, addressing the child labour and education challenges of indigenous peoples in most cases requires continuous follow-up, dialogue and innovation that stretches well beyond the typical life-time of international support.

6

Right to Education

The right to education has several different facets, both quantitative and qualitative.

Article 26 of the Universal Declaration of Human Rights states that:

1. Everyone has the right to education. Education shall be free, at least in the elementary and fundamental stages. Elementary education shall be compulsory. Technical and professional education shall be made generally available and higher education shall be equally accessible to all on the basis of merit.

2. Education shall be directed to the full development of the human personality and to the strengthening of respect for human rights and fundamental freedoms. It shall promote understanding, tolerance and friendship among all nations, racial or religious groups, and shall further the activities of the United Nations for the maintenance of peace.

3. Parents have a prior right to choose the kind of education that shall be given to their children.

Articles 13 and 14 of the International Covenant on Economic, Social and Cultural Rights (1966) are given below:

Article 13

1. The States Parties to the present Covenant recognize the right of everyone to education. They agree that education shall be directed to the full development of the human personality and the sense of its dignity, and shall strengthen the respect for human rights and fundamental freedoms. They further agree that education shall enable all persons to participate effectively in a free society, promote understanding, tolerance and friendship among all nations and all racial, ethnic or religious groups, and further the activities of the United Nations for the maintenance of peace.

2. The States Parties to the present Covenant recognize that, with a view to achieving the full realization of this right:

   (a) Primary education shall be compulsory and available free to all;

   (b) Secondary education in its different forms, including technical and vocational secondary education, shall be made generally available and accessible to all by every appropriate means, and in particular by the progressive introduction of free education;

(c) Higher education shall be made equally accessible to all, on the basis of capacity, by every appropriate means, and in particular by the progressive introduction of free education;

(d) Fundamental education shall be encouraged or intensified as far as possible for those persons who have not received or completed the whole period of their primary education;

(e) The development of a system of schools at all levels shall be actively pursued, an adequate fellowship system shall be established, and the material conditions of teaching staff shall be continuously improved.

3. The States Parties to the present Covenant undertake to have respect for the liberty of parents and, when applicable, legal guardians to choose for their children schools, other than those established by the public authorities, which conform to such minimum educational standards as may be laid down or approved by the State and to ensure the religious and moral education of their children in conformity with their own convictions.

4. No part of this article shall be construed so as to interfere with the liberty of individuals and bodies to establish and direct educational institutions, subject always to the observance of the principles set forth in paragraph 1 of this article and to the requirement that the education given in such institutions shall conform to such minimum standards as may be laid down by the State.

Article 14

Each State Party to the present Covenant which, at the time of becoming a Party, has not been able to secure in its metropolitan territory or other territories under its jurisdiction compulsory primary education, free of charge, undertakes, within two years, to work out and adopt a detailed plan of action for the progressive implementation, within a reasonable number of years, to be fixed in the plan, of the principle of compulsory education free of charge for all.

Article 28 of the Convention on the Rights of the Child (1989) states that:

1. States Parties recognize the right of the child to education, and with a view to achieving this right progressively and on the basis of equal opportunity, they shall, in particular:

   (a) Make primary education compulsory and available free to all;

   (b) Encourage the development of different forms of secondary education, including general and vocational education, make them available and accessible to every child, and take appropriate measures such as the introduction of free education and offering financial assistance in case of need;

   (c) Make higher education accessible to all on the basis of capacity by every appropriate means;

   (d) Make educational and vocational information and guidance available and accessible to all children;

(e) Take measures to encourage regular attendance at schools and the reduction of dropout rates.

2. States Parties shall take all appropriate measures to ensure that school discipline is administered in a manner consistent with the child's human dignity and in conformity with the present Convention.

3. States Parties shall promote and encourage international cooperation in matters relating to education, in particular with a view to contributing to the elimination of ignorance and illiteracy throughout the world and facilitating access to scientific and technical knowledge and modern teaching methods. In this regard, particular account shall be taken of the needs of developing countries.

When the Universal Declaration of Human Rights was drawn up, only a minority of the world's young people had access to any kind of formal education, let alone a choice among different kinds, and little more than half of the world's adults could read and write a simple passage about their everyday lives. For those who drew up and adopted the Declaration, it was vital to ensure first that access to and participation in education should be universal: 'Education shall be free, at least in the elementary and fundamental stages', and 'Elementary education shall be compulsory'. At the same time, 'Technical and professional education shall be made generally available and higher education shall be equally accessible to all on the basis of merit'.

Educational opportunities have greatly increased in the years since the Declaration was proclaimed. A majority of the world's young people now go to school, and participation in formal education beyond the elementary and fundamental stages has expanded. Four out of five adults in the world today are estimated to have at least some simple literacy skills. Although the absolute number of illiterate adults in the world is larger than it was in 1948, it is now estimated to be falling, and the percentage of illiterate adults in every region of the world has significantly declined. Despite these advances, it is uncertain how much real progress has been made. The problem is not just one of assessing trends in opportunities for access to education. The right to education was conceived from the beginning as having a qualitative as well as a quantitative aspect.

'Education shall be directed to the full development of the human personality and to the strengthening of respect for human rights and fundamental freedoms', proclaims the second paragraph of Article 26. 'It shall promote understanding, tolerance and friendship among all nations, racial or religious groups and shall further the activities of the United Nations for the maintenance of peace'. How well have these purposes been fulfilled? Are people's literacy skills, for example, whether in industrial or developing countries, adequate to enable them to participate fully in the political, economic, social and cultural life of their society? And what of 'tolerance and friendship among all nations, racial or religious groups'?

Memory of the abuse of education for the purposes of political propaganda and stirring up racial and national hatreds in the period before the Second World War was still fresh when the Declaration was drawn up. How much better is the situation today? Are schools doing all that they can to counter problems of social exclusion and discrimination? In sum, mere access to education still leaves open the question of whether the education is directed to good purposes, for the individual and society.

Education is coming to occupy an ever larger place in people's lives as its role among the forces at work in modern societies increases. There are several reasons this. The traditional division of life into separate periods – childhood and youth devoted to schooling, adulthood and working life, and retirement – no longer corresponds to things as they are today and corresponds still less to the demands of the future.

Today, one can hope to amass during his or her youth an initial fund of knowledge which will serve for a lifetime. The swift changes taking place in the world call knowledge to be continuously updated, and at the same time, the initial education of young people is tending to become more protracted. A shorter working shorter working hours and a longer expectancy of after retirement are also increasing the time available for other activities.

Education, too, is changing fast. More and more opportunities for learning out of school are occurring all fields, while skills, in the traditional sense of the term, are giving way in many modern sectors of activity to the ideas of developing competence and adaptability. The traditional distinction between initial education and continuing education therefore needs to be reconsidered.

Continuing education that is really in harmony with the needs of modern societies can no longer be defined in relation to a particular time of life (adult education as opposed to the education of the young, for instance) or to too specific a purpose (vocational as opposed to general).

The time to learn is now the whole lifetime, and each field of knowledge spreads into and enriches the others.

Today education is so varied in its tasks and forms that it covers all the activities that enable people, from childhood to old age, to acquire a living knowledge of the world, of other people and themselves. A key to the new millennium, learning throughout life will be essential for adapting to the evolving requirements of the labour market and for better mastery of the changing time-frames and rhythms of individual existence.

Every person – child, youth and adult – shall be able to benefit from educational opportunities designed to meet their basic learning needs. These needs comprise both essential learning tools (such as literacy, oral expression, numeracy, and problem-solving) and the basic learning content (such as knowledge, skills, values and attitudes) required by human beings to be able to survive, to develop their full capacities, to live and work in dignity, to participate fully in development, to improve the quality of their lives, to make informed decisions, and to continue learning. The scope of basic learning needs and how they should be met varies with individual countries and cultures, and inevitably, changes with the passage of time.

The satisfaction of these needs empowers individuals in any society and confers upon them a responsibility to respect and build upon their collective cultural, linguistic and spiritual heritage, to promote the education of others, to further the cause of social justice, to achieve environmental protection, to be tolerant towards social, political and religious systems which differ from their own, ensuring that commonly accepted humanistic values and human rights are upheld, and to work for international peace and solidarity in an interdependent world. Another and no less fundamental aim of educational development is the transmission and enrichment of common cultural and moral values. It is in these values that the individual and society find their identity and worth.

Basic education is more than an end in itself. It the foundation for lifelong learning and human development on which countries may build, systematically, further levels and types of education and training.

The international community's commitment to implement the rights and freedoms set out in the Universal Declaration, i.e. to adopt measures designed to ensure their effective recognition and observance, has over the years taken various forms ranging from international treaties to internationally agreed Programmes and Frameworks for Action. The most important are the multilateral treaties. The Universal Declaration itself, although of historic importance in setting out standards of achievement in human rights, does not have the force of law. It is not a treaty but an internationally endorsed statement of principles. The transformation of the principles into treaty provisions establishing legal obligations on the part of each ratifying state was undertaken in two covenants prepared after the Declaration was adopted: the International Covenant on Economic, Social and Cultural Rights, and the International Covenant on Civil and Political Rights.

In contrast to the preparation of the Declaration, the preparation of the Covenants was a much longer process undertaken over a period of eighteen years. The two

Covenants were adopted by the United Nations' General Assembly in 1966, but another ten years were to pass before a sufficient number of States (thirty-five) had ratified them to bring them into force, i.e. make them legally binding on the ratifying States.

The right to education is dealt with in Articles 13 and 14 of the International Covenant on Economic, Social and Cultural Rights, and is also mentioned in Article 18(4) of the International Covenant on Civil and Political Rights. The latter affirms the 'liberty of parents and, when applicable, legal guardians to ensure the religious and moral education of their children in conformity with their own convictions', as stated in paragraph 3 of Article 13 of the International Covenant on Economic, Social and Cultural Rights.

Besides the Covenants, which together aim at a comprehensive coverage of the rights and freedoms set out in the Universal Declaration, a large number of other international treaties have been adopted over the years in regard to specific rights, or specific aspects of some or all of the rights, e.g. the Convention on the Elimination of All Forms of Discrimination against Women (1979). The five principal international treaties relating directly to education are:

- International Covenant on Economic, Social and Cultural Rights (1966);
- Convention against Discrimination in Education (1960);
- Protocol Instituting a Conciliation and Good Offices Commission to be Responsible for Seeking the Settlement of any Disputes which may arise between

States Parties to the Convention against Discrimination in Education (1962);

— Convention on the Rights of the Child (1989); and

— Convention on Technical and Vocational Education (1989).

While the number of countries which have ratified a given treaty can be taken as a fair measure of the international community's overall degree of 'commitment' to its provisions, it should be noted that the ratification process allows countries, if they wish, to include with their instruments of ratification a formal declaration on how the country intends to interpret one or more of the treaty's provisions, or alternatively a reservation that it does not intend to implement one or more provisions at all. For example, in respect to Article 13 of the International Covenant on Economic, Social and Cultural Rights, Ireland made the following Reservation:

— Ireland recognizes the inalienable right and duty of parents to provide for the education of children, and, while recognizing the State's obligation to provide for free primary education and requiring that children receive a certain minimum education, nevertheless reserves the right to allow parents to provide for the education of their children in their homes provided that these minimum standards are observed.

— In regard to the same article, Japan indicated that it 'reserves the right not to be bound by "in particular by the progressive introduction of free education"

> referred to in the said provisions', while Zambia indicated that although it 'fully accepts the principles embodied in the same article and undertakes to take the necessary steps to apply them in their entirety, the problems of implementation, and particularly the financial implications, are such that full application of the principles in question cannot be guaranteed at this stage'. With particular reference to paragraphs 3 and 4 of Article 13, the government of the former People's Republic of the Congo declared: 'In our country, such provisions are inconsistent with the principle of nationalization of education and with the monopoly granted to the State in that area'.

Nevertheless, the number of States which have made formal interpretative Declarations and/or Reservations in regard to Article 13 and/or Article 14 of the Covenant is relatively minor: 16 out of a grand total of 139 ratifying States.

Ratifying the Covenant or any of the other treaties is one thing; concrete measures by countries to implement their provisions is another matter altogether. With the exception of the special case of the UNESCO Protocol, each of the treaties provides for a procedure or mechanism to monitor implementation: basically the submission of periodic reports by countries to the United Nations or UNESCO, as the case may be, on the measures taken to implement the provisions of the treaty in question. In the case of the Covenant, for example, the national reports are examined by the Committee on Economic, Social and Cultural Rights of the United Nations' Economic and Social Council (ECOSOC).

The effectiveness of the monitoring is highly dependent on the quality of the national reports submitted by countries. There are no sanctions of course for failure to implement the treaties. Nevertheless, the monitoring bodies can exert moral pressure on countries by issuing reports and making recommendations. The ECOSOC Committee mentioned above, for example, has also developed the practice of periodically issuing General Comments on the implementation of particular Articles; a General Comment in regard to Article 13 was issued in 1999 (General Comment No. 13, The Right to Education [Article 13 of the Covenant], United Nations, Economic and Social Council, Committee on Economic, Social and Cultural Rights, Twenty first session, 15 November–3 December 1999, Document No. E/C.12/1999/10). In addition, the United Nations' Commission on Human Rights – the body which originally drafted the Universal Declaration – decided in 1998 to appoint for a period of three years a Special Rapporteur on the right to education, with the mandate specifically 'to report on the status, throughout the world, of the progressive realization of the right to education', as well as to carry out several other tasks.

Besides these official monitoring arrangements, it also remains open to individual citizens in each ratifying country, depending on the legal system in the country, to challenge their own State on noncompliance with the provisions of a given treaty if they believe that to be the case. In countries with highly developed legal systems, as in Western Europe for example, there now exists a substantial body of case law in regard to the right to education. All these considerations point to the need for caution in taking the ratification of a given treaty as a clear signal of 'commitment' – in other than a legal sense – to implement its provisions.

In addition to treaties, countries have adopted many other forms of commitment to implementation of the right to education or particular aspects of it, ranging from agreed Recommendations of international conferences of States. While the Recommendations formally agreed by international conferences of States do not have the legally binding force of treaties, they are normally adopted by consensus on the understanding that States will make best efforts to implement their provisions.

ROLE OF EDUCATION IN PROTECTING CHILDREN IN CONFLICT

A child's right to education is enshrined in a number of declarations and conventions. The Universal Declaration of Human Rights of 1948 outlines the right to free, compulsory elementary education, and states that education should work to strengthen respect for human rights and promote peace. Parents have the right to choose the kind of education provided to their child.

The Fourth Geneva Convention of 1949 states that, in situations of military occupation, the occupying power must facilitate institutions devoted to the care and education of children. Protocol I states that schools and other buildings used for civil purposes are guaranteed protection from military attacks. Protocol II states that children shall receive an education in keeping with the wishes of their parents.

The rights of refugee children are protected in the 1951 Convention Relating to the Status of Refugees, which guarantees the right to elementary education, and states that they should be accorded the same opportunities as nationals from the host country. Beyond primary school, refugee children are treated as other aliens, allowing for the recognition of foreign school certificates and the awarding of scholarships.

The Convention on the Rights of the Child of 1989 calls for states to make primary education compulsory and free to all, and to encourage the development of accessible secondary and other forms of education. The Convention mandates an education that builds on a child's potential and supports their cultural identity. The Convention emphasises psychosocial support for conflict-affected children, and outlines the principle of non-discrimination, including access for the disabled, gender equity and the protection of the linguistic and cultural rights of ethnic minorities. The Convention also protects a child's right to recreation and culture.

The Rome Statute of 1998 outlining the legal jurisdiction of the International Criminal Court (ICC) includes protection for educational institutions under Article 8, which covers war crimes. The ICC protects against 'intentionally driven attacks against buildings dedicated to religion, education, art, science, or charitable purposes'.A number of regional agreements also address issues of education. References to the right to education are found in the Protocol to the European Convention for the Protection of Human Rights and Fundamental Freedoms (1952); the American Declaration on the Rights and Duties of Man (1998); and the African Charter on the Rights and Welfare of the Child (1999).

Education has also been subject to a series of international conferences and agreements. In 1990, the

World Conference on Education for All (EFA) in Jomtien, Thailand, agreed to universalise education and reduce illiteracy. Aggressive targets were set aimed at achieving universal basic education by the end of the decade. The global commitment to basic education was revisited ten years later, at the World Education Forum in Dakar, Senegal. When considering EFA, the Forum's 1,100 participants clearly meant education that went beyond merely formal schooling. Thus, according to the Dakar Framework for Action, delegates committed themselves and their governments to:

— 'expanding and improving comprehensive early childhood care and education, especially for the most vulnerable and disadvantaged children;

— ensuring that by 2015 all children, particularly girls, children in difficult circumstances and those belonging to ethnic minorities, have access to and complete free and compulsory primary education of good quality;

— ensuring that the learning needs of all young people and adults are met through equitable access to appropriate learning and life skills programmes; achieving a 50% improvement in levels of adult literacy by 2015, especially for women, and equitable access to basic and continuing education for all adults; eliminating gender disparities in primary and secondary education by 2005, and achieving gender equality in education by 2015, with a focus on ensuring girls' full and equal access to and achievement in basic education of good quality; and improving all aspects of the quality of education and ensuring excellence of all so that recognised and measurable learning outcomes are achieved by all, especially in literacy, numeracy and essential life skills'.

Education in emergencies is primarily carried out in situations where children lack access to their national and community education systems due to the occurrence of complex emergencies or natural disasters. Because modern conflicts are chronic and recurring, the sector tends to use the word 'emergency' in its broadest sense, encompassing not only the first days or months after an event, but also the effort to deal with the on-going effects of the crisis, and reconstruction.

Within the context of EFA, emergency education does not negate states' responsibility to educate their people; rather, it provides the space for the international community to assist where the government is unable or unwilling to provide education.

Attacks on schools are one of the most easily quantifiable ways of gauging the effect of a conflict on education. During 2001, for instance, Israeli soldiers shot at nearly 100 schools in the Occupied Territories, using rubber bullets, live ammunition and tear gas. Another 71 schools came under attack through tank shelling or rockets fired from helicopters.

In East Timor, the violence of September 1999 destroyed between 80% and 90% of school buildings and related infrastructure. Iain Levine, Chief of Humanitarian Policy at UNICEF, suggests that such attacks can occur because education represents state authority; in some circumstances, such as in southern Sudan, schools along with health centres may be the only public buildings in rural areas which can be targeted.

The impact of conflict on education may also be felt more indirectly, as part of a wider pattern of disruption and dislocation and the effects of state collapse. The Machel study notes that formal education is at risk during war 'because it relies on consistent funding and administrative support that is difficult to sustain during political turmoil. During the fighting in Somalia and under the Khmer Rouge regime in Cambodia, public expenditure on education was reduced to nearly nothing'. In Mozambique, wartime damage to schools left two-thirds of the country's two million primary-school children with no access to education.

Children's reduced enrolment and attendance at schools is another potential measure of conflict's impact on education. Emily Vargas-Baron of the RISE Institute claims that, of the approximately 115m children worldwide who are out of school, a large majority are living in nations affected by complex crises. The Oxfam Education Report states that two-thirds of countries in Africa that are experiencing or recovering from conflict have enrolment rates of less than 50%. Just 3% of refugee adolescents –some 50,000 children – attend anything beyond primary school.

For internally-displaced children, the prospects can often be worse; access to education in parts of Angola, the Democratic Republic of Congo, Somalia and southern Sudan are minimal. In Somalia, it is estimated that only 9% of school-age children are attending school.

Detailed information in areas of conflict is rarely available, and these figures should be treated with caution. Enrolment ratios are based on comparisons of registered children against often inaccurate figures of the numbers eligible for schooling.

Moreover, they give a poor reflection of actual attendance patterns. Existing measures of the impact of conflict on education also say nothing about quality. Where children in areas of conflict are lucky enough to go to school, their learning is often hindered by trauma or hunger, untrained or ill-prepared teachers, or the lack of sufficient learning materials and infrastructure. Even when officially open, schools can be closed down periodically, and days and terms can be shortened.

In a review exploring wars' effect on global attempts to achieve EFA, Marc Sommers, a research fellow at Boston University, concludes that imprecise data 'presents a serious constraint on the ability to accurately estimate war's impact on education systems, administrators, teachers and students'.

While education is generally considered a force for good, conflict can distort its benefits and introduce additional risks. Schools may not always be safe: for example, Chechen schools have been bombed during class hours because they were deemed to be sheltering military targets, and grenades have been thrown into classrooms.Teachers too may be at risk; in Colombia and Sudan, teachers have been threatened and killed.

Education may be connected to recruitment by facilitating access to children; in southern Sudan, for instance, schools have been used as a convenient way of assembling young men for military service. In the Democratic Republic of Congo (DRC), schools have been a common site of child recruitment by Rwandan-backed rebel groups. Propaganda teams from the Liberation Tigers of Tamil Eelam (LTTE) in Sri Lanka have positioned recruitment booths near schools, and used street theatre to induce children into joining the military.

In northern Uganda, fighting forces have kidnapped schoolchildren directly from classrooms. One rebel group in Burundi abducted more than 150 students from two schools in November 2001, setting fire to several classrooms as they did so. The prospect of education may itself serve as a rationale for joining an armed group. In southern Sudan during the 1980s, boys were lured hundreds of kilometres from their homes by promises of education, only to find that the 'schools' promised to them were also military training camps.

The stress that conflict places on communities can make the school environment itself more threatening. Corporal punishment, for instance, seems to become more common in schools during times of conflict. While teachers in many countries may see caning and slapping as an appropriate disciplinary tool, war can exacerbate its use as teachers take out their frustrations and stress on their pupils.

In conflict areas of West Timor, Buton and Ambon, for example, teachers' use of physical punishment, ridicule and humiliation to control and discipline children appears to be connected to the stresses they themselves experience.The risk of violence or abuse in an educational context may be particularly acute for girls; in West African refugee camps, teachers regularly ask female students for sexual favours in exchange for good grades.

In Kosovo after 1999, fear of rape or abduction kept many Kosovar minority children, especially girls, away from school. The broader economic pressures people affected by conflict face may also inhibit schooling.War-affected children from the most economically disadvantaged backgrounds are discouraged from attending school due to the expense. In extreme cases, such as the exploitation found in West Africa, young people may deliberately put themselves at risk, for example through prostitution, to pay school fees. Even when officially 'free', hidden costs remain, such as for uniforms, books and transport.

Survival pressures may cause children to be removed from school and set to productive work; girls may be married off earlier than usual, or parents may be forced to exclude one child from school for the sake of the education of other family members. Bedreldin Shutta of Save the Children recounts one instance in Sri Lanka where a mother reported that she would not hesitate to encourage her elder child to join an armed group if it meant money to pay for the education of her two remaining children.

In societies in conflict, education systems may themselves be politicised. A UNICEF study highlights a variety of ways in which education can be manipulated to the detriment of children:

— the uneven distribution of education as a means of creating or preserving positions of economic, social and political privilege;

— education as a weapon in cultural repression;

— the denial of education as a weapon of war;

— education as a means of manipulating history for political purposes;

— education as a means of diminishing self-worth and encouraging hate;

— segregation in education as a means of ensuring inequality and inferiority; and

— using textbooks to inhibit children from dealing with conflict constructively.

Thus, during the crisis in Rwanda and Burundi education was used to heighten ethnic tensions between Hutu and Tutsi, conditioning the population to accept ethnic discrimination and propagating a culture of mutual fear and pre-emptive self-defence. In Serbia, the education system was used to subjugate the Kosovar Albanians; in Sri Lanka in the 1970s and 1980s, government textbooks presented Tamils as the historical enemy of the Sinhalese.

Governments may deliberately block access to education for certain groups. In the mid-1990s, for example, the Zairean government sought to prevent Rwandan refugees from having access to schooling. Many young Palestinians in schools in Lebanon have a 'distorted and unclear perception' of their own history because curricula are required to teach from a Lebanese perspective.

In recent years, protection has occupied an increasingly important position on the humanitarian agenda, with agencies going 'beyond the conventional view of how people are dying, to embrace how people are living'. This humanitarian concern for protection arose out of the horrors of the 1990s: ethnic cleansing in Bosnia, the Rwandan genocide, atrocities in Sierra Leone. Since then, humanitarians have begun to explore what kinds of practical actions can be taken to protect civilians both from physical harm, and from wider violations of their human rights.

Children constitute a particularly vulnerable group in times of war by virtue of their dependence on adult care. Conflict and displacement can present particular threats, such as separation from family, abduction or recruitment by fighting forces, or exposure to targeted violence or landmines. At the same time, pre-existing threats, such as sexual or gender-based violence, labour exploitation or malnutrition and disease,may increase.

Efforts to protect children in times of war date back to the early years of the twentieth century; in 1924, for instance, the League of Nations adopted the Geneva Declaration on the Rights of the Child. Today, the standards for child protection during times of conflict are largely based on the Convention on the Rights of the Child (1989) and its Optional Protocols (2000); the Convention Relating to the Status of Refugees (1951) and its Protocols (1967); and the Geneva Conventions (1949) and Additional Protocols (1977).

Declaration of Human Rights (1948) and the subsequent International Covenant on Civil and Political Rights and the International Covenant on Economic, Social and Cultural Rights (1966). Regional instruments such as the European Convention on Human Rights (1950) also make specific reference to children. Following Machel's landmark UN study in 1996, a number of key initiatives have been taken.

— The appointment in 1997 of a Special Representative of the UN Secretary-General for Children and Armed Conflict.

— The UN's adoption of the CRC's Optional Protocol prohibiting the participation in hostilities of those below 18 years of age.This was spearheaded by the Coalition to Stop the Use of Child Soldiers, a network of humanitarian agencies.

— High-level meetings to focus attention on the plight of children in war, such as the Oslo/Hadeland

Conference 'Protection of Children and Adolescents in Complex Emergencies' in 1998 and the 'International Conference on War-Affected Children', held in Winnipeg, Canada, in 2000.

— Action for the Rights of the Child (ARC), a rights-based training initiative by UNHCR, Save the Children, the UN High Commissioner for Human Rights (OHCHR) and UNICEF, which has developed a series of resource packs on conflict-affected children's rights and needs.

— The Watchlist on Children and Armed Conflict, an NGO initiative that prepares reports on the situation of children in specific conflicts, and makes recommendations to UN and international actors to improve child protection.

— A set of Inter-agency Guiding Principles on Separated Children developed by the Working Group on Separated Children, as a means to strengthen the tracing and reuniting of separated children.

— The Sphere Project, which has established minimum standards in disaster response as a way to improve the quality and accountability of humanitarian action. The particular needs of children are being incorporated as a cross-cutting sector in current revisions.

— A number of innovative agency-based initiatives, including the Emergency Stand-by Teams of Save the Children Sweden and Norway, and the Norwegian Refugee Council (NRC); UNICEF's Child Friendly Spaces initiative; and the series of participatory adolescent field studies led by the Women's Commission for Refugee Women and Children.

In practice, children's protection is variously seen as a legal, social and physical concern. Defining its scope beyond the legal framework is, however, difficult. In an external evaluation of UNHCR's efforts to protect refugee children, for instance, there was confusion among staff as to what child protection meant, and what the agency's policy actually entailed. Few written definitions of child protection exist.

The Oslo/Hadeland Conference described the international protection of children and adolescents as 'the gamut of activities through which ... rights are secured by the international community'. Save the Children has developed a draft definition of child protection as 'action to prevent or address harm caused to children because their rights to security, survival or development are threatened –directly or indirectly – by the acts of third parties, including armed groups'.

Child protection is a continuum.At one end lie efforts to address violations of a child's rights, such as tracing and reuniting separated children, demobilising child soldiers and ensuring that schools are safe zones for children. Other protection activities focus on securing governmental and community respect for children's rights through training, advocacy and strengthening local mechanisms of enforcement and dissemination.

These activities are often combined with the delivery of assistance and services to address gaps in the rights of specific groups, such as girls, minorities and children with disabilities. Protection-related elements are often included in these activities, but not as their primary aim.

Within the international humanitarian community, there are increasing calls for education to play a role in enhancing child protection, both as a service to be supported and delivered, and as an 'enabling right' which assists children in accessing their other rights. The Oslo/Hadeland conference on child protection in November 1998 claimed that 'Experience shows that education has a preventive effect on recruitment, abduction and gender based violence, and thereby serves as an important protection tool'.

In UNHCR's Global Consultations on International Protection, education is similarly described as 'an important protection tool'. Materials produced by the ARC declare that education has a 'direct protection function in monitoring the development and progress of children.'

Certain aspects of education can inherently protect children: the sense of self-worth that comes from being identified as a student and a learner; the growth and development of social networks; the provision of adult supervision and access to a structured, ordered schedule. Maintaining education and its 'built-in' protective components can thus provide vital continuity and support for children living through crisis.

At the same time, education can offer an adaptive response, addressing some of the particular conditions that arise from conflict. Thus, teaching in a conflictaffected environment can pass on potentially lifesaving information, or impart basic skills in literacy and numeracy that may be crucial to a child's survival.

Child-focused humanitarian activity in conflict situations tends to assist a relatively limited number of children most affected by the crisis.Vulnerable groups might include child soldiers, separated children, children living on the streets, the sick or malnourished, those with a disability and child-headed households.

The urgency of their predicament, along with their high profile and discrete numbers, makes them an appealing focus. However, efforts that target vulnerable groups without taking into account the needs of their peers tend to create inequity and foster resentment. Jane Lowicki of the Women's Commission for Refugee Women and Children points out, for example, that in Sierra Leone a number of demobilisation projects have provided free education to former child soldiers. Non-combatant young people who are not able to attend school seem to resent this; they see themselves as the real victims and as more deserving.

The international community is increasingly aware that all children living in the midst of war are vulnerable and need protection. Schools and recreational activities can bring some elements of physical protection to the majority of children – providing a safe place to play, offering an alternative to destructive behaviour, giving access to nutritious meals or providing regular adult supervision.

For children who have been especially victimised by the conflict, coming together for educational activities may make it easier to identify those needing special help, and programmes can be tailored to their specific needs. Follow-up work to find children who do not attend school will further aid in identifying the at-risk, while education staff from the community can be invaluable in identifying children facing threats due to separation from their families, susceptibility to military recruitment or experience of sexual exploitation.They will also understand the impact of gender, ethnicity or disability on children in their own community.

In terms of a child's psychosocial health, education offers a regular routine, opportunities for self-expression and the chance to engage with peers. The very status of 'student' can be valuable, protecting a child from forced recruitment, or bolstering a sense of identity and inclusion; in Liberia, for instance, former combatants sought to attend school to redefine themselves as something other than soldiers.

By gathering children together, education programmes can support socialisation, establish peer networks and encourage children to understand and accept views other than their own. Regular routines enhance children's development and assist in their recovery from conflict.

Education activities are important in establishing daily schedules that create a familiar and comfortable rhythm and establish a sense of structure and purpose. For families, schooling provides a schedule for the week, while also marking special times such as weekends, holidays and school breaks.A child's attendance at school also grants parents the time and space to rebuild their livelihoods, re-establish sources of income, or simply come to terms with their experiences.

School attendance also encourages children to regain some hope in the prospect of a better future. Goals such as completing homework, preparing for exams or completing a school certificate, regular assignments and tests and rewards such as gold stars and celebrations at the end of term provide children with achievable short-term and long-term objectives. These can be essential when finding a reason to continue the struggle to live in a conflict-affected society. This sense of hope can extend into a child's relationship to the community.

During conflicts, children lose the sense of what it means to be a good citizen and how to live in a non-confrontational way. In places where war has lasted for years, some children will never have seen how a stable family or community functions. Education can respond to this need through building children's skills in listening, problem-solving and conflict resolution.

Instruction also transmits vital basic skills, such as literacy and numeracy and the capacity for critical thinking, as well as imparting important information. In circumstances of crisis, academic learning is not a luxury. Knowing how to read, write and do basic maths is essential for children in protecting themselves.

Reading skills enable children to gather information about their environment – whether from signs, newspapers, health brochures or medicine bottles. Writing skills enable children to sign for services and write letters seeking assistance. Children may need basic mathematical skills to manage their household's flow of money.

Children and adolescents in war do not see themselves as passive victims, but as 'active survivors of experience.' Every day, children make decisions about what is in their best interests based upon their knowledge and life experience. Deciding to volunteer for the military or to venture into a heavily landmined area may be logical decisions, based on need.

Children's responsibilities can also extend to caring for younger siblings, especially when separated from their parents. Providing children with accurate information from sources that they can trust strengthens their ability to cope with conflict at a practical level, to analyse situations and make decisions. In crisis situations, thousands of children fall victim to dangers which simple health and hygiene education could have prevented.

In most cases, these children are living in a new environment; they do not know the location of landmines, the importance of immunisation or hygiene or how to minimise the risk of a disease like HIV/AIDS and cholera. They might not understand the consequences of sexual activity or drug use. Education in schools is one of the most practical means of conveying the kind of messages that enable children to make safe decisions.

7

Child Development

Developmental psychologists and policy researchers alike think of the child as the locus of development. But others have begun to focus more on the contexts provided to children. For example, among the rights listed in the United Nations' Convention on the Rights of the Child is an obligation of the state to provide assistance to parents, such as income supports, child care services, children's health care services, and education.

A consortium of state policymakers recently brought together to select a common set of indicators to evaluate welfare reform also focused on contexts, nominating outcomes that included many aspects of children's environments, such as reduced child poverty and adequate housing. Such indicators reflect the view that a policy's effects on the home environment, for example, are as relevant as effects on a child's school performance. These contrasting perspectives illustrate the multiple and sometimes contradictory criteria and objectives for public policies affecting children.

The most reasonable approach to assessing the impact of welfare and income support policies on children would keep various objectives in balance:

— emphasizing a child's present well-being as well as his or her future as an adult;

— considering a child's well-being as well as his or her productivity;

— expecting policies to promote positive development as well as prevent harm; and

— defining child outcomes to include healthy contexts as well as skills and behaviours.

Following are the goals for healthy child development:

— Health and physical comfort, including shelter, nourishment, freedom from pain and abuse, and medical care.

— Family or adults who care, are reasonably constant and reliable, and who provide love and encouragement. Consistency of care givers and settings.

— Development of intellectual and other capabilities to their fullest, such as language skill; school achievement; and skill in athletics, music, or art.

— Emotional well-being and mental health, including self-worth, sense of personal control, and freedom from depression and anxiety.

— Skills in relating to others, both adults and peers, including, for example, assertiveness without violence, sociability, cooperation, understanding others' perspectives, complying with adult expectations, and leadership.

— Responsibility and morality, including the ability to guide one's own behaviour and act in accord with societal standards of right and wrong.

— In adulthood, ability to support self and family, be a good parent, contribute to society, be mentally and physically healthy, and not commit crimes or abuse substances.

Changes in employment, resources, and family structure are likely in turn to influence children's physical and material environment, family environment, and child care, school, neighbourhood, and community environments. Environmental contexts and child characteristics are both potentially important, albeit indirect, outcomes of public policy directed at families. Environmental contexts that support a decent quality of life can be justified on that basis alone, but they are also important because they can affect children's physical, intellectual, and socioemotional development. Random-assignment experiments, which randomly assign some participants to the program and others to a control group have established the causal influences in some instances-that is, whether the context affects the child, the child affects the context, or both are caused by other factors. But it is also recognized that children often play a role in both selecting and responding to available contexts, and they in turn are influenced by their experiences. Thus, most current child development theories maintain that effects on children and context are bidirectional-that is, they are mutual and intertwined.

There are three key elements contribute to a healthy physical and material environment for children:

— an adequate standard of living (particularly sufficient food, clothing, and housing);

— health care services, including prevention and treatment (such as immunization); and

— safety from injury, violence, and environmental hazards.

The physical and material environments that poor children experience are often characterized by hardship, hunger, homelessness, exposure to toxins and other dangerous substances, exposure to violence and other hazards to physical safety, and inadequate preventive health care. When families and communities do not have-or do not provide-the necessary preventive resources, children are at greater risk of injuries, failure to thrive, mortality, untreated medical and dental conditions, and health problems such as asthma. Policies that improve family income or provide assistance with food, housing, and child care increase families' material resources. Income is often used as a proxy for material resources, but it is not a direct index of the material goods and services available to children. Although intensive qualitative interviews with mothers living in poverty show that most families budget money in ways that will benefit children, families vary in how much of their income they spend on children.

For healthy development, children need adult family members and other adults who are mentally healthy, responsible, constant, and reliable to provide them with love and encouragement. The parent-child relationship should be characterized by warmth, open communication, and firm (but not harsh) discipline. And children benefit when both parents assume responsibility for their emotional and financial support.

Welfare and income support policies that change parents' employment status, family resources, and family structure could affect children's home environments by changing parents' time at home, parents' personal sense of well-being, and the relationships among family members. Experimental evidence has shown that the quality of the home environment can be improved by interventions that teach mothers about child rearing, but no evidence documents the effects of interventions less directly focused on child rearing.

In the very large amount of research relating parenting and the home environment to children's cognitive and intellectual development, some consistent patterns have emerged. First, although children who develop strong intellectual skills also tend to demonstrate positive social and emotional behaviour, the home and family characteristics associated with intellectual versus social development are somewhat different. For infants and preschool children, the cognitive and social environment provided in the home predicts children's language development, intelligence, school readiness, and school achievement in reading and math, even when controlling for numerous other family and demographic characteristics. Maternal intellectual ability also is a strong predictor of children's academic performance, a finding that suggests both genetic and environmental contributions to a child's performance.

Children's social behaviour and emotional well-being are more strongly related to the quality of parent-child interactions, and less strongly to income and cognitive environment. Maternal depression is associated with behavioural problems much more consistently than with problems in cognitive or intellectual functioning, probably because of its effects on parenting practices. Children and youth who demonstrate positive social behaviour and low levels of psychological distress perceive their relations with parents positively, and they tend to have mothers who are warm and who avoid harsh punishment.

Young people who engage in deviant and delinquent behaviour tend to have parents who provide low levels of supervision, monitoring, and control. Virtually all of this literature is subject to some methodological problems that should be of concern in evaluating policy effects. First, links between parent and child characteristics are probably due, at least in part, to genetic similarities. Second, children's behaviour elicits and influences parenting and parent well-being as well as responds to it, so the association of parent and child behaviours probably indicates bidirectional causation.

For example, in one recent series of studies, better "outcomes" were found among adolescents whose parents monitor their whereabouts. Investigators argue persuasively that these outcomes are not due to parents' vigilant supervision, but instead are due largely to the fact that better-adjusted adolescents volunteer such information about their whereabouts. Finally, in many of the studies evaluating welfare policies, children's social behaviour is measured by maternal report only, so the measure reflects the mother's reaction to the child as well as the child's behaviour.

Child care, schools, out-of-school activities, mass media, social supports, and neighbourhoods are sources of formative experiences for children in general. Such resources may be especially important for children with a single, employed parent. Research suggests that healthy development can be promoted by child care that is reliable, safe, and of high quality; by education and out-of-school activities appropriate to a child's ability and culture; and by neighbourhood and communities that are safe and that have resources for serving children. From the time children are infants through their school-age and teen years, the environments they experience while their parents work can play an important role in their development. The impact of these policies depends on the age of the child, and the quality, type, and stability of care. Even very young children are now spending a large amount of time in child care.

Current welfare policies permits states to require parents' participation in work-related activities when children are infants, leading to concerns that a mother's time away from her infant will interfere with early development of a positive mother-child relationship and a secure attachment. Some evidence suggests that mothers who return to work very early in their infants' lives or whose infants have extensive early child care are less sensitive to their children than are their counterparts. Maternal sensitivity is associated with the development of secure attachments for infants, but there is little evidence that time with a child per se affects the development of secure attachment.

An abundance of evidence shows that high-quality child care—care that provides intellectual stimulation, social involvement of adults with children, and language interactions-can have a positive influence on Children's intellectual development, particularly among children in low-income families. Longitudinal, correlational studies consistently show a relationship between high quality of care and small but significant gains in children's cognitive and language development, even with controls for demographic characteristics and parenting behaviour.

These results could be due to unobserved characteristics that differentiate families who choose high-and low-quality care, and that some of the results do not endure into later childhood and adolescence.

Experimental studies show that high-quality programs for low-income infants and pre-schoolers lead to short-term and, in some cases, long-term improvements in school performance. Preschool children who receive care in formal center-based settings show better cognitive and language development on average than do those cared for by relatives or nonrelatives in home-based settings. Similarly, somewhat older children, especially those living in low-income areas, who participate in formal after-school programs have been shown to perform better in school compared with those in other types of after-school arrangements.

Between about third and fifth grade, many children phase out of formal child care programs and spend less and less time under the direct supervision of their parents. During this transition, organized youth activities offer opportunities to build skills and interact with peers with at least some adult supervision. Youths who participate in structured activities approved by adults have better school performance and less deviant behaviour than do those who spend after-school time in unsupervised activities with peers, especially in low-income families and neighbourhoods. Stability of care appears to be more consistently related to social and emotional well-being than is quality or type of care. Low-income children who experience unstable child care-frequent changes and multiple arrangements-tend to have more behavioural problems than do those with more stable child care.

Changing child care arrangements may be a sign of instability in other facets of family life, including housing, parental employment, and family composition-a pattern that has been described as "turbulence." Also, counting evidence suggests that children who enter care early or spend many hours in care throughout the preschool years may have more behavioural problems than do those who spend more time in the care of parents. As children get older, they have increasing control over where they spend their time, whom they associate with, and what activities they experience. Thus, the links between their out-of-school environments and any positive development probably reflects bidirectional influences-that is, youths who are more attached to school and nondeviant peers select more positive activities, which in turn reinforce positive behaviour.

The effects of neighbourhoods and communities are considerably smaller than family influences, children's development nevertheless is influenced by where they live. Young children and adolescents who live in middle-class neighbourhoods perform better in school than do children from comparable families living in less affluent neighbourhoods, even with controls for individual family characteristics. Safety and school quality are neighbourhood features with important potential consequences for children's development.

Children and youths in the experimental groups had lower levels of behavioural problems, fewer asthma attacks and injuries, and were less often the victims of violence than were the children in the control group. Parents reported less gunfire and less drug activity in the neighbourhood. No measures of cognitive or academic performance were reported, but in an earlier quasi-experiment in which families moved from inner-city public housing to suburban communities, positive effects on children's school performance were found.

The evidence linking environmental contexts to child development, especially among low-income families, is quite strong. Children who are deprived of adequate physical and material resources, who lack attention from a warm and loving family, or who spend lengthy hours in low-quality child care settings tend to show negative intellectual and behavioural outcomes. Thus, policies that work to ameliorate these conditions are likely to have a positive impact on children's development. In 1996, major welfare policy strategies include work requirements, time limits on welfare receipt, sanctions for failing to participate in work-related activities, casework, financial incentives such as increased income disregards, which allow recipients to earn more before losing benefits, quotas and incentives for states, and transitional Medicaid and child care assistance.

The effects of maternal employment on children in low-income families probably depend on whether overall family resources increase, characteristics of the job(s) (benefits, stimulation, schedule), characteristics of the child (age, sex, temperament), characteristics of the mother (health, mental health, attitudes and beliefs), and available support (family, child care, community programs). If maternal employment increases material resources, its effects on children are likely to be positive. Data indicate, however, that trading welfare assistance for employment earnings does not always change family income, and resources may decline when the costs of employment, such as transportation, child care, payroll taxes, and clothing, are considered.

Mandatory employment in conjunction with time limits could result in reduced disposable income in some families. Some types of employment might increase parents' skills (human capital) or contacts with adults (social capital), which in turn could have positive effects on the home environment. Proponents of welfare reform emphasize the value of parental modelling; children who see parents going to a job regularly and bringing home a paycheck will accept employment as the norm of adult life. Parents' work lives can serve as a model for their children, but both positive and negative messages could be conveyed. Mothers who have a positive attitude about combining work with family are more satisfied and report less role strain than those who believe they should be at home with their children. When parents' jobs are routine and repetitious or have very low wages, their children may infer that work is dull and boring.

Young children are in someone else's care when mothers are at work, and the quality of that care is likely to mediate effects of parental employment. But many school-age children and youths are in "self-care" while their mothers work. Although parents often monitor their children by telephone and through neighbours, children without direct supervision are vulnerable to antisocial peers or, if they stay home, to many hours in front of the television set. Self-care in late childhood and early adolescence does not appear to pose risks for middle-class children, but, for those who live in poverty and in dangerous neighbourhoods, the odds of behavioural problems increase when young adolescents are unsupervised. In fact, parents appear to recognize the differential risk; middle-class and white children are more likely than poor and minority children to be in self-care.

The effects of maternal employment vary with a child's age, but potential harmful effects do not necessarily decline as children get older. In fact, researchers have found that maternal employment during the adolescent years is associated with adolescent delinquency, lowered educational attainment, and low adolescent well-being. One reason may be that, unlike younger children, adolescents with employed mothers are generally not in supervised alternative settings. Maternal employment can also affect children's responsibilities and family routines. Policymakers often assert that employment will provide a structure for family schedules of getting up, having meals, and going to bed. If a parent has a regular work schedule, this result might occur, but many low-income jobs have irregular and unconventional hours, and many parents work more than one job.

Unconventional and extended work hours may result in children assuming more responsibility for household tasks or caring for siblings, rather than spending more time in child care. Such a shift in responsibility could lead to either positive or negative consequences for children. Most of the literature on low-income families suggests that children's cognitive and social development is more positive in families with employed mothers than in those with unemployed mothers. But it appears that much if not all of this difference is a function of preexisting differences in demographic attributes, skills, personality, and child-rearing practices between employed and unemployed mothers rather than being a product of employment.

In a large sample of mothers and infants, employed mothers provided a higher-quality home environment than unemployed mothers did, but these differences were entirely accounted for by maternal characteristics. Parents with more skills, and better psychological and physical health, are probably more likely to find and maintain paid employment. Parents with those same qualities are also more likely to provide better environments for their children. Children might benefit if the job pays decent wages and provides some opportunity for social or cognitive stimulation; if children are in good-quality child care, youth programs, or neighbourhoods that support positive development; if the mother does not feel excessive role strain, depression, or conflict about her dual roles; and if family economic or social resources are improved.

The consequences of a mother not being employed may be more negative under welfare reform because the time limits on receiving welfare threaten seriously reduced income and because people may be discouraged by their failure to meet society's expectation that they support their families. Welfare policies that include wage supplements, income disregards, and subsidies for necessary expenses such as child care increase overall family income and resources. Although there is considerable debate about the influence of income per se on children's cognitive and social development, to the extent that increased resources improve a family's material circumstances, the quality of the home and child care environments, opportunities for children to participate in beneficial activities, and the neighbourhood in which a family lives, results for children are positive.

Family income during the preschool years appears to be particularly important in predicting cognitive and educational attainment, probably because income affects the quality of the home and child care environments. The home is an important source of intellectual stimulation before children enter formal schooling, and analyses show that the degree of cognitive and social stimulation at home varies with family income. Higher-income families also are more likely than low-income families to use center-based care or higher-quality home-based care for pre-schoolers. Income guarantees led to slightly better school achievement for elementary-school- age children and to better nutrition for a very disadvantaged rural sample. Income supports also led to a higher probability of separation and divorce for couples experiencing high levels of conflict, but not for those with low levels of conflict.

Poverty and income loss affect the socioemotional climate of the home, which in turn influences children's psychological well-being and behaviour. Studies of poor families and families that experienced large reductions in income indicate that the effects on children are mediated primarily by parents' psychological distress, which may be reflected in practices such as low warmth and frequent use of harsh punishment. Comparisons of families receiving welfare with comparable poor families not receiving welfare show that long-term welfare recipients provide lower-quality home environments than do other poor families.

Although many studies show little or no relation of welfare receipt to children's cognitive and social development when differences in demographic and family characteristics are taken into account, some studies have shown that welfare predicts higher rates of grade retention, lower academic achievement, and lower completed schooling among children. By contrast, adolescents in welfare families placed more importance on school than did those in poor, non-welfare families. It is clearly important for policymakers to understand why and how families receiving welfare differ from other poor families, and why welfare income may not confer the same benefits as other income. But it is very difficult to find samples with truly comparable material resources and parental characteristics.

People receiving welfare by definition have almost no assets, whereas other people with low incomes may have more resources of various kinds. Also, unlike other income supports, welfare carries a stigma that may affect the way others treat parents and children, as well as the way they think about themselves. Such changes affect parents' and children's well-being, parenting, and the family environment. Mothers report high levels of behavioral problems among children in families who have made a transition either into or out of welfare, compared with families whose status has not changed. To understand how policies that affect family material resources also affect child development, studies are needed to examine how a family's overall resources are perceived and deployed, and how these behaviours affect the contexts experienced by children.

EARLY CHILDHOOD CARE AND DEVELOPMENT (ECCD) PROGRAMMES

Globalisation and the turn towards market economies that gained momentum in the 1980s have been accompanied by increases in poverty levels and in economic and social inequalities. To try to counter this tendency, governments and international organizations have been pushed to support 'compensatory' programmes, among which figure many early childhood care and development (ECCD) programmes. There is also a growing concern about changing values linked to globalisation, leading to calls in some countries for new initiatives to counter the advance of consumerism and individualism, beginning in the early years.

The mobilisation and emancipation of women, which began in earnest in the 1970s, has helped to foster increasing participation by women in the paid labour force, creating new demands for programmes of early childhood care.

During the last two decades, some of the above tendencies intensified and several new major developments appeared with potential effects on early childhood. The technological revolution intensified. The pace of globalisation picked up, accompanied not only by increases in inequality, poverty, exclusion and 'compensatory' programmes, but also by growth in employment in the informal sector.

The ability of low-income populations to buy services has been further reduced. Globalisation has also helped to drive a redefinition of the role of the state, with implications for the handling of all social programmes, including ECCD. Budgeting processes have been affected.

Internal strife and civil wars have increased in number, displacing many people from their homes and sometimes separating children from their families. Accelerated movement towards democracy has occurred in some areas but has receded in others, affecting priorities and policies. The Soviet Union has broken up, bringing about a decline of the socialist model which placed considerable emphasis on providing a particular kind of institutionalized childcare.

The process of decentralisation has accelerated in many countries. major blip in the pace of economic development occurred in the Asian region, provoking some rethinking. The ecology movement has gained momentum. The pandemic of HIV/AIDS has reached disastrous levels in some countries, particularly those within sub-Saharan Africa.

The important concomitant effects on the composition and structure of families, on child-rearing patterns and practices, on the welfare and quality of life of children, and on policies and programmes intended to improve that quality of life. In the knowledgeable people, frequent reference was made to poverty, unemployment, economic crises and adjustments, inequality, erosion of social values and dislocation associated with conflict as barriers to the advance of ECCD.

There are immense differences in the timing and incidence of particular trends and conditions in particular countries, with accompanying differences in their influence on early childhood care and development, both across and within countries of the 'Majority World'.

For example, it is difficult to discuss in the same tense and voice ECCD programmes in Eastern Europe and in the African subcontinent. Most countries in both regions are struggling to construct 'new' identities while preserving traditions, and both are plagued by major economic problems, but the starting points are very different, the cultures are worlds apart, and the particular conditions make it difficult to include the two regions in the same conversation.

Many criteria emerged that might be applied to defining 'advances' in the ECCD field during the 1990s. Although, a priori, one might expect the main standard for improvement to be set in terms of the well-being of children, most of the advances described refer to changes in programme coverage, to conditions that set the stage for increased availability and quality of ECCD programmes, or to actual changes in programming that, eventually, should bring improvements in the well-being of children.

In many countries, important improvements have occurred in the health and nutritional status of children. Recognizing the importance of good health and nutrition for learning, some country reports made reference to these improvements. Many, however, concentrated on educational improvements, leaving health and nutrition aside.

Over the last ten years, major advances have been made worldwide in reducing infant and child mortality. The effect of immunization programmes on infant mortality has been widely documented and the general tendency is clear. The same clarity and general advance is not so evident for nutritional status and for the results of feeding components offered as part of ECCD programmes.

Relatively high levels of undernourishment and vitamin deficiencies continue in many parts of Asia, Africa and Latin America. Moreover, feeding programmes have not always lived up to expectation. For example, two relatively recent evaluations carried out in Latin America found that there was little or no improvement in the nutritional status of participants in ECCD programmes despite a relatively high cost of feeding children in the programmes. The nutritional status of rural children in Mexico has not changed in more than twenty years.

These results are logical if one considers that feeding programmes do not necessarily change basic feeding habits at home, that they often do not provide food at weekends, that parents may reduce food provided to children at home because they are getting food elsewhere, and that diarrhoea linked to poor sanitary conditions continues to offset potential gains from food supplementation.

On the other hand, micronutrient supplementation programmes seem to have had important positive effects and intensive nutritional programmes in Argentina and Chile seem to have had good results in reducing malnutrition. Taken together, these results suggest that broad approaches need to be promoted if health and nutrition components of ECCD programmes are to be effective in improving the well-being of young children; simple supplementary feeding programmes are insufficient.

Unfortunately, very few countries provide measures of the psycho-social well-being of young children or of their advances in learning during their early years. It is therefore impossible to judge advances in this area for national populations or to link advances to the many programme initiatives that have been undertaken. There are, however, exceptions at the level of particular programmes for which indicators have been created and evaluations carried out. Unfortunately, such information rarely appears in the country reports.

Improvements are occasionally inferred from changes in subsequent school performance and retention, but these are at best indirect measures of a child's general development or psycho-social well-being.

Various reviews of the literature suggest that there are indeed long-term effects. These reviews bring together results of specific studies of specific programmes and do not report results of systematic monitoring of national changes in children's development and learning during the early years. Specific studies, and the few cases where there has been some agreement on an indicator of psycho-social development and where consistent measurement has occurred over time, show that:

- Programmes of reasonable quality do have important positive effects on early development, often with longer-term effects.
- The effects can favour rural children who are at a social disadvantage. An important improvement in the nutritional status of children does not automatically bring about the anticipated improvement in various dimensions of psycho-social development.
- The area of language development seems to show a consistent lag in development related to socio-economic conditions as well as to first language differences.

In addition to changes in the demographic, economic, social and political contexts, a host of more immediate changes affecting ECCD were noted in country programmes and by knowledgeable people. These include changes in:

- knowledge and its dissemination;
- the conceptual and scientific bases available to be drawn upon and the formation of communication networks;
- attitudes and awareness of political leaders, funders, planners and the population at large about the importance of ECCD and its potential benefits;
- policies and legal and legislative frameworks for programming, internationally and nationally;
- the availability of resources, both financial and human;
- organizational bases, strengthened and consolidated, both governmental and non-governmental.

The most frequently mentioned advance in knowledge related to ECCD during the 1990s was an advance in understanding how the brain develops and functions. New discoveries in neuroscience and their dissemination through scientific, professional and popular channels have had an important influence on the demand for, and the willingness to consider support for, early childhood education and development programmes.

It is now possible to point to longitudinal studies in various countries of the Majority World as well as studies in Europe, the United States and elsewhere in the Minority World, that show clearly how ECCD programmes can have effects on children in primary school. A prime example of such Majority World research is the excellent work done in Turkey in which children cared for in different settings, and whose mothers participated in a parent education programme, were shown to benefit in later life. These studies have helped to convince policy-makers and programmers of the value of investing in ECCD. They reinforce the Jomtien commitment to including early education within basic education. Other new avenues of research that are beginning to influence practice include studies of 'resilience', conditions under which programmes can have a negative effect on child development.

Influence of ecological and transactional models that gained prominence in the 1980s continues to provide a basis for complementary approaches to ECCD that work towards changing the family, community and broader institutional and cultural environments with which a child interacts in the process of developing and learning. The search for 'best practices' which took off in the 1980s continues, but the chorus of those who question the search for universals and the base for best practices in developmental psychology has grown ever louder. Additional importance is being attached to discovering, respecting, and incorporating cultural differences into thinking about how early childhood education and care 'should' occur.

Viewpoints grounded in anthropology, sociology, ethics and other fields are being brought to bear on ECCD, highlighting the need to begin with the cultural and social definitions of childhood and education held by those who are the participants in early childhood programmes rather than with a predetermined set of definitions and models imposed from outside.

This tendency is consistent with a strand of thinking about social and economic development that is grounded in local participation, and in 'putting the first last'.Interestingly, while few of the people surveyed pointed directly to lack of funding as a barrier to advance in the ECCD field, there is a widespread feeling that the field is underfunded, that public financial support is low and unstable, and that the lack of resources is an important problem.

During the 1980s and the early 1990s, financing within the international community for programmes related to young children was focused on survival, and, more specifically on health and nutrition. Guided by a consortium of donors and by the energetic promotion efforts of a Child Survival Revolution by UNICEF and the World Health Organization, major lending agencies, bilateral organizations, major foundations and the larger international NGOs emphasized immunization, oral rehydration, feeding, and other actions that were directed primarily at reducing infant and child mortality rates. Very little attention was given to child development. Donors seemed to accept the half-truth that attending to health and nutrition would automatically benefit mental, social and psychological development.

At the beginning of the decade, the Bernard van Leer Foundation was the only international institution with a history of consistent and significant support to early childhood development programmes located within the Majority World. That assistance was provided primarily within a child-centred, community-based development framework. UNICEF, because of its decentralized nature, but without much support from the centre. International educational assistance was seldom provided for pre-school or child development projects but was concentrated increasingly on primary schooling, representing a shift from an earlier tendency to favour support for university development.

During the 1990s, however, the picture began to change. Indeed, there is no doubt that the overall level of international financing available for ECCD has increased a great deal since 1990. The picture is less clear with respect to national budgets. The country's dealing with finances reveal that few have presented information specifically on the funding of early childhood programmes. There are several reasons for the gap in information, related to budget conventions and to the difficulty of bringing together information from the many administrative entities responsible for ECCD programmes. In a very few countries, funding for ECCD constitutes a significant part of the education budget.

Estimates are not available for the financial support that falls to the private and social sectors. In some countries, however, it is clear that an important part of the resource burden falls on non-governmental sources. In Latin America and elsewhere, a large variety of 'non-formal' programmes draw heavily on the involvement of community members who 'volunteer' their services, thereby reducing the main cost of most ECCD programmes—salaries.

Discussions of the contribution to ECCD of the 'for-profit private sector' must be divided into at least two parts, involving (a) entrepreneurial institutions or individuals who offer ECCD services in order to make a profit, and (b) profit-making companies organized for other purposes, which may provide resources from their profits to support early childhood, by offering ECCD services on the premises to employees, providing financial incentives to their employees to seek services elsewhere, or making contributions to ECCD through special taxes or related philanthropic efforts.

In many countries, entrepreneurs make an important contribution to ECCD. But sometimes it is difficult to determine whether or not such private efforts are really closer to community service than to profit-seeking behaviour. Indeed, when individuals set up centres catering for families with relatively low incomes, it is difficult for them to make ends meet let alone make a profit. At the same time, there is concern that the growth of private, for-profit centres attending to young children is a problem because it is chaotic and unregulated, creating greater disparities and providing services of poor quality for low-income families unable to pay for a better programme.

The contribution of the second for-profit group—the non-ECCD part of the private sector—to the field of ECCD has been minimal. Some governments and international organizations such as the World Bank wish to seek greater support for ECCD from this part of the private sector. The early efforts have had little real effect so far, but the tendency is present, and careful thought must be given to evaluating the different ways in which the sector might be involved in order to avoid discrimination or a lowering of programme quality, when the hope is that quality will be enhanced. In all likelihood, the greatest source of support for ECCD still comes from parents.

This is clearly true for the earliest years during which the overwhelming majority of children remain at home. But even in the countries with a relatively high enrolment for children age 4 or above, parents often contribute through payments of quotas, uniforms, or materials required in official as well as in private programmes. Clearly, in cases where the growth of ECCD is demand-driven and largely run by private entrepreneurs or community, these costs to parents will be higher, with greater possibilities of discrimination related to the ability to pay.

In some of the country's knowledgeable people, organizational changes were frequently mentioned as 'advances' in the ECCD field during the 1990s. The particular advance cited might involve bringing the field under the control of the Education Ministry and sector, presumably to give greater attention to the educational quality of programmes. Advances were also cited relating to the creation of coordinating mechanisms reaching across sectors, parts of the same sector, or agencies responsible for 'care' as contrasted with 'education'.

Another organizational change that has occurred in many countries during the 1990s has been the decentralization of programmes. This change is seen by some as important in opening up the possibility for greater diversity related to local circumstances and cultural differences, increasing the level of local participation, and facilitating accountability. Others see decentralization as a new form of maintaining control from the centre, as a barrier to the important redistributional role that states should play, and as a formula for diminished quality related to the lack of adequately trained human resources at the local level. How decentralization is in fact affecting ECCD will have to be looked at closely in the coming years and the tendency will require greater attention to advocacy and training at local levels.

Moving closer to the heart of the ECCD process, many countries noted as advances in quality the initiation or expansion of training courses for early childhood caregivers and teachers. Important advances in the formation of ECCD agents were noted in a review of initial education in Latin America International support for ECCD has often focused on training.Many programmes also mentioned curricular reforms during the period, generally oriented towards making the process more active, exploratory, democratic, culturally adjusted, etc. There was evidence of some importing of curricula, such as Step-by-Step, related to grants made by the Soros Foundation in Central Asia, or Montessori programmes in Africa, presumably with the assumption that tried and tested curricula will result in programmes of better quality. The proportion of adults to children was also used in a few cases as an indicator of quality, again under the assumption that fewer children per adult improves the interaction between the education agent and the child. The ratio of technical-pedagogical supervisors to preschool teachers was also mentioned as an indicator of quality.

In many countries, the need continues to convince politicians, policymakers, programmers and education officials, often now at local levels, of the importance of ECCD. In order to create political will, there is a need to develop:

— better strategies of communicating, lobbying and advocating.

— strategies directed to groups that have not always been called upon to help in the process and groups that are emerging as important potential actors.

— a better information base, with systematic descriptions of programmes thought to be effective, improved indicators, more solid statistics, strengthened monitoring and evaluation systems, and greater attention to local research.

In order to formulate and strengthen policy there is a need to:

— undertake analytical studies of existing policies affecting children, looking beyond narrowly conceived education policies to, for example, social welfare, health, and labour policies that affect childcare and development during the early years.

— seek conformity with the Convention on the Rights of the Child, incorporating principles of the best interests of the child, non-discrimination and participation.

— work closely with the legal profession.

— establish norms and standards which are not so rigid or high as to be unworkable but which will assure positive attention to children.

— provide a clearer legal base for assigning budget allocations.

ECCD programmes generally command a small portion of government budgets, relative to percentage of young children in the population. In budgetary terms, children are clearly not placed first. There is therefore a need to:

— increase allocations to ECCD in national budgets and make more permanent commitments to such funding

— strengthen the capacity of states and municipalities to obtain resources for ECCD

— seek cost-effective approaches, including quality community-based non-formal approaches to ECCD

— explore more vigorously such alternative avenues of funding as debt swaps, philanthropic contributions, and private-sector involvement.

— co-ordinate the increase of financial resources with attention to the capacity to handle such resources and the strengthening of human resources.

— provide local organization access to central pools of money in order to better respond to demand originating in local communities.

The bureaucratically convenient tendency to extend the same programme to all children conflicts with the need to tailor ECCD programmes to cultural, geographical, economic and age differences. This tendency is reinforced by the notion that ECCD is the same as 'pre-school' which, in turn, is simply an extension downward of primary schooling. There is therefore a need to:

— think in terms of complementary and varied approaches to ECCD that include family and community-based programmes

— involve NGOs more actively as partners

— decentralize programme responsibility as well as administrative responsibility, with attention to building local capacity

— construct culturally relevant programmes with local communities rather than impose ECCD practices from the centre.

There is a pressing need to:

— re-examine training and supervision and provide sound training (both pre-service and in-service) at all levels, with respect to a diversity of ECCD approaches.

— reduce the number of children (or families) per education/ care agent.

— improve and reformulate curricula, taking into account not only 'best practices' but also local definition of what constitutes 'best practices'.

— draw upon existing experience in a more systematic way.

— establish better systems for monitoring and evaluating both children and programmes.

The following 'disadvantaged' populations need to be given greater attention: low-income, rural, indigenous, girls, HIV/AIDS, children age 0 to 3, pregnant and lactating mothers, working mothers, fathers.

If a holistic and integrated notion of learning and development is to be honoured and if resources are to be used more effectively, greater co-ordination is needed (a) among government programmes of health, welfare, social security, nutrition, education, rural or community development, etc.; (b) within the education sector, especially between ECCD and primary schooling; and (c) between governmental and non-governmental organizations. There is a need to:

— create intersectoral, interorganizational co-ordinating bodies.

— construct joint programmes crossing bureaucratic boundaries.

— strengthen the ability of families and communities to call upon and bring together services that are currently offered in an uncoordinated fashion.

— seek agreement on the populations that are most in need of attention and direct services to those populations in a converging manner.

— build partnerships.

The conceptual frameworks guiding programmes intended to improve early childhood care and development and early learning have come primarily from developmental psychology and formal education. There is a need to go beyond the knowledge that these fields can provide to incorporate broader views with cultural, social and ethical dimensions brought to bear.

There is also a need to relate ECCD programming, conceptually and operationally, to other programme lines that begin from analyses of children's rights, poverty, working mothers, rural development, special needs, street children, refugees, adolescents, gender, etc. Starting from the premise that the quality of programmes will be only as good as the people who operate them, it is logical to place emphasis on assuring that ECCD people at various levels are well motivated and are part of a continuous process of training. This does not mean that all those who attend to, care for, and educate young children or who work with parents and communities to improve care need to have university degrees. It does mean that they need both pre-service and in-service training.

Early childhood programmes often suffer from weak systems of administrative supervision linked to 'inspection', when what is really needed is a strong system of technical supervision tied to improving continuous learning, including opportunities to interact with and learn from peers. Such training, done well, motivates as well as providing essential information and improving methods. A priority for many countries, then, might be to strengthen their pre-service and (especially) inservice training in combination with a reconstituted system of supervision that builds on participation of education, care and development agents. In addition, training will be needed for administrators, supervisors, planners, evaluators and others who form part of an ECCD system. Increasingly, there is a need to assist local administrators, planners and functionaries to work in the ECCD field.

Perhaps the greatest and most lasting effects on a child's learning and development can come from improvements in the capacity of parents to provide a supportive environment for learning and development. There are many possible ways to support and work with parents and family members and the particular combination of how to go about this work will vary with conditions.

There is a tendency to view parent education as a kind of quick and cheap way of dealing with the early childhood area. There is also a tendency for some ECCD programmers to look at parents as instruments rather than as people. In addition, parent education is often thought of as mothers' education. A concerted effort will be needed to moderate these tendencies, providing more prolonged and better-funded programmes in this area, with the emphasis on those that help parents to grow as people, not just as parents, and involving fathers as well as mothers. In institutional environments there is a tendency to keep parents at the margin, at best providing them with periodic 'talks', rather than seeking ways of involving them directly in setting the direction of an institution and in its functioning.

Among the lessons learned from successful programmes is that effectiveness is fostered if programmes develop slowly and are monitored and adjusted regularly. The information from monitoring and evaluation will serve advocacy as well as policy and administrative purposes, and it should help the process of reconceptualization that many results respondents feel is necessary. The fact that countries did not provide information on how the well-being of their children has, or has not, progressed. This gap needs to be filled by supporting countries to define the particular outcomes and measures that they feel will provide essential feedback about how well they are doing with respect to the learning and development of their young children. Within the International Consultative Forum on Education for All, run by international organizations, it seems appropriate to reflect on the role that has been, and can be, played by international organizations in promoting and supporting programmes directed at improving the care and development of young children.

International organizations have been given credit for and have played several important roles in helping ECCD to extend and improve. These include assistance in providing frameworks for analysis and action, strengthening the knowledge base and disseminating information, advocating, as well as by providing technical and financial support. At the same time, it is important to recognise that these forms of assistance represent interventions that imply certain value positions, and that their results depend as much on the manner in which the assistance is offered as on the amount of assistance provided, which can have negative as well as positive consequences.

MILLENNIUM GOALS OF CHILD DEVELOPMENT

In the Millennium Declaration of September 2000, Member States of the United Nations made a most passionate commitment to address the crippling poverty and multiplying misery that grip many areas of the globe. "We will spare no effort," they affirmed, "to free our fellow men, women and children from the abject and dehumanizing conditions of extreme poverty, to which more than a billion of them are currently subjected."

Governments set a date of 2015 by which they would meet the Millennium Development Goals: eradicate extreme poverty and hunger, achieve universal primary education, promote gender equality and empower women, reduce child mortality, improve maternal health, combat HIV/AIDS, malaria and other diseases, ensure environmental sustainability, and develop a global partnership for development. While achieving each goal is critical to development, two are considered by leaders in the international community to be central to all others – universal education, and gender equality and empowering women.

Universal education might seem a relatively straightforward goal but it has proven as difficult as any to achieve. Decades after commitments and reaffirmations of those commitments have been made to ensure a quality education for every child, some 121 million children are still denied this right. Despite thousands of successful projects in countries around the globe, gender parity in education –in access to school, successful achievement and completion – is as elusive as ever and girls continue to systematically lose out on the benefits that an education affords. As a result, the children whose lives would have been saved if their mothers had been educated continue to die. Those boys and girls who would have been healthier had their mothers been educated continue to suffer needlessly. The reduction in poverty, hunger and HIV/AIDS that would follow if all children were educated remains an idealist's dream. It doesn't have to be that way.

Universal education, and all the good that it will bring, is possible. Investing in girls' education today – not just with money but with energy and enthusiasm, commitment and concern, focus and intensity –is a strategy that will protect the rights of all children to a quality education, and a strategy that will jump-start all other development goals. But, the signs in the first three years since the Millennium Declaration are not encouraging for universal education, or gender parity in education or for any of the other Millennium Development Goals.

The events of 11 September 2001 and the battle against terrorism around the globe have occupied much of the world's headline attention and soaked up resources that could have been devoted to human development. Now, the world will have to strain to the utmost to meet the commitments of the Goals. If progress is not accelerated, the levels of hunger that threaten survival will persist in some regions of the world for an inconceivable 100 years. Millions of children under five will continue to die needlessly over the same time.

More immediately than the 2015 date, the Millennium Development Goal of gender parity in primary and secondary education is set to be achieved by 2005 – a full 10 years before the others. Not only an end in itself but also part of the broader goal of education for all, the 2005 goal is the first test of the world's commitment to break poverty's stranglehold.

Many countries, however, will fall short of the 2005 target for gender parity in education if nothing is done now to accelerate change.

Without the foundation of gender parity in education as the necessary step towards the equality of women, any achievements towards the later goals will not be sustainable. Thus the 2005 goal of eliminating gender disparity in primary and secondary education becomes the first step toward meeting the 2015 goals – and the most urgent one of all.

The international community's commitment to universal education was first set down in the 1948 Universal Declaration of Human Rights and later reiterated in the 1989 Convention on the Rights of the Child. At the 1990 World Summit for Children, world leaders not only reaffirmed their commitment that girls and boys alike should have a quality basic education, they also pledged to place their emphasis on reducing the disparities that had existed between rates of school enrolment for decades.

Despite these commitments, the ideal of universal education remains unfulfilled and gender gaps persist until today. The 2005 target date for gender parity is attached not only to the Millennium Development Goals, but to the goals that were first put forth at the World Conference on Education For All in Jomtien, Thailand in 1990, and then reaffirmed at the 2000 World Education Forum in Dakar, Senegal. Here, too, girls' education was afforded first attention: "The most urgent priority is to ensure access to, and improve the quality of education for girls and women, and to remove every obstacle that hampers their active participation...."

So it is that for more than a decade, the Education For All (EFA) campaign, led by UNESCO, has embraced a mission that includes both advocacy and "a sense of accountability towards commitments." Through its Global Monitoring Reports, EFA assesses individual countries' yearly progress and champions educational policies that will increase enrolment rates and success in school. In its 2002 Report,EFA noted that although 86 countries have already achieved gender parity in primary enrolment, and another 36 appear close to meeting that goal, 31 countries, the majority of which are located in sub-Saharan Africa, are at high risk of not achieving the goal by 2015.

Following Dakar, 13 agencies formed the United Nations Girls' Education Initiative in the EFA spirit to mount a "sustained campaign to improve the quality and availability of girls' education" that works at both the global and country levels. It is in its capacity as lead agency of this Initiative that UNICEF embraces the urgency of the 2005 Millennium Development Goal to eliminate gender disparity in education.

These commitments to universal education and eliminating gender disparities in primary and secondary education by 2005 were avowed once again by the Heads of States and Government who convened at the UN General Assembly Special Session on Children in May 2002 and pledged to make education for all children an essential part of building a 'World Fit for Children'.

Despite decades of attention to the issue, some 121 million children are out of school, and 65 million of them are girls. At any moment, they are being denied their right to a basic education, as nations fail to make primary education compulsory, free, available, accessible, acceptable – and adaptable to girls and boys alike. And scores of countries are without the talent, energy and creativity these millions of children could bring to the development of their societies.

Think for a moment of a nine-year-old girl who is currently denied her right to an education. The two years until the end of 2005 may not seem like much time to those responsible for delivering gender parity by that date. It may seem reasonable to accept that the target is impossible, and to settle for only an incremental improvement.

But to that girl the next two years are vital and irreplaceable. Once lost, they cannot be reclaimed. Going to school will transform her life. It will offer her learning and an expanded sense of her own potential, increasing her selfconfidence, her social and negotiation skills, her earning power and her ability to protect herself against violence and ill health. Education will open up the world to her.

If the school gates remain shut and barred to this young girl, the gulf between her and the woman she could have become will widen with every passing month. Once she misses her chance to attend primary school, she also loses out on secondary education and beyond. The price of losing two school years would be catastrophic to any child but is even higher for a girl – and it will be paid not only by the girl herself but also by her family, her society and her country.

The negative effects of not attending school are greater for girls than for boys – and their impact transfers to the next generation of both boys and girls. Whether educated or not, girls are more at risk than boys from HIV/AIDS, sexual exploitation and child trafficking. Without the knowledge and life skills that school can provide, these risks are multiplied. So it is that school allows girls and their families multiple protections and its absence means multiple exposures.

Why are girls systematically left out of school, women excluded from political processes, and countries left behind as development advances in some places and not in others? The answers, summarized here are interrelated.

Failure of accountability. Rather than recognized as the right of every child, education is too often seen simply as a 'good thing' for most children. As a result, while it is considered desirable to have as many children in school as a country can afford, it is not considered obligatory or necessary that governments mobilize the needed resources so that all children can complete a quality education.

Parents often do not realize that governments have the obligation to make education available to all children, and attribute their children's failure to attend school as some failure of their own. They are not likely to demand that governments fulfil this fundamental obligation to their younger citizens.

In the face of competing demands on public resources and political will, education loses out. In times of fiscal constraints or social crises – for example, HIV/AIDS and the upheavals that attend violent conflicts or natural disasters – education for some children is easily sacrificed. And because of the persistent and often subtle gender discrimination that runs through most societies, it is girls who are sacrificed first, being the last enrolled and first withdrawn from schools when times get tough.

Failure of understanding. Human rights principles have not been integrated into economic development programmes, and the ultimate objective of development – human well-being instead of economic performance – has thus been lost. Those who are the most marginalized – women, girls and the poor – lose out the most. Such discrimination, unrecorded, leaves the rights of the marginalized far from the thoughts of development policy makers. In addition, how educated women contribute to any country's development has yet to be widely recognized. Despite the scientific evidence, educating girls is rarely discussed in policy circles as a way to ensure social progress. As a result, investment in girls' education is often bypassed when budget decisions are being negotiated.

Historically, the predominant views of development and the financing mechanisms accompanying them have focused on single-factor motors of development: economic growth and structural adjustment, which underestimate the value of social development, education in general and girls' education in particular.

Such approaches do not begin by asking what resources are required to fund education, health, nutrition and shelter for children. They never get to the question of how to raise required resources without destabilizing macroeconomic parameters. The macroeconomic parameters are set first, with resources for people-centred investments, including those that address gender equality, as only a residual consideration.

Just as importantly, development paradigms have generally failed to address the unequal relationships between men and women, and failed to take into account women's potential to contribute in the private and public sectors to a country's development. As a result, issues affecting women and girls are nearly invisible in the theories, policies and practices of development.

Even among those committed to the goal of Education For All, there is often a traditional perspective that looks only to the education sector when identifying problems and developing solutions. As a result, policies and programmes are often narrow and singlefocused, though it is a multisectoral approach that is needed to overcome the obstacles barring girls from school.

Traditional perspectives often fail to take into account the gender issues that affect children's access to school, those related to the differences between the needs of girls and boys, and the inequities in their roles, responsibilities and identities. Without a recognition of such differences, educational policies and practices are gender blind, when they should be gender sensitive. In such cases, the behaviour and attitudes of policy makers and practitioners at best fail to meet the particular needs of boys and girls and at worst sabotage their right to an education.

With the rights of 65 million girls unmet and the Millennium Development Goals in peril, change is clearly needed. But it is needed at many levels and will not be achieved through enrolment drives alone. To successfully remove the barriers that prevent girls from accessing an education, and succeeding in and completing school, societies will inevitably have to deal with factors that are fundamental to the quality of life of the whole community.

Girls' education is so inextricably linked with the other facets of human development that to make it a priority is to also make change on a range of other fronts, from the health and status of women to early childhood care, from nutrition, water and sanitation to community empowerment, from the reduction of child labour and other forms of exploitation to the peaceful resolution of conflicts.

A concerted global push is now needed to meet the Millennium Development Goals and the education goals of Dakar – as well as to realize the vision of the Special Session on Children to create a world fit for children. The effort is morally imperative; it must also be practical and it must be catalytic.

It is within this context that UNICEF's longstanding commitment to girls' education has assumed greater urgency and why we now call on all those concerned with human rights and the Millennium Development Goals to:

1. Accelerate actions in countries that display specific and flagrant gender discrimination against girls and boys, especially in those where either group is significantly at risk of being left out of school.
2. Embrace a human rights-based, multisectoral approach to development, in order to redress the multiple discriminatory situations that deny children their right to quality primary education.

By using a human rights model and a multisectoral approach to ensuring that all girls are educated, the world will necessarily have to address underlying inequities and gender discrimination. The results of such a global initiative will cover a broad landscape. It will create by 2005 a vanguard generation of children who are living a lesson in equality. It will mean that schools, curricula and teachers are changing to become truly child-friendly, thereby offering a better education to all children equally. It will mean that all countries have acknowledged that education is an urgent priority and that developing countries have shifted their resources to attract and retain girls and boys in school. It will mean that donor countries have lived up to their pledges to support development. It will be a powerful global expression of commitment to children's rights.

The multiple global efforts to ensure the right of every girl and boy to an education – including the Education For All movement, the United Nations Girls' Education Initiative, the World Bank's Fast-Track Initiative and the Global Movement for Children – must step up their work. The international community has committed itself, time and again, to fulfilling the education rights of girls as well as boys. The research community has demonstrated, in study after study, the social value of providing girls with an education.

Having 65 million more girls in school, alongside millions of boys – each learning, growing and thriving – will put new life into development and help create the healthier, fairer and more democratic world we have been striving towards for decades.

8

Child Protection: Role of UNICEF

UNICEF uses the term 'child protection' to refer to protection from violence, exploitation, abuse and neglect. Violations of the child's right to protection, in addition to being human rights violations, are also massive, under-recognized and underreported barriers to child survival and development. Children subjected to violence, exploitation, abuse and neglect are at risk of:

— shortened lives;

— poor physical and mental health;

— educational problems (including dropping out of school);

— poor parenting skills later in life;

— homelessness, vagrancy and displacement.

Conversely, successful protection increases a child's chances of growing up physically and mentally healthy, confident and self-respecting, and less likely to abuse or exploit others, including his or her own children.

Child protection is closely linked to other aspects of a child's well-being. An immunized child who is constantly beaten is not a healthy child; a school-going child taunted and abused for his or her ethnicity does not enjoy a good learning environment; and an adolescent sold into prostitution will not be empowered to participate in and contribute to society. Child protection is an integral part of the business of development.

Child protection is an issue for children in every country of the world:

— more than 1 million children worldwide are living in detention as a result of being in conflict with the law. In Central and Eastern Europe alone, about 1.5 million children were living in public care at the end of the 1990s;

— about 14 million children under 15 are estimated to have been orphaned as a result of AIDS alone;

— aproximately 246 million children work, with about 180 million engaged in the worst forms of child labour;

— an estimated 1.2 million children are trafficked every year;

— 2 million children are believed to be exploited through prostitution and pornography;

— at any given time over 300,000 child soldiers, some as young as eight, are exploited in armed conflicts in over 30 countries. More than 2 million children are estimated to have died as a direct result of armed conflicts during the 1990s;

— an estimated 100 million to 130 million women and girls alive today have undergone some form of genital mutilation/cutting;

— 40 million children below the age of 15 suffer from abuse and neglect, and require health and social care.

BUILDING A PROTECTIVE ENVIRONMENT FOR CHILDREN

Children are entitled to grow up in an environment that protects them. UNICEF identifies and responds to eight key aspects of a protective environment:

— *attitudes, traditions, customs, behaviour and practices*: In societies where attitudes or traditions facilitate abuse – for example, regarding sex with minors, the appropriateness of severe corporal punishment, the application of harmful traditional practices or differences in the perceived status and value of boys and girls – the environment will not be protective. In societies where all forms of violence against children are taboo, and where the rights of children are broadly respected by custom and tradition, children are more likely to be protected;

— *governmental commitment to fulfilling protection rights*: Government interest in,recognition of and commitment to child protection is an essential element for a protective environment;

— *open discussion of, and engagement, with child protection issues*: At the most immediate level, children need to be free to speak up about child protection concerns affecting them or other children. At the national level, both media attention and civil society engagement with the issue contribute to child protection. Partnerships among actors at all levels are essential for an effective and coordinated response;

— *legislation and enforcement*: An adequate legislative framework, its consistent implementation, accountability and a lack of impunity are essential elements of a protective environment;

— *capacity*: Health workers, teachers, police, social workers and many others who deal with children need to be equipped with the skills, knowledge, authority and motivation to identify and respond to child protection problems. The capacity of families and communities to protect their children is also essential. There are other broader types of capacity that relate to the protective environment, including the provision of education and safe areas for play;

— *children's life skills, knowledge and participation:* If children are unaware of their right not to be abused, or are not warned of the dangers of, for example, trafficking, they are more vulnerable to abuse. Children need information and knowledge to be equipped to protect themselves. Children also need to be provided with safe and protective channels for participation and self-expression;

— *monitoring and reporting:* A protective environment for children requires an effective monitoring system that records the incidence and nature of child protection abuses and allows for informed and strategic responses. Such systems can be more effective when they are participatory and locally based;

— *services for recovery and reintegration*: Child victims of any form of neglect, exploitation or abuse are entitled to care and non-discriminatory access to basic social services. These services must be provided in an environment that fosters the health, self-respect and dignity of the child.

Some elements of the protective environment will overlap. For example, governmental commitment may dictate whether services for victims of abuse are provided, or whether investment is made in monitoring mechanisms. Similarly, media attention can be a key factor in influencing attitudes.

UNICEF'S APPROACH

In its work with partners, UNICEF seeks to strengthen the web of elements that make up a protective environment for the child. Prevention is the priority and we also support and advocate for mitigating the effects of abuse.

To achieve this, UNICEF employs a number of child protection strategies, including:

- national advocacy and initiating dialogue at all levels – from government to communities, families and children themselves;
- international advocacy, including the use of international human rights mechanisms;
- seeking societal behaviour change, challenging attitudes and traditions that can underpin child protection abuses and supporting those that are protective;
- strengthening capacity to assess and analyse protection issues;
- using law-based approaches, recognizing that legal standards are particularly important to child protection and that they need to be known, understood, accepted and enforced;

- working for and prioritizing child protection in and after conflict and instability;
- working with communities for child protection;
- ensuring access to services for recovery and reintegration for children who have suffered child protection abuses;
- promoting child participation and strengthening children's own resilience.

UNICEF seeks to mainstream protection throughout all its work. For example:

- in education, UNICEF promotes safe schools and discourages the use of corporal punishment;
- in its integrated approach to early childhood, UNICEF discourages violent forms of discipline and promotes early birth registration;
- in its work on HIV/AIDS, UNICEF tackles the stigma that is often attached to children affected by HIV/AIDS, and provides protection for vulnerable children who have been orphaned as a result of AIDS.

UNICEF IN ACTION

In Angola, UNICEF has worked with NGOs to demobilize children through a programme for the reintegration of underage soldiers. Children returning from war received assistance to trace their relatives, and were transferred back to their home villages to be reunited. The programme also identified appropriate school and job training opportunities. Work in the communities was conducted by *catequistas*, trained local church members who provided psychosocial assistance. The group drew upon traditional beliefs and practices to aid local communities to accept former child soldiers and to facilitate their reintegration. UNICEF continues to be involved in current efforts to demobilize child soldiers and reunite them with their families.

In Bangladesh, UNICEF supported a major communications campaign on child rights addressing a number of protection issues including domestic child labour and violence against children. This involved a focused media campaign with television, radio and print media inputs, linked with NGO interventions in these areas.

In East Asia, UNICEF supports projects aimed at increasing the status of and opportunities for women and adolescent girls, while ensuring their protection. Activities include forums for the exchange of materials and information-sharing through street drama, songs and other community-based approaches. Materials warn of the dangers of travelling abroad for employment and provide additional information on HIV/AIDS and other sexually transmitted infections. Projects also provide skills training for communitybased support groups, non-formal education programmes and cross-border initiatives.

In Indonesia, UNICEF facilitated a consultative process and provided technical support for the drafting of new and comprehensive legislation on children's issues. The new legislation was adopted by the Indonesian parliament in 2002.

In Romania, UNICEF has sought to prevent child abandonment through a project in eight maternity hospitals. It provided counselling and material support for 765 pregnant women and mothers in difficult circumstances in order to encourage them to keep their babies. Support for foster families and family-like homes has prevented some children from being institutionalized.

In Timor-Leste, UNICEF and its partners support NGO initiatives in psychosocial support and counselling, with a special focus on victims of violence and/or sexual abuse. A shelter for sexually abused women is also being established. UNICEF also supported a review of laws relating to juvenile justice and conducted training of police officers, judges and public defenders on relevant international standards. This led to a series of legal revisions.

In Thailand, UNICEF supported the Office of the National Commission on Women's Affairs in organizing a 'Youth Camp for Ending Violence against Children and Women'. The aim is to build up youth networks and strengthen the capacity of local agencies to provide protection against domestic violence to children and women. After the training, participants were appointed as youth volunteers to monitor violence against children, youth and women in their communities.

Internationally, UNICEF is the lead agency for the realization of the goals and targets of 'A World Fit for Children', the outcome document of the United Nations General Assembly Special Session on Children, held in New York in May 2002. This includes key provisions relating to child protection in all areas.

PARTNERSHIPS

UNICEF's protection work begins with partnerships. UNICEF's partners include governments, NGOs, other UN agencies, religious organizations, professional associations, children and youth, and the media. One important partner is the United Nations Committee on the Rights of the Child, which regularly highlights the importance of child protection and provides detailed recommendations and guidance to governments on how to effectively protect children.

9

Convention on the Right of Child

The Convention on the Right of Child was adopted by the General Assembly of United Nations on 20 November 1989. The details of the Convention are given below.

PREAMBLE

The States Parties to the present Convention,

Considering that, in accordance with the principles proclaimed in the Charter of the United Nations, recognition of the inherent dignity and of the equal and inalienable rights of all members of the human family is the foundation of freedom, justice and peace in the world,

Bearing in mind that the peoples of the United Nations, have, in the Charter, reaffirmed their faith in fundamental human rights and in the dignity and worth of the human person, and have determined to promote social progress and better standards of life in larger freedom,

Recognising that the United Nations has, in the Universal Declaration of Human Rights and in the International Covenants on Human Rights, proclaimed and agreed that everyone is entitled to all the rights and freedoms set forth therein, without distinction of any kind, such as race, colour, sex, language religion, political or other opinion, national or social origin, property, birth or other status,

Recalling that, in the Universal Declaration of Human Rights, the United Nations has proclaimed that childhood is entitled to special care and assistance,

Convinced that the family, as the fundamental group of society and the natural environment for the growth and well-being of all its members and particularly children, should be afforded the necessary protection and assistance so that it can fully assume its responsibilities within the community,

Recognising that the child, for the full and harmonious development of his or her personality, should grow up in a family environment, in an atmosphere of happiness, love and understanding,

Considering that the child should be fully prepared to live an individual life in society, and brought up in the spirit of the ideals proclaimed in the Charter of the United Nations, and in particular in the spirit of peace, dignity, tolerance, freedom, equality and solidarity,

Bearing in mind the need to extend particular care to the child has been stated in the Geneva Declaration of the Rights of the Child of 1924 and in the Declaration of the

Rights of the Child adopted by the General Assembly on 20 November 1959 and recognised in the Universal Declaration of Human Rights, in the International Covenant on Civil and Political Rights (in particular in articles 23 and 24), in the International Covenant on Economic, Social and Cultural Rights (in particular in Article 10) and in the statutes and relevant instruments of specialised agencies and international organisations concerned with the welfare of children,

Bearing in mind as indicated in the Declaration of the Rights of the Child, "the child, by reason of his physical and mental immaturity, needs special safeguards and care, including appropriate legal protection, before as well as after birth",

Recalling the provisions of the Declaration on Social and Legal Principles relating to Protection and Welfare of Children, with Special Reference to Foster Placement and Adoption Nationally and Internationally; the United Nations Standard Minimum Rules for the Administration of Juvenile Justice (The Beijing Rules); and the Declaration on the Protection of Women and Children in Emergency and Armed Conflict,

Recognising that, in all countries in the world, there are children living in exceptionally difficult conditions, and the such children need special consideration,

Taking due account of the importance of the traditions and cultural values of each people for the protection and harmonious development of the child,

Recognising the importance of international cooperation for improving the living conditions of children in every country, in particular in the developing countries,

Have agreed as follows:

PART I

ARTICLE 1

For the purposes of the present Convention, a child means every human being below the age of eighteen years unless under the law applicable to the child, majority is attained earlier.

ARTICLE 2

1. States Parties shall respect and ensure the rights set forth in the present Convention to each child within their jurisdiction without discrimination of any kind, irrespective of the child's or his or her parent's or legal guardian's race, colour, sex, language, religion, political or other opinion, national ethnic or social origin, property, disability, birth or other status.
2. States Parties shall take all appropriate measures to ensure that the child is protected against all forms of discrimination or punishment on the basis of the status, activities, expressed opinions, or beliefs of the child's parents, legal guardians, or family members.

ARTICLE 3

1. In all actions concerning children, whether undertaken by public or private social welfare institutions, courts of law, administrative authorities or legislative bodies, the best interests of the child shall be a primary consideration.

2. States Parties undertake to ensure the child such protection and care as is necessary for his or her well-being, taking into account the rights and duties of his or her parents, legal guardians, or other individuals legally responsible for him or her, and to this end, shall take all appropriate legislative and administrative measures.

3. States Parties shall ensure that the institutions, services and facilities responsible for the care or protection of children shall conform with the standards established by competent authorities, particularly in the areas of safety, health, in the number and suitability of their staff, as well as competent supervision.

ARTICLE 4

States Parties shall undertake all appropriate legislative, administrative, and other measures for the implementation of the rights recognised in the present Convention. With regard to economic, social and cultural rights, States Parties shall undertake such measures to the maximum extent of their available resources and, where needed, within the framework of international cooperation.

ARTICLE 5

States Parties shall respect the responsibilities, rights and duties of parents or, where applicable, the members of the extended family or community as provided for by local custom, legal guardians or other persons legally responsible for the child, to provide, in a manner consistent with the evolving capacities of the child, appropriate direction and guidance in the exercise by the child, appropriate direction and guidance in the exercise by the child of the rights recognised in the present Convention.

ARTICLE 6

1. States Parties recognise that every child has the inherent right to life.
2. States Parties shall ensure to the maximum extent possible the survival and development of the child.

ARTICLE 7

1. The child shall be registered immediately after birth and shall have the right from birth to a name, the right to acquire a nationality and, as far as possible, the right to know and be cared for by his or her parents.
2. States Parties shall ensure the implementation of these rights in accordance with their national law and their obligations under the relevant international instruments in this field, in particular where the child would otherwise be stateless.

ARTICLE 8

1. States Parties undertake to respect the right of the child to preserve his or her identity, including nationality, name and family relations as recognised by law without unlawful interference.

2. Where a child is illegally deprived of some or all of the elements of his or her identity, States Parties shall provide appropriate assistance and protection, with a view to re-establishing speedily his or her identity.

ARTICLE 9

1. States Parties shall ensure that a child shall not be separated from his or her parents against their will, except when competent authorities subject to judicial review determine, in accordance with applicable law and procedures, that such separation is necessary for the best interests of the child. Such determination may be necessary in a particular case such as one involving abuse or neglect of the child by the parents, or one where the parents are living separately and a decision must be made as to the child's place of residence.

2. In any proceedings pursuant to paragraph 1 of the present Article, all interested parties shall be given an opportunity to participate in the proceeding and make their views known.

3. States Parties shall respect the right of the child who is separated from one or both parents to maintain personal relations and direct contact with both parents on a regular basis, except if it is contrary to the child's best interests.

4. Where such separation results from any action initiated by a States Party, such as the detention, imprisonment, exile, deportation or death (including death arising from any cause while the person is in the custody of the State) of one or both parents or of the child, that State Party shall, upon request,

provide the parents, the child or, if appropriate, another member of the family with the essential information concerning the whereabouts of the absent member(s) of the family unless the provision of the information would be detrimental to the well-being of the child. States Parties shall further ensure that the submission of such a request shall of itself entail no adverse consequences for the person(s) concerned.

ARTICLE 10

1. In accordance with the obligation of States Parties under article 9, paragraph 1, applications by a child or his or her parents to enter or leave a State party for the purpose of family reunification shall be dealt with by States Parties in a positive, humane and expeditious manner. States Parties shall further ensure that the submission of such a request shall entail no adverse consequences for the applicants and for the members of their family.

2. A child whose parents reside in different States shall have the right to maintain on a regular basis, save in exceptional circumstances personal relations and direct contacts with both parents. Towards that end and in accordance with the obligation of States Parties under article 9, paragraph 1, States Parties shall respect the right of the child and his or her parents to leave any country, including their own, and to enter their own country. The right to leave any country shall be subject only to such restrictions as are prescribed by law and which are necessary to protect the national security, public order (order public), public health or morals or the rights and

freedoms of others and are consistent with the other rights recognised in the present Convention.

ARTICLE 11

1. States Parties shall take measures to combat the illicit transfer and non-return of children abroad.
2. To this end, States Parties shall promote the conclusion of bilateral or multilateral agreements or accession to existing agreements.

ARTICLE 12

1. States Parties shall assure to the child who is capable of forming his or her own views the right to express those views freely in all matters affecting the child, the views of the child being given due weight in accordance with the age and maturity of the child.
2. For this purpose, the child shall in particular be provided the opportunity to be heard in any judicial and administrative proceedings affecting the child, either directly, or through a representative or an appropriate body, in a manner consistent with the procedural rules of national law.

ARTICLE 13

1. The child shall have the right to freedom of expression; this right shall include freedom to seek, receive and impart information and ideas of all kinds, regardless of frontiers, either orally, in writing

or in print, in the form of art, or through any other media of the child's choice.

2. The exercise of this right may be subject to certain restrictions, but these shall only be such as are provided by law and are necessary:

   a) For respect of the rights or reputations of others, or

   b) For the protection of national security or of public order (order public), or of public health or morals.

ARTICLE 14

1. States Parties shall respect the right of the child to freedom of thought, conscience and religion.

2. States Parties shall respect the rights and duties of the parents and when applicable, legal guardians, to provide direction to the child in the exercise of his or her right in a manner consistent with the evolving capacities of the child.

3. Freedom to manifest one's religion or beliefs may be subject only to such limitations as are prescribed by law and are necessary to protect public safety, order, health or morals, or the fundamental rights and freedoms of others.

ARTICLE 15

1. States Parties recognise the rights of the child to freedom of association and to freedom of peaceful assembly.

2. No restrictions may be placed on the exercise of these rights other than those imposed in conformity with the law and which are necessary in a democratic society in the interests of national security or public safety, public order (order public), the protection of public health or morals or the protection of the rights and freedoms of others.

ARTICLE 16

1. No child shall be subjected to arbitrary or unlawful interference with his or her privacy, family, home or correspondence, nor to unlawful attacks on his or her honour and reputation;

2. The child has the right to the protection of the law against such interference or attacks.

ARTICLE 17

States Parties recognise the important function performed by the mass media and shall ensure that the child has access to information and material from a diversity of national and international sources, especially those aimed at the promotion of his or her social, spiritual and moral well-being and physical and mental health. To this end, States Parties shall:

a) Encourage the mass media to disseminate information and material of social and cultural benefit to the child and in accordance with the spirit of Article 29;

b) Encourage international co-operation in the production, exchange and dissemination of such information and material from a diversity of cultural, national and international sources;

c) Encourage the production and dissemination of children's books;

d) Encourage the mass media to have particular regard to the linguistic needs of the child who belongs to a minority group or who is indigenous.

e) Encourage the development of appropriate guidelines for the protection of the child from information and material injurious to his or her well-being, bearing in mind the provisions of Articles 13 and 18.

ARTICLE 18

1. States Parties shall use their best efforts to ensure recognition of the principles that both parents have common responsibilities for the upbringing and development of the child. Parents or, as the case may be, legal guardians, have the primary responsibility for the upbringing and development of the child. The best interests of the child will be their basic concern.

2. For the purpose of guaranteeing and promoting the rights set forth in the present Convention, States Parties shall render appropriate assistance to parents and legal guardians in the performance of their child-rearing responsibilities and shall ensure the development of institutions, facilities and services of the care of children.

3. States Parties shall take all appropriate measures to ensure that children of working parents have the right to benefit from child-care services and facilities for which they are eligible.

ARTICLE 19

1. States Parties shall take all appropriate legislative, administrative social and educational measures to protect the child from all forms of physical or mental violence, injury or abuse, neglect or negligent treatment, maltreatment or exploitation, including sexual abuse, while in the care of parent(s), legal guardian(s) or any other person who has the care of the child.

2. Such protective measures should, as appropriate, include effective procedures for the establishment of social programmes to provide necessary support for the child and for those who have the care of the child, as well as for other forms of prevention and for identification, reporting, referral, investigation, treatment and follow-up of instances of child maltreatment described heretofore, and, as appropriate, for judicial involvement.

ARTICLE 20

1. A child temporarily or permanently deprived of his or her family environment, or in whose own best interests cannot be allowed to remain in that environment shall be entitled to special protection and assistance provided by the State.

2. States Parties shall in accordance with their national laws ensure alternative care for such a child.

3. Such care could include, *inter alia,* foster placement *kafalah of Islamic law,* adoption or if necessary placement in suitable institutions for the care of children. When considering solutions, due regard shall be paid to the desirability of continuity in a child's upbringing and to the child's ethnic, religious, cultural and linguistic background.

ARTICLE 21

States Parties that recognise and/or permit the system of adoption shall ensure that the best interests of the child shall be the paramount consideration and they shall:

a) Ensure that the adoption of a child is authorised only by competent authorities who determine, in accordance with applicable law and procedures and on the basis of all pertinent and reliable information, that the adoption is permissible in view of the child's status concerning parents, relatives and legal guardians and that, if required, the persons concerned have given their informed consent to the adoption on the basis of such counselling as may be necessary;

b) Recognised that inter-country adoption may be considered as an alternative means of child's care, if the child cannot be placed in a foster or an adoptive family or cannot in any suitable manner be cared for in the child's country of origin;

c) Ensure that the child concerned by inter-country adoption enjoys safeguards and standards equivalent to those existing in the case of national adoption;

d) Take all appropriate measures to ensure that, in inter-country adoption, the placement does not result in improper financial gain for those involved in it;

e) Promote, where appropriate, the objectives of the present article by concluding bilateral or multilateral arrangements or agreements, and endeavour, within this framework, to ensure that the placement of the child in another country is carried out by competent authorities or organs.

ARTICLE 22

1. States Parties shall take appropriate measures to ensure that a child who is seeking refugee status or who is considered a refugee in accordance with applicable international or domestic law and procedures shall, whether unaccompanied or accompanied by his or her parents or by any other person, receive appropriate protection and humanitarian assistance in the enjoyment of applicable rights set forth in the present Convention and in other international human rights or humanitarian instruments to which the said States are Parties.

2. For this purpose, States Parties shall provide, as they consider appropriate, co-operation in any efforts by

the United Nations and other competent inter-governmental organisations or non-governmental organisations co-operating with the United Nations to protect and assist such a child and to trace the parents or other members of the family of any refugee child in order to obtain information necessary for reunification with his or her family. In cases where no parents or other members of the family can be found, the child shall be accorded the same protection as any other child permanently or temporarily deprived of his or her family environment for any reason, as set forth in the present Convention.

ARTICLE 23

1. States Parties recognise that a mentally or physically disabled child should enjoy a full and decent life, in conditions which ensure dignity, promote self-reliance and facilitate the child's active participation in the community.

2. States Parties recognise the right of the disabled child to special care and shall encourage and ensure the extension, subject to available resources, to the eligible child and those responsible for his or her care, of assistance for which application is made and which is appropriate to the child's condition and to the circumstances of the parents or others caring for the child.

3. Recognising the special needs of a disabled child, assistances extended in accordance with paragraph 2 of the present article shall be provided free of charge, whenever possible, taking into account the financial

resources of the parents or others caring for the child, and shall be designed to ensure that the disabled child has effective access to and receives education, training, health care services, rehabilitation services, preparation for employment and recreation opportunities in a manner conducive to the child's achieving the fullest possible social integration and individual development, including his or her cultural and spiritual development.

4. States Parties shall promote, in the spirit of international cooperation, the exchange of appropriate information in the field of preventive health care and of medical psychological and functional treatment of disabled children, including dissemination of and access to information concerning methods of rehabilitation, education and vocational services, with the aim of enabling States Parties to improve their capabilities and skills and to widen their experience in these areas. In this regard, particular account shall be taken of the needs of developing countries.

ARTICLE 24

1. States Parties recognise the right of the child to the enjoyment of the highest attainable standard of health and to facilities for the treatment of illness and rehabilitation of health. States Parties shall strive to ensure that no child is deprived of his or her right of access to such health care services.
2. States Parties shall pursue full implementation of this right and, in particular, shall take appropriate measures:

a) To diminish infant and child mortality;

b) To ensure the provision of necessary medical assistance and health care to all children with emphasis on the development of primary health care;

c) To combat disease and malnutrition, including within the framework of primary health care, through, *inter alia*, the application of readily available technology and through the provision of adequate nutritious foods and clean drinking water, taking into consideration the dangers and risks of environmental pollution;

d) To ensure appropriate pre-natal and post-natal health care for mothers;

e) To ensure that all segments of society, in particular parents and children, are informed, have access to education and are supported in the use of basic knowledge of child health and nutrition, the advantages of breastfeeding, hygiene and environmental sanitation and the prevention of accidents;

f) To develop preventive health care, guidance for parents and family planning education and services.

3. States Parties shall take all effective and appropriate measures with a view to abolishing traditional practices prejudicial to the health of children.

4. States Parties undertake to promote and encourage international cooperation with a view to achieving progressively the full realisation of the right recognised in the present article. In this regard, particular account shall be taken of the needs of developing countries.

ARTICLE 25

States Parties recognise the right of a child who has been placed by the competent authorities for the purposes of care, protection or treatment of his or her physical or mental health, to a periodic review of the treatment provided to the child and all other circumstances relevant to his or her placement.

ARTICLE 26

1. States Parties shall recognise for every child the right to benefit from social security, including social insurance, and shall take the necessary measures to achieve the full realisation of this right in accordance with their national law.
2. The benefits should, where appropriate, be granted, taking into account the resources and the circumstances of the child and persons having responsibility for the maintenance of the child, as well as any other consideration relevant to an application for benefits made by or on behalf of the child.

ARTICLE 27

1. States Parties recognise the right of every child to a standard of living adequate for the child's physical, mental, spiritual, moral and social development.

2. The parent(s) or others responsible for the child have the primary responsibility to secure, within their abilities and financial capacities, the conditions of living necessary for the child's development;

3. States Parties, in accordance with national conditions and within their means, shall take appropriate measures to assist parents and others responsible for the child to implement this right and shall in case of need provide material assistance and support programmes, particularly with regard to nutrition, clothing and housing.

4. States Parties shall take all appropriate measures to secure the recovery of maintenance for the child from the parents of other persons having financial responsibility for the child, both within the State Party and from abroad. In particular, where the person having financial responsibility for the child lives in a State different from that of the child, States Parties shall promote the accession to international agreements of the conclusion of such agreements, as well as the making of other appropriate arrangements.

ARTICLE 28

1. States Parties recognise the right of the child to education, and with a view to achieving this right progressively and on the basis of equal opportunity, they shall, in particular:

   a) Make primary education compulsory and available free to all;

b) Encourage the development of different forms of secondary education, including general and vocational education, make them available and accessible to every child, and take appropriate measures such as the introduction of free education and offering financial assistance in case of need;

c) Make higher education accessible to all on the basis of capacity by every appropriate means;

d) Make educational and vocational information and guidance available and accessible to all children;

e) Take measures to encourage regular attendance at schools and the reduction of dropout rates.

2. States Parties shall take all appropriate measures to ensure that school discipline is administered in a manner consistent with the child's human dignity and in conformity with the present Convention.

3. States Parties shall promote and encourage international cooperation in matters relating to education, in particular with a view to contributing to the elimination of ignorance and illiteracy throughout the world and facilitating access to scientific and technical knowledge and modern teaching methods. In this regard, particular account shall be taken of the needs of developing countries.

ARTICLE 29

1. States Parties agree that the education on the child shall be directed to:

   a) The development of the child's personality, talents and mental and physical abilities to their fullest potential;

   b) The development of respect for human rights and fundamental freedoms, and for the principles enshrined in the Charter of the United Nations.

   c) The development of respect for the child's parents, his or her own cultural identity, language and values, for the national values of the country in which the child is living, the country from which he or she may originate, and for civilisations different from his or her own;

   d) The preparation of the child for responsible life in a free society, in the spirit of understanding, peace tolerance equality of sexes, and friendship among all peoples, ethnic, national and religious groups and persons of indigenous origin;

   e) The development of respect for the natural environment.

2. No part of the present Article or article 28 shall be construed so as to interfere with the liberty of individuals and bodies to establish and direct educational institutions, subject always to the

observance of the principle set forth in paragraph 1 of the present article and to the requirements that the education given in such institutions shall confirm to such minimum standards as may be laid down by the State.

ARTICLE 30

In those States in which ethnic, religious or linguistic minorities or persons of indigenous origin exist, a child belonging to such a minority or who is indigenous shall not be denied the right, in community with other members of his or her group, to enjoy his or her own culture, to profess and practise his or her own religion, or to use his or her own language.

Article 31

1. States Parties recognise the right of the child to rest and leisure, to engage in play and recreational activities appropriate to the age of the child and to participate freely in cultural life and the arts.
2. States Parties shall respect and promote the right of the child to participate fully in cultural and artistic life and shall encourage the provision of appropriate and equal opportunities for cultural, artistic, recreational and leisure activity.

Article 32

1. States Parties recognise the right of the child to be protected from economic exploitation and from performing any work that is likely to be hazardous or to interfere with the child's education, or to be

harmful to the child's health or physical, mental, spiritual, moral or social development.

2. States Parties shall take legislative, administrative, social and educational measures to ensure the implementation of the present article. To this end, and having regard to the relevant provisions of other international instruments, States Parties shall in particular:

   a) Provide for a minimum age or minimum ages for admission to employment;

   b) Provide for appropriate regulation of the hours and conditions of employment; and

   c) Provide for appropriate penalties or other sanctions to ensure the effective enforcement of the present article.

ARTICLE 33

States Parties shall take all appropriate measures, including legislative, administrative, social and educational measures, to protect children from the illicit use of narcotic drugs and psychotropic substances as defined in the relevant international treaties, and to prevent the use of children in the illicit production and trafficking of such substances.

ARTICLE 34

States Parties undertake to protect the child from all forms of sexual exploitation and sexual abuse. For these purposes, States Parties shall in particular take all appropriate national, bilateral and multilateral measures to prevent:

a) The inducement or coercion of a child to engage in any unlawful sexual activity;

b) The exploitative use of children in prostitution or other unlawful sexual practices; and

c) The exploitative use of children in pornographic performances and materials.

ARTICLE 35

States Parties shall take all appropriate national, bilateral and multilateral measures to prevent the abduction of the sale of or traffic in children for any purpose or in any form.

ARTICLE 36

States Parties shall protect the child against all other forms of exploitation prejudicial to any aspects of the child's welfare.

ARTICLE 37

States Parties shall ensure that:

a) No child shall be subjected to torture or other cruel, inhuman or degrading treatment or punishment. Neither capital punishment nor life imprisonment without possibility of release shall be imposed for offences committed by persons below eighteen years of age;

b) No child shall be deprived of his or her liberty unlawfully or arbitrarily. The arrest, detention or imprisonment of a child shall be in conformity with the law and shall be used only as a measure of last resort and for the shortest appropriate period of time;

c) Every child deprived of liberty shall be treated with humanity and respect for the inherent dignity of the human person, and in a manner which takes into account the needs of persons of his or her age. In particular, every child deprived of liberty shall be separated from adults unless it is considered in the child's best interest not to do so and shall have the right to maintain contact with his or her family through correspondence and visits, save in exceptional circumstances; and

d) Every child deprived of his or her liberty shall have the right to prompt access to legal and other appropriate assistance, as well as the right to challenge the legality of the deprivation of his or her liberty before a court or other competent, independent and impartial authority, and to a prompt decision on any such action.

ARTICLE 38

1. States Parties undertake to respect and to ensure respect for rules of international humanitarian law applicable to them in armed conflicts which are relevant to the child.

2. States Parties shall take all feasible measures to ensure that persons who have not attained the age of fifteen years do not take a direct part in hostilities.

3. States Parties shall refrain from recruiting any person who has not attained the age of fifteen years into their armed forces. In recruiting among those persons

who have attained the age of fifteen years but who have not attained the age of eighteen years, States Parties shall endeavour to give priority to those who are oldest.

4. In accordance with their obligations under international humanitarian law to protect the civilian population in armed conflicts, States Parties shall take all feasible measures to ensure protection and care of children who are affected by an armed conflict.

ARTICLE 39

States Parties shall take all appropriate measures to promote physical and psychological recovery and social reintegration of a child victim of: any form of neglect, exploitation, or abuse; torture or any other form of cruel, inhuman or degrading treatment or punishment; or armed conflicts. Such recovery and reintegration shall take place in an environment which fosters the health, self-respect and dignity of the child.

ARTICLE 40

1. States Parties recognise the right of every child alleged as, accused of, or recognised as having infringed the penal law to be treated in a manner consistent with the promotion of the child's sense of dignity and worth, which reinforces the child's respect for the human rights and fundamental freedoms of others and which takes into account the child's age and the desirability of promoting the child's reintegration and the child's assuming a constructive role in society.

2. To this end, and having regard to the relevant provisions of international instruments, States Parties shall, in particular, ensure that:

   a) No child shall be alleged as, be accused of, or recognised as having infringed the penal law by reason of acts or omissions that were not prohibited by national or international law at the time they were committed;

   b) Every child alleged as or accused of having infringed the penal law has at least the following guarantees:

      i) To be presumed innocent until proven guilty according to law;

      ii) To be informed promptly and directly of the charges against him or her, and, if appropriate, through his or her parents of legal guardians, and to have legal or other appropriate assistance in the preparation and presentation of his or her defence;

      iii) To have the matter determined without delay by a competent, independent and impartial authority or judicial body in a fair hearing according to law, in the presence of legal or other appropriate assistance and, unless it is considered not to be in the best interest of the child, in particular, taking into account his or her age or situation, his or her parents or legal guardians;

      iv) Not to be compelled to give testimony or to confess guilt; to examine or have examined adverse witnesses and to obtain the participation and examination of witnesses on his or her behalf under conditions of equality;

v) If considered to have infringed the penal law to have this decision and any measures imposed in consequence thereof reviewed by a higher competent, independent and impartial authority or judicial body according to law;

vi) To have the free assistance of an interpreter if the child cannot understand or speak the language used; and

vii) To have his or her privacy fully respected at all stages of the proceedings.

3. States Parties shall seek to promote the establishment of laws, procedures, authorities and institutions specifically applicable to children alleged as, accused of or recognised as having infringed the penal law, and, in particular:

a) The establishment of a minimum age below which children shall be presumed not to have the capacity to infringe the penal law; and

b) Whenever appropriate and desirable measures for dealing with such children without resorting to judicial proceedings, providing that human rights and legal safeguards are fully respected.

4. A variety of dispositions, such as care, guidance and supervision orders; counselling; probation; foster care; education and vocational training programmes and other alternatives to institutional care shall be available to ensure that children are dealt with in a manner appropriate to their well being and

proportionate both to their circumstances and the offence.

ARTICLE 41

Nothing in the present Convention shall affect any provisions which are more conducive to the realisation of the rights of the child and which may be contained in:

a) The law of a State Party; or

b) International law in force for that State.

PART II

ARTICLE 42

States Parties undertake to make the principles and provisions of the Convention widely known, by appropriate and active means, to adults and children alike.

ARTICLE 43

1. For the purpose of examining the progress made by States Parties in achieving the realisation of the obligations undertaken in the present Convention, there shall be established a Committee in the Rights of the Child, which shall carry out the functions hereinafter provided.

2. The Committee shall consist of ten experts of high moral standing and recognised competence in the field covered by this Convention. The members of the Committee shall be elected by States Parties from among their nationals and shall serve in their

personal capacity, consideration being given to equitable geographical distribution, as well as to the principal legal systems.

3. The members of the Committee shall be elected by secret ballot from a list of persons nominated by States Parties. Each State Party may nominate one person from among its own nationals.

4. The initial election to the Committee shall be held no later than six months after the date of the entry into force of the present Convention and thereafter every second year. At least four months before the date of each election, the Secretary-General of the United Nations shall address a letter to States Parties inviting them to submit their nominations within two months. The Secretary-General shall subsequently prepare a list in alphabetical order of all persons thus nominated, indicating States Parties which have nominated them, and shall submit it to the States Parties to the present Convention.

5. The elections shall be held at meetings of States Parties convened by the Secretary-General at United Nations Headquarters. At those meetings, for which two thirds of States Parties shall constitute a quorum, the persons elected to the Committee shall be those who obtain the largest number of votes and an absolute majority of the votes of the representatives of States Parties present and voting.

6. The members of the Committee shall be elected for a term of four years. They shall be eligible for re-election if renominated. The term of five of the members elected at the first election, shall expire at the end of two years; immediately after the first

election the names of these five members shall be chosen by lot by the Chairman of the meeting.

7. If a member of the Committee dies or resigns or declares that for any other cause he or she can no longer perform the duties of the Committee, the State Party which nominated the member shall appoint another expert from among its nationals to serve for the remainder of the term, subject to the approval of the Committee.

8. The Committee shall establish its own rules of procedure.

9. The Committee shall elect its officers for a period of two years.

10. The meetings of the Committee shall normally be held at United Nations Headquarters or at any other convenient place as determined by the Committee. The Committee shall normally meet annually. The duration of the meetings of the Committee shall be determined, and reviewed, subject to the approval of the General Assembly.

11. The Secretary-General of the United Nations shall provide the necessary staff and facilities for the United Nations shall provide the necessary staff and facilities for the effective performance of the functions of the Committee under the present Convention.

12. With the approval of the General Assembly, the members of the Committee established under the present Convention shall receive emoluments from United Nations resources on such terms and conditions as the Assembly may decide.

ARTICLE 44

1. States Parties undertake to submit to the Committee, through the Secretary-General of the United Nations, reports on the measures they have adopted which give effect to the rights recognised herein and on the progress made on the enjoyment of those rights:

   a) Within two years of the entry into force of the Convention for the State Party concerned; and

   b) Thereafter every five years.

2. Reports made under the present article shall indicate factors and difficulties, if any affecting the degree of fulfilment of the obligations under the present Convention. Reports shall also contain sufficient information to provide the Committee with a comprehensive understanding of the implementation of the Convention in the country concerned.

3. A State Party which has submitted a compre-hensive initial report to the Committee need not, in its subsequent reports submitted in accordance with paragraph 1 (b) of the present article, repeat basic information previously provided.

4. The Committee may request from States Parties further information relevant to the implementation of the Convention.

5. The Committee shall submit to the General Assembly, through the Economic and Social Council, every two years, reports on its activities.

6. States Parties shall make their reports widely available to the public in their own countries.

ARTICLE 45

In order to foster the effective implementation of the Convention and to encourage international cooperation in the field covered by the Convention:

a) The specialised agencies, the United Nations Children's Fund, and other United Nations organs shall be entitled to be represented at the consideration of the implementation of such provisions of the present Convention as fall within the scope of their mandate. The Committee may invite the specialised agencies, the United Nations Children's Fund and other competent bodies as it may consider appropriate to provide expert advice on the implementation of the Convention in areas falling within the scope of their respective mandates. The Committee may invite the specialised agencies, the United Nations Children's Fund, and other United Nations organs to submit reports on the implementation of the Convention in areas falling within the scope of their activities;

b) The Committee shall transmit, as it may consider appropriate to the specialised agencies, the United Nations Children's Fund and other competent bodies, any reports from States Parties that contain a request, or indicate a need, for technical advice or assistance, along with the Committee's observations and suggestions, if any, on these requests or indications;

c) The Committee may recommend to the General Assembly to request the Secretary-General to undertake on its behalf studies on specific issues relating to the rights of the child;

d) The Committee may make suggestions and general recommendations based on information received pursuant to articles 44 and 45 of the present Convention. Such suggestions and general recommen-dations shall be transmitted to any State Party concerned and reported to the General Assembly, together with comments, if any, from States Parties.

PART III

ARTICLE 46

The present Convention shall be open for signature by all States.

ARTICLE 47

The present Convention is subject to ratification. Instruments of ratification shall be deposited with the Secretary-General of the United Nations.

ARTICLE 48

The present Convention shall remain open for accession by any State. The instruments of accession shall be deposited with the Secretary-General of the United Nations.

ARTICLE 49

1. The present Convention shall enter into force on the thirtieth day following the date of deposit with the Secretary-General of the United Nations of the twentieth instrument of ratification or accession.

2. For each State ratifying or acceding to the Convention after the deposit of the twentieth instrument of ratification or accession, the Convention shall enter into force on the thirtieth day after the deposit by such State of its instrument of ratification or accession.

ARTICLE 50

1. Any State Party may propose an amendment and file it with the Secretary-General of the United Nations. The Secretary-General shall thereupon communicate the proposed amendment to States Parties, with a request that they indicate whether they favour a conference of States Parties for the purpose of considering and voting upon the proposal. In the event that, within four months from the date of such communication, at least one third of the States Parties favour such a conference, the Secretary-General shall convene the conference under the auspices of the United Nations. Any amendment adopted by a majority of States Parties present and voting at the conference shall be submitted to the General Assembly for approval.

2. An amendment adopted in accordance with paragraph 1 of the present article shall enter into force when it has been approved by the General Assembly of the United Nations and accepted by a two-thirds majority of States Parties.

3. When an amendment enters into force, it shall be binding on those States Parties which have accepted it, other States Parties still being bound by the

provisions of the present Convention and any earlier amendments which they have accepted.

ARTICLE 51

1. The Secretary-General of the United Nations shall receive and circulate to all States the text of reservations made by States at the time of ratification or accession.

2. A reservation incompatible with the object and purpose of the present Convention shall not be permitted.

3. Reservations may be withdrawn at any time by notification to that effect addressed to the Secretary-General of the United Nations, who shall then inform all states. Such notification shall take effect on the date on which it is received by the Secretary-General.

ARTICLE 52

A State Party may denounce the present Convention by written notification to the Secretary-General of the United Nations. Denunciation becomes effective one year after the date of receipt of the notification by the Secretary-General.

ARTICLE 53

The Secretary-General of the United Nations is designated as the depositary of the present Convention.

ARTICLE 54

The original of the present Convention, of which the Arabic, Chinese, English French, Russian and Spanish text are equally authentic, shall be deposited with the Secretary-General of the United Nations.

In Witness Whereof the undersigned plenipotentiaries, being duly authorised thereto by their respective Governments have signed the present Convention.

10

A World Fit for Children

Declaration Adopted by the UN General Assembly at Twenty Seven Special Session, 10 May 2992

I. Declaration

1. Eleven years ago, at the World Summit for Children, world leaders made a joint commitment and issued an urgent, universal appeal to give every child a better future.

2. Since then, much progress has been made, as documented in the report of the Secretary-General entitled "We the Children".1 Millions of young lives have been saved, more children than ever are in school, more children are actively involved in decisions concerning their lives and important treaties have been concluded to protect children. However, these achievements and gains have been uneven, and many obstacles remain, particularly in developing countries. A brighter future for all has proved elusive, and overall gains have fallen short of national obligations and international commitments.

3. We, the Heads of State and Government and representatives of States participating in the special session of the General Assembly on children, reaffirming our commitment to the purposes and principles enshrined in the Charter of the United Nations are determined to seize this historic opportunity to change the world for and with children. Accordingly, we reaffirm our commitment to complete the unfinished agenda of the World Summit for Children and to address other emerging issues vital to the achievement of the longer-term goals and objectives endorsed at recent major United Nations summits and conferences, in particular, the United Nations Millennium Declaration,2 through national action and international cooperation.

4. We reaffirm our obligation to take action to promote and protect the rights of each child — every human being below the age of 18 years including adolescents. We are determined to respect the dignity and to secure the well-being of all children. We acknowledge that the Convention on the Rights of the Child,3 the most universally embraced human rights treaty in history, and its Optional Protocols contain a comprehensive set of international legal standards for the protection and well-being of children. We also recognize the importance of other international instruments relevant for children.

5. We stress our commitment to create a world fit for children in which sustainable human development, taking into account the best interests of the child, is founded on principles of democracy, equality, nondiscrimination, peace and social justice and the universality, indivisibility, interdependence and

interrelatedness of all human rights, including the right to development.

6. We recognize and support parents and families or, as the case may be, legal guardians as the primary caretakers of children, and we will strengthen their capacity to provide the optimum care, nurturing and protection.

7. We hereby call on all members of society to join us in a global movement that will help build a world fit for children through upholding our commitments to the following principles and objectives:

   (1) *Put children first.* In all actions related to children, the best interests of the child shall be a primary consideration.

   (2) *Eradicate poverty*: invest in children. We reaffirm our vow to break the cycle of poverty within a single generation, united in the conviction that investments in children and the realization of their rights are among the most effective ways to eradicate poverty. Immediate action must be taken to eliminate the worst forms of child labour.

   (3) *Leave no child behind.* Each girl and boy is born free and equal in dignity and rights; therefore, all forms of discrimination affecting children must end.

   (4) *Care for every child.* Children must get the best possible start in life. Their survival, protection, growth and development in good health and with proper nutrition is the essential foundation of human development. We will make concerted efforts to fight infectious diseases, tackle major

causes of malnutrition and nurture children in a safe environment that enables them to be physically healthy, mentally alert, emotionally secure, socially competent and able to learn.

(5) *Educate every child.* All girls and boys must have access to and complete primary education that is free, compulsory and of good quality as a cornerstone of an inclusive basic education. Gender disparities in primary and secondary education must be eliminated.

(6) *Protect children from harm and exploitation.* Children must be protected against any acts of violence, abuse, exploitation and discrimination, as well as all forms of terrorism and hostagetaking.

(7) *Protect children from war.* Children must be protected from the horrors of armed conflict. Children under foreign occupation must also be protected, in accordance with the provisions of international humanitarian law.

(8) *Combat HIV/AIDS.* Children and their families must be protected from the devastating impact of human immunodeficiency virus/acquired immunodeficiency syndrome (HIV/AIDS).

(9) *Listen to children and ensure their participation.* Children and adolescents are resourceful citizens capable of helping to build a better future for all. We must respect their right to express themselves and to participate in all matters affecting them, in accordance with their age and maturity.

(10) *Protect the Earth for children.* We must safeguard our natural environment, with its diversity of life,

its beauty and its resources, all of which enhance the quality of life, for present and future generations. We will give every assistance to protect children and minimize the impact of natural disasters and environmental degradation on them.

8. We recognize that the implementation of the present Declaration and Plan of Action require not only renewed political will, but also the mobilization and allocation of additional resources at both the national and international levels, taking into account the urgency and gravity of the special needs of children.

9. In line with these principles and objectives, we adopt the Plan of Action contained in section III below, confident that together we will build a world in which all girls and boys can enjoy childhood — a time of play and learning, in which they are loved, respected and cherished, their rights are promoted and protected, without discrimination of any kind, where their safety and well-being are paramount and where they can develop in health, peace and dignity.

II. Review of Progress and Lessons Learned

10. The World Declaration and the Plan of Action of the World Summit for Children4 are among the most rigorously monitored and implemented international commitments of the 1990s. Annual reviews were held at the national level and progress reports presented to the General Assembly. A mid-decade review and an extensive global end-decade review were conducted. The latter included high-level regional meetings in Beijing, Berlin, Cairo, Kathmandu and

Kingston, which reviewed progress; ensured follow-up to the Summit and other major conferences; promoted renewed commitment to the achievement of the goals of the World Summit; and guided actions for the future. Complementing efforts by Governments, a wide range of actors participated in the reviews, including children, young people's organizations, academic institutions, religious groups, civil society organizations, parliamentarians, the media, United Nations agencies, donors and major national and international non-governmental organizations.

11. As documented in the end-decade review of the Secretary-General on follow-up to the World Summit for Children, the 1990s was a decade of great promises and modest achievements for the world's children. On the positive side, the Summit and the entry into force of the Convention on the Rights of the Child helped accord political priority to children. A record 192 countries ratified, acceded to or signed the Convention. Some 155 countries prepared national programmes of action to implement the Summit goals. Regional commitments were made. International legal provisions and mechanisms strengthened the protection of children. Pursuit of the Summit goals has led to many tangible results for children: this year, 3 million fewer children will die than a decade ago; polio has been brought to the brink of eradication; and, through salt iodization, 90 million newborns are protected every year from a significant loss of learning ability.

12. Yet much more needs to be done. The resources that were promised at the Summit at both the national and international levels have yet to fully materialize

Critical challenges remain: more than 10 million children die each year although most of those deaths could be prevented; 100 million children are still out of school, 60 per cent of them girls; 150 million children suffer from malnutrition; and HIV/AIDS is spreading with catastrophic speed. There is persistent poverty, exclusion and discrimination, and inadequate investment in social services. Also, debt burdens, excessive military spending, inconsistent with national security requirements, armed conflict, foreign occupation, hostagetaking and all forms of terrorism, as well as the lack of efficient use of resources, among other factors, can constrain national efforts to combat poverty and to ensure the well-being of children. The childhood of millions continues to be devastated by hazardous and exploitative labour; the sale and trafficking of children, including adolescents, and other forms of abuse, neglect, exploitation and violence.

13. The experience of the past decade has confirmed that the needs and rights of children must be a priority in all development efforts. There are many key lessons: change is possible — and children's rights are an effective rallying point; policies must address both the immediate factors affecting or excluding groups of children and the wider and deeper causes of inadequate protection and rights violations; targeted interventions that achieve rapid successes need to be pursued, with due attention to sustainability and participatory processes; and efforts should build on children's own resilience and strength. Multisectoral programmes focusing on early childhood and support to families, especially in high-risk conditions, merit special support because they provide lasting

benefits for child growth, development and protection.

III. Plan of Action

A. *Creating a world fit for children*

14. A world fit for children is one in which all children get the best possible start in life and have access to a quality basic education, including primary education that is compulsory and available free to all, and in which all children, including adolescents, have ample opportunity to develop their individual capacities in a safe and supportive environment. We will promote the physical, psychological, spiritual, social, emotional, cognitive and cultural development of children as a matter of national and global priorities.

15. The family is the basic unit of society and as such should be strengthened. It is entitled to receive comprehensive protection and support. The primary responsibility for the protection, upbringing and development of children rests with the family. All institutions of society should respect children's rights and secure their well-being and render appropriate assistance to parents, families, legal guardians and other caregivers so that children can grow and develop in a safe and stable environment and in an atmosphere of happiness, love and understanding, bearing in mind that in different cultural, social and political systems, various forms of the family exist.

16. We also recognize that a considerable number of children live without parental support, such as orphans, children living on the street, internally

displaced and refugee children, children affected by trafficking and sexual and economic exploitation and children who are incarcerated. Special measures should be taken to support such children and the institutions, facilities and services that care for them, and to build and strengthen children's own abilities to protect themselves.

17. We are determined to promote access by parents, families, legal guardians, caregivers and children themselves to a full range of information and services to promote child survival, development, protection and participation.

18. Chronic poverty remains the single biggest obstacle to meeting the needs, protecting and promoting the rights of children. It must be tackled on all fronts, from the provision of basic social services to the creation of employment opportunities, from the availability of microcredit to investment in infrastructure, and from debt relief to fair trade practices. Children are hardest hit by poverty because it strikes at the very roots of their potential for development — their growing bodies and minds. Eradication of poverty and reduction of disparities must therefore be a key objective of development efforts. The goals and strategies agreed upon at recent major United Nations conferences and their follow-ups, in particular the Millennium Summit, provide a helpful international framework for national strategies for poverty reduction to fulfil and protect the rights and promote the well-being of children.

19. We recognize that globalization and interdependence are opening new opportunities through trade,

investment and capital flows and advances in technology, including information technology, for the growth of the world economy, development and improvement of living standards around the world. At the same time, there remain serious challenges, including serious financial crises, insecurity, poverty, exclusion and inequality within and among societies. Considerable obstacles to further integration and full participation in the global economy remain for developing countries, in particular the least developed countries, as well as for some countries with economies in transition. Unless the benefits of social and economic development are extended to all countries, a growing number of people in all countries and even entire regions will remain marginalized from the global economy. We must act now in order to overcome those obstacles affecting peoples and countries and to realize the full potential of opportunities presented for the benefit of all, in particular children. We are committed to an open, equitable, rule-based, predictable and non-discriminatory multilateral trading and financial system. Investment in, inter alia, education and training will assist in enabling children to partake of the benefits of the breakthroughs in information and communication technologies. Globalization offers opportunities and challenges. The developing countries and countries with economies in transition face special difficulties in responding to those challenges and opportunities. Globalization should be fully inclusive and equitable, and there is a strong need for policies and measures at the national and international levels, formulated and implemented with the full and effective participation of developing countries and countries with economies in transition to help them respond effectively to those challenges and opportunities, giving high priority to achieving progress for children.

20. Discrimination gives rise to a self-perpetuating cycle of social and economic exclusion and undermines children's ability to develop to the fullest. We will make every effort to eliminate discrimination against children, whether rooted in the child's or his or her parent's or legal guardian's race, colour, sex, language, religion, political or other opinion, national, ethnic or social origin, property, disability, birth or other status.

21. We will take all measures to ensure the full and equal enjoyment of all human rights and fundamental freedoms, including equal access to health, education and recreational services, by children with disabilities and children with special needs; to ensure the recognition of their dignity; to promote their self-reliance; and to facilitate their active participation in the community.

22. Indigenous children, children belonging to minorities and vulnerable groups, are disproportionately disadvantaged in many countries due to all forms of discrimination, including racial discrimination. We shall take appropriate measures to end discrimination, to provide special support, and to ensure equal access to services for these children.

23. The achievement of goals for children, particularly for girls, will be advanced if women fully enjoy all human rights and fundamental freedoms, including the right to development, are empowered to participate fully and equally in all spheres of society and are protected and free from all forms of violence,

abuse and discrimination. We are determined to eliminate all forms of discrimination against the girl child throughout her life cycle and to provide special attention to her needs in order to promote and protect all her human rights, including the right to be free from coercion and from harmful practices and sexual exploitation. We will promote gender equality and equal access to basic social services, such as education, nutrition, health care, including sexual and reproductive health care, vaccinations, and protection from diseases representing the major causes of mortality, and will mainstream a gender perspective in all development policies and programmes.

24. We also recognize the need to address the changing role of men in society, as boys, adolescents and fathers, and the challenges faced by boys growing up in today's world. We will further promote the shared responsibility of both parents in education and in the raising of children, and will make every effort to ensure that fathers have opportunities to participate in their children's lives.

25. It is vital that national goals for children include targets for reducing disparities, in particular those which arise from discrimination on the basis of race, between girls and boys, rural and urban children, wealthy and poor children and those with and without disabilities.

26. A number of environmental problems and trends, such as global warming, ozone layer depletion, air pollution, hazardous wastes, exposure to hazardous chemicals and pesticides, inadequate sanitation, poor hygiene, unsafe drinking water and food and

inadequate housing, need to be addressed to ensure the health and well-being of children.

27. Adequate housing fosters family integration, contributes to social equity and strengthens the feeling of belonging, security and human solidarity, which are essential for the well-being of children. Accordingly, we will attach a high priority to overcoming the housing shortage and other infrastructure needs, particularly for children in marginalized peri-urban and remote rural areas.

28. We will take measures to manage our natural resources and protect and conserve our environment in a sustainable manner. We will work to change unsustainable patterns of production and consumption, bearing in mind principles, including, inter alia, the principle that, in view of different contributions to global and environmental degradation, States have common but differentiated responsibilities. We will help to educate all children and adults to respect the natural environment for their health and well-being.

29. The Convention on the Rights of the Child and its Optional Protocols contain a comprehensive set of international legal standards for the protection and well-being of children. We also recognize the importance of other international instruments relevant for children. The general principles of, inter alia, the best interests of the child, non-discrimination, participation and survival and development provide the framework for our actions concerning children, including adolescents. We urge all countries to consider, as a matter of priority, signing and ratifying or acceding to the Convention

on the Rights of the Child, its Optional Protocols, as well as the International Labour Organization Conventions 138 and 182. We urge States Parties to fully implement their treaty obligations and to withdraw reservations incompatible with the object and purpose of the Convention and to consider reviewing reservations with a view to withdrawing them.

30. We welcome the entry into force of the Optional Protocols to the Convention on the Rights of the Child on the involvement of children in armed conflict and on the sale of children, child prostitution and child pornography, and urge States Parties to fully implement them.

31. We, the Governments participating in the special session, commit ourselves to implementing the Plan of Action through consideration of such measures as:

(a) Putting in place, as appropriate, effective national legislation, policies and action plans and allocating resources to fulfil and protect the rights and to secure the well-being of children;

(b) Establishing or strengthening national bodies, such as, inter alia, independent ombudspersons for children, where appropriate, or other institutions for the promotion and protection of the rights of the child;

(c) Developing national monitoring and evaluation systems to assess the impact of our actions on children;

(d) Enhancing widespread awareness and understanding of the rights of the child.

PARTNERSHIPS AND PARTICIPATION

32. In order to implement the present Plan of Action, we will strengthen our partnership with the following actors, who have unique contributions to make, and encourage the use of all avenues for participation to advance our common cause — the well-being of children and the promotion and protection of their rights:

(1) Children, including adolescents, must be enabled to exercise their right to express their views freely, according to their evolving capacity, and build self-esteem, acquire knowledge and skills, such as those for conflict resolution, decision-making and communication, to meet the challenges of life. The right of children, including adolescents, to express themselves freely must be respected and promoted and their views taken into account in all matters affecting them, the views of the child being given due weight in accordance with the age and maturity of the child. The energy and creativity of children and young people must be nurtured so that they can actively take part in shaping their environment, their societies and the world they will inherit. Disadvantaged and marginalized children, including adolescents in particular, need special attention and support to access basic services, build self-esteem and to prepare them to take responsibility for their own lives. We will strive to develop and implement programmes to promote meaningful participation by children, including adolescents, in decision-making processes, including in families and schools and at the local and national levels.

(2) Parents, families, legal guardians and other caregivers have the primary role and responsibility for the well-being of children, and must be supported in the performance of their child-rearing responsibilities. All our policies and programmes should promote the shared responsibility of parents, families, legal guardians and other caregivers, and society as a whole in this regard.

(3) Local governments and authorities, through, inter alia, strengthened partnerships at all levels, can ensure that children are at the centre of agendas for development. By building on ongoing initiatives, such as child-friendly communities and cities without slums, mayors and local leaders can significantly improve the lives of children.

(4) Parliamentarians or members of legislatures are key to the implementation of this plan of action, the success of which will require that they promote awareness raising; adopt necessary legislation; facilitate and appropriate the financial resources needed for this purpose; and monitor their effective utilization.

(5) Non-governmental organizations and community-based organizations will be supported in their work and mechanisms should be established, where appropriate, to facilitate the participation of civil society in matters relating to children. Civil society actors have a special role to play in promoting and supporting positive behaviour and creating an environment that is conducive to the well-being of children.

(6) The private sector and corporate entities have a special contribution to make, from adopting and adhering to practices that demonstrate social responsibility to providing resources, including innovative sources of financing and community improvement schemes that benefit children, such as microcredits.

(7) Religious, spiritual, cultural and indigenous leaders, with their tremendous outreach, have a key role as front-line actors for children to help translate the goals and targets of this Plan of Action into priorities for their communities and to mobilize and inspire people to take action in favour of children.

(8) The mass media and their organizations have a key role to play in raising awareness about the situation of children and the challenges facing them; they should also play a more active role in informing children, parents, families and the general public about initiatives that protect and promote the rights of children, and should also contribute to educational programmes for children. In this regard, the media should be attentive to their influence on children.

(9) Regional and international organizations, in particular all United Nations bodies, as well as the Bretton Woods institutions and other multilateral agencies, should be encouraged to collaborate and play a key role in accelerating and achieving progress for children.

(10) People who work directly with children have great responsibilities. It is important to enhance their status, morale and professionalism.

B. *GOALS, STRATEGIES AND ACTIONS*

33. Since the World Summit for Children, many goals and targets relevant to children have been endorsed by major United Nations summits and conferences and their review processes. We strongly reaffirm our commitment to achieve these goals and targets, and to offer this and future generations of children the opportunities denied to their parents. As a step towards building a strong foundation for attaining the 2015 international development targets and Millennium Summit goals, we resolve to achieve the unmet goals and objectives as well as a consistent set of intermediate targets and benchmarks during the course of this decade (2000-2010) in the following priority areas of action.

34. Taking into account the best interests of the child, we commit ourselves to implement the following goals, strategies and actions with appropriate adaptations to the specific situation of each country and the diverse situations and circumstances in different regions and countries throughout the world.

1. *PROMOTING HEALTHY LIVES*

35. Due to poverty and lack of access to basic social services, more than 10 million children under five years of age, nearly half of them in their neonatal period, die every year of preventable diseases and malnutrition. Complications related to pregnancy and childbirth and maternal anaemia and malnutrition kill more than half a million women and adolescents each year, and injure and disable many more. More than one billion people cannot obtain safe drinking

water; 150 million children under five years of age are malnourished; and more than two billion people lack access to adequate sanitation.

36. We are determined to break the intergenerational cycle of malnutrition and poor health by providing a safe and healthy start in life for all children; providing access to effective, equitable, sustained and sustainable primary health care systems in all communities, ensuring access to information and referral services; providing adequate water and sanitation services; and promoting a healthy lifestyle among children and adolescents. Accordingly, we resolve to achieve the following goals in conformity with the outcomes of recent United Nations conferences, summits and special sessions of the General Assembly, as reflected in their respective reports:

    (a) Reduction in the infant and under-five mortality rate by at least one third, in pursuit of the goal of reducing it by two thirds by 2015;

    (b) Reduction in the maternal mortality ratio by at least one third, in pursuit of the goal of reducing it by three quarters by 2015;

    (c) Reduction of child malnutrition among children under five years of age by at least one third, with special attention to children under two years of age, and reduction in the rate of low birth weight by at least one third of the current rate;

    (d) Reduction in the proportion of households without access to hygienic sanitation facilities and affordable and safe drinking water by at least one third;

(e) Development and implementation of national early childhood development policies and programmes to ensure the enhancement of children's physical, social, emotional, spiritual and cognitive development;

(f) Development and implementation of national health policies and programmes for adolescents, including goals and indicators, to promote their physical and mental health;

(g) Access through the primary health-care system to reproductive health for all individuals of appropriate ages as soon as possible and no later than 2015.

37. To achieve these goals and targets, taking into account the best interests of the child, consistent with national laws, religious and ethical values and cultural backgrounds of its people, and in conformity with all human rights and fundamental freedoms, we will carry out the following strategies and actions:

(1) Ensure that the reduction of maternal and neonatal morbidity and mortality is a health sector priority and that women, in particular adolescent expectant mothers, have ready and affordable access to essential obstetric care, well-equipped and adequately staffed maternal health-care services, skilled attendance at delivery, emergency obstetric care, effective referral and transport to higher levels of care when necessary, post-partum care and family planning in order to, inter alia, promote safe motherhood.

(2) Provide access to appropriate, user-friendly and high-quality health-care services, education and information to all children.

(3) Address effectively, for all individuals of appropriate age, the promotion of their healthy lives, including their reproductive and sexual health, consistent with the commitments and outcomes of recent United Nations conferences and summits, including the World Summit for Children, the United Nations Conference on Environment and Development, the International Conference on Population and Development, the World Summit for Social Development and the Fourth World Conference on Women, their five-year reviews and reports.

(4) Promote child health and survival and reduce disparities between and within developed and developing countries as quickly as possible, with particular attention to eliminating the pattern of excess and preventable mortality among girl infants and children.

(5) Protect, promote and support exclusive breastfeeding of infants for six months and continued breastfeeding with safe, appropriate and adequate complementary feeding up to two years of age or beyond. Provide infant-feeding counselling for mothers living with HIV/AIDS so that they can make free and informed choices.

(6) Special emphasis must be placed on prenatal and post-natal care, essential obstetric care and care for newborns, particularly for those living in areas without access to services.

(7) Ensure full immunization of children under one year of age at 90 per cent nationally, with at least 80 per cent coverage in every district or equivalent administrative unit; reduce deaths due

to measles by half by 2005; eliminate maternal and neonatal tetanus by 2005; and extend the benefits of new and improved vaccines and other preventive health interventions to children in all countries.

(8) Certify by 2005 the global eradication of poliomyelitis.

(9) Eradicate guinea worm disease.

(10) Strengthen early childhood development by providing appropriate services and support to parents, including parents with disabilities, families, legal guardians and caregivers, especially during pregnancy, birth, infancy and early childhood, so as to ensure children's physical, psychological, social, spiritual and cognitive development.

(11) Intensify proven, cost-effective actions against diseases and malnutrition that are the major causes of child mortality and morbidity, including reducing by one third deaths due to acute respiratory infections; reducing by one half deaths due to diarrhoea among children under the age of five; reducing by one half tuberculosis deaths and prevalence; and reducing the incidence of intestinal parasites, cholera, sexually transmitted infections, HIV/AIDS and all forms of hepatitis, and ensure that effective measures are affordable and accessible, particularly in highly marginalized areas or populations.

(12) Reduce by one half the burden of disease associated with malaria and ensure that 60 per cent of all people at risk of malaria, especially

children and women, sleep under insecticide-treated bednets.

(13) Improve the nutrition of mothers and children, including adolescents, through household food security, access to basic social services and adequate caring practices.

(14) Support populations and countries suffering from severe food shortages and famine.

(15) Strengthen health and education systems and expand the social security systems to increase access to integrated and effective health, nutrition and childcare in families, communities, schools and primary health-care facilities, including prompt attention to marginalized boys and girls.

(16) Reduce child injuries due to accidents or other causes through the development and implementation of appropriate preventive measures.

(17) Ensure effective access by children with disabilities and children with special needs to integrated services, including rehabilitation and health care, and promote family-based care and appropriate support systems for parents, families, legal guardians and caregivers of these children.

(18) Provide special help to children suffering from mental illnesses or psychological disorders.

(19) Promote physical, mental and emotional health among children, including adolescents, through play, sports, recreation, artistic and cultural expression.

(20) Develop and implement policies and programmes for children, including adolescents, aimed at preventing the use of narcotic drugs, psychotropic substances and inhalants, except for medical purposes, and at reducing the adverse consequences of their abuse as well as support preventive policies and programmes, especially against tobacco and alcohol.

(21) Develop policies and programmes aimed at children, including adolescents, for the reduction of violence and suicide.

(22) Achieve sustainable elimination of iodine deficiency disorders by 2005 and vitamin A deficiency by 2010; reduce by one third the prevalence of anaemia, including iron deficiency, by 2010; and accelerate progress towards reduction of other micronutrient deficiencies, through dietary diversification, food fortification and supplementation.

(23) In efforts to ensure universal access to safe water and adequate sanitation facilities, pay greater attention to building family and community capacity for managing existing systems and promoting behavioural change through health and hygiene education, including in the school curriculum.

(24) Address any disparities in health and access to basic social services, including health-care services for indigenous children and children belonging to minorities.

(25) Develop legislation policies and programmes, as appropriate, at the national level and enhance

international cooperation to prevent, inter alia, the exposure of children to harmful environmental contaminants in the air, water, soil and food.

2. PROVIDING QUALITY EDUCATION

38. Education is a human right and a key factor to reducing poverty and child labour and promoting democracy, peace, tolerance and development. Yet more than 100 million children of primary school age, the majority of them girls, are not enrolled in school. Millions more are taught by untrained and underpaid teachers in overcrowded, unhealthy and poorly equipped classrooms. And one third of all children do not complete five years of schooling, the minimum required for basic literacy.

39. As agreed at the World Education Forum in Dakar, which reconfirmed the mandated role of the United Nations Educational, Scientific and Cultural Organization in coordinating Education For All partners and maintaining their collective momentum within the process of securing basic education, we will accord high priority to ensuring by 2015 that all children have access to and complete primary education that is free, compulsory and of good quality. We will also aim at the progressive provision of secondary education. As a step towards these goals, we resolve to achieve the following targets:

    (a) Expand and improve comprehensive early childhood care and education, for girls and boys, especially for the most vulnerable and disadvantaged children;

(b) Reduce the number of primary school-age children who are out of school by 50 per cent and increase net primary school enrolment or participation in alternative, good quality primary education programmes to at least 90 per cent by 2010;

(c) Eliminate gender disparities in primary and secondary education by 2005; and achieve gender equality in education by 2015, with a focus on ensuring girls' full and equal access to and achievement in basic education of good quality;

(d) Improve all aspects of the quality of education so that children and young people achieve recognized and measurable learning outcomes especially in numeracy, literacy and essential life skills;

(e) Ensure that the learning needs of all young people are met through access to appropriate learning and life skills programmes;

(f) Achieve a 50 per cent improvement in levels of adult literacy by 2015, especially for women.

40. To achieve these goals and targets, we will implement the following strategies and actions:

(1) Develop and implement special strategies to ensure that schooling is readily accessible to all children and adolescents, and that basic education is affordable for all families.

(2) Promote innovative programmes that encourage schools and communities to search more actively for children who have dropped out or are excluded from school and from learning,

especially girls and working children, children with special needs and children with disabilities, and help them enrol, attend, and successfully complete their education, involving governments as well as families, communities and non-governmental organizations as partners in the educational process. Special measures should be put in place to prevent and reduce drop out due to, inter alia, entry into employment.

(3) Bridge the divide between formal and non-formal education, taking into account the need to ensure good quality of the educational services, including the competence of providers, and acknowledging that non-formal education and alternative approaches provide beneficial experiences. In addition, develop complementarity between the two delivery systems.

(4) Ensure that all basic education programmes are accessible, inclusive and responsive to children with special learning needs and for children with various forms of disabilities.

(5) Ensure that indigenous children and children belonging to minorities have access to quality education on the same basis as other children. Efforts must be directed to providing this education in a manner that respects their heritage. Efforts must also be directed at providing educational opportunities so that indigenous children and children belonging to minorities can develop an understanding of, and sustain their cultural identity, including significant aspects such as language and values.

(6) Develop and implement special strategies for improving the quality of education and meeting the learning needs of all.

(7) Create, with children, a child-friendly learning environment, in which they feel safe, are protected from abuse, violence and discrimination, and are healthy and encouraged to learn. Ensure that education programmes and materials fully reflect the promotion and protection of human rights and the values of peace, tolerance and gender equality, using every opportunity presented by the International Decade for a Culture of Peace and Non-Violence for the Children of the World (2001-2010).

(8) Strengthen early childhood care and education by providing services, developing and supporting programmes directed to families, legal guardians, caregivers and communities.

(9) Provide education and training opportunities to adolescents to help them acquire sustainable livelihoods.

(10) Design, where appropriate, and implement programmes that enable pregnant adolescents and adolescent mothers to continue to complete their education.

(11) Urge the continued development and implementation of programmes for children, including adolescents, especially in schools, to prevent/discourage the use of tobacco and alcohol; detect, counter and prevent trafficking, and the use of narcotic drugs and psychotropic substances except for medical purposes, by, inter

alia, promoting mass media information campaigns on their harmful effects as well as the risk of addiction and taking necessary actions to deal with the root causes.

(12) Promote innovative programmes to provide incentives to lowincome families with school-age children to increase the enrolment and attendance of girls and boys and to ensure that they are not obliged to work in a way that interferes with their schooling.

(13) Develop and implement programmes that specifically aim to eliminate gender disparities in enrolment and gender-based bias and stereotypes in education systems, curricula and materials, whether derived from any discriminatory practices, social or cultural attitudes or legal and economic circumstances.

(14) Enhance the status, morale, training and professionalism of teachers including early childhood educators, ensuring appropriate remuneration for their work and opportunities and incentives for their development.

(15) Develop responsive, participatory and accountable systems of educational governance and management at the school, community and national levels.

(16) Meet the specific learning needs of children affected by crises, by ensuring that education is provided during and after crises, and conduct education programmes to promote a culture of peace in ways that help to prevent violence and conflict and promote the rehabilitation of victims.

(17) Provide accessible recreational and sports opportunities and facilities at schools and in communities.

(18) Harness the rapidly evolving information and communication technologies to support education at an affordable cost, including open and distance education, while reducing inequality in access and quality.

(19) Develop strategies to mitigate the impact of HIV/AIDS on education systems and schools, students and learning.

3. *PROTECTING AGAINST ABUSE, EXPLOITATION AND VIOLENCE*

41. Hundreds of millions of children are suffering and dying from war, violence, exploitation, neglect and all forms of abuse and discrimination. Around the world children live under especially difficult circumstances: permanently disabled or seriously injured by armed conflict; internally displaced or driven from their countries as refugees; suffering from natural and man-made disasters, including such perils as exposure to radiation and dangerous chemicals; as children of migrant workers and other socially disadvantaged groups; as victims of racism, racial discrimination, xenophobia and related intolerance. Trafficking, smuggling, physical and sexual exploitation and abduction, as well as the economic exploitation of children, even in its worst forms, are daily realities for children in all regions of the world, while domestic violence and sexual violence against women and children remain serious problems. In several countries, there have been social

and humanitarian impacts from economic sanctions on the civilian population, in particular women and children.

42. In some countries, the situation of children is adversely affected by unilateral measures not in accordance with international law and the Charter of the United Nations that create obstacles to trade relations among States, impede the full realization of social and economic development and hinder the well-being of the population in the affected countries, with particular consequences for women and children, including adolescents.

43. Children have the right to be protected from all forms of abuse, neglect, exploitation and violence. Societies must eliminate all forms of violence against children. Accordingly, we resolve to:

(a) Protect children from all forms of abuse, neglect, exploitation and violence;

(b) Protect children from the impact of armed conflict and ensure compliance with international humanitarian law and human rights law;

(c) Protect children from all forms of sexual exploitation including paedophilia; trafficking, and abduction;

(d) Take immediate and effective measures to eliminate the worst forms of child labour as defined in International Labour Organization Convention No. 182, and elaborate and implement strategies for the elimination of child labour that is contrary to accepted international standards;

(e) Improve the plight of millions of children who live under especially difficult circumstances.

44. To achieve these goals, we will implement the following strategies and actions:

GENERAL PROTECTION

(1) Develop systems to ensure the registration of every child at or shortly after birth, and fulfil his or her right to acquire a name and a nationality, in accordance with national laws and relevant international instruments.

(2) Encourage all countries to adopt and enforce laws, and improve the implementation of policies and programmes to protect children from all forms of violence, neglect, abuse and exploitation, whether at home, in school or other institutions, in the workplace, or in the community.

(3) Adopt special measures to eliminate discrimination against children on the basis of race, colour, sex, language, religion, political or other opinion, national, ethnic or social origin, property, disability, birth or other status and ensure their equal access to education, health and basic social services.

(4) End impunity for all crimes against children by bringing perpetrators to justice and publicizing the penalties for such crimes.

(5) Take steps with a view to the avoidance of and refrain from any unilateral measure not in accordance with international law and the Charter of the United Nations that impedes the

full achievement of economic and social development by the population of the affected countries, in particular children and women, that hinders their well-being and that creates obstacles to the full enjoyment of their human rights, including the right of everyone to a standard of living adequate for their health and well-being and their right to food, medical care and the necessary social services. Ensure that food and medicine are not used as tools for political pressure.

(6) Raise awareness about the illegality and harmful consequences of failing to protect children from violence, abuse and exploitation.

(7) Promote the establishment of prevention, support and caring services as well as justice systems specifically applicable to children, taking into account the principles of restorative justice and fully safeguard children's rights and provide specially trained staff that promote children's reintegration in society.

(8) Protect children from torture and other cruel, inhuman or degrading treatment or punishment. Call upon the Governments of all States, in particular States in which the death penalty had not been abolished, to comply with the obligations they have assumed under relevant provisions of international human rights instruments, including in particular articles 37 and 40 of the Convention on the Rights of the Child and articles 6 and 14 of the International Covenant on Civil and Political Rights.

(9) End harmful traditional or customary practices, such as early and forced marriage and female genital mutilation, which violate the rights of children and women.

(10) Establish mechanisms to provide special protection and assistance to children without primary caregivers.

(11) Adopt and implement policies for the prevention, protection, rehabilitation and reintegration, as appropriate, of children living in disadvantaged social situations and who are at risk, including orphans, abandoned children, children of migrant workers, children working and/or living on the street and children living in extreme poverty, and ensure their access to education, health, and social services as appropriate.

(12) Protect children from adoption and foster care practices that are illegal, exploitative or that are not in their best interest.

(13) Address cases of international kidnapping of children by one of the parents.

(14) Combat and prevent the use of children, including adolescents, in the illicit production and trafficking of narcotic drugs and psychotropic substances.

(15) Promote comprehensive programmes to counter the use of children, including adolescents, in the production and trafficking of narcotic drugs and psychotropic substances.

(16) Make appropriate treatment and rehabilitation accessible for children, including adolescents,

dependent on narcotic drugs, psychotropic substances, inhalants and alcohol.

(17) Provide protection and assistance to refugees and internally displaced persons, the majority of whom are women and children, in accordance with international law, including international humanitarian law.

(18) Ensure that children affected by natural disasters receive timely and effective humanitarian assistance through a commitment to improved contingency planning and emergency preparedness, and that they are given all possible assistance and protection to help them resume a normal life as soon as possible.

(19) Encourage measures to protect children from violent or harmful web sites, computer programmes and games that negatively influence the psychological development of children, taking into account the responsibilities of the family, parents, legal guardians and caregivers.

Protection from armed conflict

(20) Strengthen the protection of children affected by armed conflict and adopt effective measures for the protection of children under foreign occupation.

(21) Ensure that issues pertaining to the rights and protection of children are fully reflected in the agendas of peacemaking processes and in ensuing peace agreements, and are incorporated, as appropriate, into United Nations peacekeeping operations and peace-building programmes; and involve children where possible in these processes.

(22) End the recruitment and use of children in armed conflict contrary to international law and ensure their demobilization and effective disarmament, and implement effective measures for their rehabilitation, physical and psychological recovery and reintegration into society.

(23) Put an end to impunity, prosecute those responsible for genocide, crimes against humanity, and war crimes and exclude, where feasible, these crimes from amnesty provisions and amnesty legislation, and ensure that whenever post-conflict truth and justice-seeking mechanisms are established, serious abuses involving children are addressed and that appropriate childsensitive procedures are provided.

(24) Take concrete action against all forms of terrorism, which causes serious obstacles to the development and well-being of children.

(25) Provide appropriate training and education in children's rights and protection as well as in international humanitarian law to all civilian, military and police personnel involved in peacekeeping operations.

(26) Curb the illicit flow of small arms and light weapons and protect children from landmines, unexploded ordnances and other war matériel that victimize them and provide assistance to victimized children during and after armed conflict.

(27) Resolve to strengthen international cooperation, including burdensharing in and coordination of

humanitarian assistance to countries hosting refugees, and to help all refugees and displaced persons, including children and their families, to return voluntarily to their homes in safety and dignity and to be smoothly reintegrated in their societies.

(28) Develop and implement policies and programmes, with necessary international cooperation, for the protection, care and well-being of refugee children and children seeking asylum and for the provision of basic social services, including access to education, in addition to health care and food.

(29) Give priority to programmes for family tracing and reunification, and continue to monitor the care arrangements for unaccompanied and/or separated refugee and internally displaced children.

(30) Assess and monitor regularly the impact of sanctions on children and take urgent and effective measures in accordance with international law with a view to alleviating the negative impact of economic sanctions on women and children.

(31) Take all necessary measures to protect children from being taken as hostages.

(32) Develop specific strategies to protect and provide for the special needs and particular vulnerabilities of girls affected by armed conflict.

Combating child labour

(33) Take immediate and effective measures to secure the prohibition and elimination of the worst

forms of child labour as a matter of urgency. Provide for the rehabilitation and social integration of children removed from the worst forms of child labour through inter alia ensuring access to free basic education and, whenever possible and appropriate, vocational training.

(34) Take appropriate steps to assist one another in the elimination of the worst forms of child labour through enhanced international cooperation and/or assistance including support for social and economic development, poverty eradication programmes and universal education.

(35) Elaborate and implement strategies to protect children from economic exploitation and from performing any work that is likely to be hazardous or to interfere with the child's education or to be harmful to the child's health or physical, mental, spiritual, moral or social development.

(36) In this context, protect children from all forms of economic exploitation by mobilizing national partnerships and international cooperation, and improve the conditions of children through, inter alia, providing working children with free basic education and with vocational training and their integration into the education system in every way possible and encourage support for social and economic policies aimed at poverty eradication and at providing families, particularly women, with employment and income-generating opportunities.

(37) Promote international cooperation to assist developing countries upon request in addressing

child labour and its root causes, inter alia, through social and economic policies aimed at poverty eradication, while stressing that labour standards should not be used for protectionist trade purposes.

(38) Strengthen the collection and analysis of data on child labour.

(39) Mainstream action relating to child labour into national poverty eradication and development efforts, especially in policies and programmes in the areas of health, education, employment and social protection.

ELIMINATION OF TRAFFICKING AND SEXUAL EXPLOITATION OF CHILDREN

(40) Take concerted national and international actions as a matter of urgency to end the sale of children and their organs, sexual exploitation and abuse, including the use of children for pornography, prostitution and paedophilia, and to combat existing markets.

(41) Raise awareness of the illegality and harmful consequences of sexual exploitation and abuse, including through the Internet, and the trafficking of children.

(42) Enlist the support of the private sector, including the tourism industry and the media, for a campaign against sexual exploitation and trafficking of children.

(43) Identify and address the underlying causes and the root factors, including external factors,

leading to sexual exploitation and trafficking of children and implement preventive strategies against sexual exploitation and trafficking of children.

(44) Ensure the safety, protection, and security of victims of trafficking and sexual exploitation and provide assistance and services to facilitate their recovery and social reintegration.

(45) Take necessary action, at all levels, as appropriate, to criminalize and penalize effectively, in conformity with all relevant and applicable international instruments, all forms of sexual exploitation and sexual abuse of children, including within the family or for commercial purposes, child prostitution, paedophilia, child pornography, child sex tourism, trafficking, the sale of children and their organs and engagement in forced child labour and any other form of exploitation, while ensuring that, in the treatment by the criminal justice system of children who are victims, the best interests of the child shall be a primary consideration.

(46) Monitor and share information regionally and internationally on the cross-border trafficking of children; strengthen the capacity of border and law enforcement officials to stop trafficking and provide or strengthen training for them to respect the dignity, human rights and fundamental freedoms of all those, particularly women and children who are victims of trafficking.

(47) Take necessary measures, including through enhanced cooperation between governments, intergovernmental organizations, the private

sector and non-governmental organizations to combat the criminal use of information technologies, including the Internet, for purposes of the sale of children, for child prostitution, child pornography, child sex tourism, paedophilia and other forms of violence and abuse against children and adolescents.

4. COMBATING HIV/AIDS

45. The HIV/AIDS pandemic is having a devastating effect on children and those who provide care for them. This includes the 13 million children orphaned by AIDS, the nearly 600,000 infants infected every year through mother-to-child transmission and the millions of HIV-positive young people living with the stigma of HIV but without access to adequate counselling, care and support.

46. To combat the devastating impact of HIV/AIDS on children, we resolve to take urgent and aggressive action as agreed at the special session of the General Assembly on HIV/AIDS, and to place particular emphasis on the following agreed goals and commitments:

    (a) By 2003, establish time-bound national targets to achieve the internationally agreed global prevention goal to reduce by 2005 HIV prevalence among young men and women aged 15 to 24 in the most affected countries by 25 per cent and by 25 per cent globally by 2010, and to intensify efforts to achieve these targets as well as to challenge gender stereotypes and attitudes, and gender inequalities in relation to HIV/AIDS, encouraging the active involvement of men and boys;

(b) By 2005, reduce the proportion of infants infected with HIV by 20 per cent, and by 50 per cent by 2010, by: ensuring that 80 per cent of pregnant women accessing antenatal care have information, counselling and other HIV prevention services available to them, increasing the availability of and by providing access for HIV-infected women and babies to effective treatment to reduce mother-to-child transmission of HIV, as well as through effective interventions for HIV-infected women, including voluntary and confidential counselling and testing, access to treatment, especially anti-retroviral therapy and, where appropriate, breast milk substitutes and the provision of a continuum of care;

(c) By 2003, develop and by 2005 implement national policies and strategies to: build and strengthen governmental, family and community capacities to provide a supportive environment for orphans and girls and boys infected and affected by HIV/AIDS including by providing appropriate counselling and psycho-social support; ensuring their enrolment in school and access to shelter, good nutrition, health and social services on an equal basis with other children; to protect orphans and vulnerable children from all forms of abuse, violence, exploitation, discrimination, trafficking and loss of inheritance.

47. To achieve these goals, we will implement the following strategies and actions:

(1) By 2003, ensure the development and implementation of multisectoral national strategies and financing plans for combating HIV/AIDS that: address the epidemic in forthright terms; confront stigma, silence and denial; address gender and age-based dimensions of the epidemic; eliminate discrimination and marginalization; involve partnerships with civil society and the business sector and the full participation of people living with HIV/AIDS, those in vulnerable groups and people mostly at risk, particularly women and young people; are resourced to the extent possible from national budgets without excluding other sources, inter alia, international cooperation; fully promote and protect all human rights and fundamental freedoms, including the right to the highest attainable standard of physical and mental health; integrate a gender perspective; and address risk, vulnerability, prevention, care, treatment and support and reduction of the impact of the epidemic; and strengthen health, education and legal system capacity;

(2) By 2005, ensure that at least 90 per cent, and by 2010, at least 95 per cent of young men and women aged 15 to 24 have access to the information, education, including peer education and youthspecific HIV education, and services necessary to develop the life skills required to reduce their vulnerability to HIV infection; in full partnership with youth, parents, families, educators and health-care providers;

(3) By 2005, develop and make significant progress in implementing comprehensive care strategies

to: strengthen family and community-based care including that provided by the informal sector, and health care systems to provide and monitor treatment to people living with HIV/AIDS, including infected children, and to support individuals, households, families and communities affected by HIV/AIDS; improve the capacity and working conditions of health care personnel, and the effectiveness of supply systems, financing plans and referral mechanisms required to provide access to affordable medicines, including anti-retroviral drugs, diagnostics and related technologies, as well as quality medical, palliative and psycho-social care;

(4) By 2005, implement measures to increase capacities of women and adolescent girls to protect themselves from the risk of HIV infection, principally through the provision of health care and health services, including sexual and reproductive health, and through prevention education that promotes gender equality within a culturally and gender sensitive framework;

(5) By 2003, develop and/or strengthen strategies, policies and programmes that recognize the importance of the family in reducing vulnerability, inter alia, in educating and guiding children and taking account of cultural, religious and ethical factors, in order to reduce the vulnerability of children and young people by: ensuring access of both girls and boys to primary and secondary education, including on HIV/AIDS in curricula for adolescents; ensuring safe and secure environments, especially for young girls; expanding good quality youth-friendly

information and sexual health education and counselling service; strengthening reproductive and sexual health programmes; and involving families and young people in planning, implementing and evaluating HIV/AIDS prevention and care programmes, to the extent possible;

(6) By 2003, develop and begin to implement national strategies that incorporate HIV/AIDS awareness, prevention, care and treatment elements into programmes or actions that respond to emergency situations, recognizing that populations destabilized by armed conflict, humanitarian emergencies and natural disasters, including refugees, internally displaced persons and, in particular, women and children, are at increased risk of exposure to HIV infection; and, where appropriate, factor HIV/AIDS components into international assistance programmes;

(7) Ensure non-discrimination and full and equal enjoyment of all human rights through the promotion of an active and visible policy of de-stigmatization of children orphaned and made vulnerable by HIV/AIDS;

(8) Urge the international community to complement and supplement efforts of developing countries that commit increased national funds to fight the HIV/AIDS epidemic through increased international development assistance, particularly those countries most affected by HIV/AIDS, particularly in sub-Saharan Africa, the Caribbean, countries at high risk of expansion of the HIV/AIDS epidemic and other affected regions whose

resources to deal with the epidemic are seriously limited.

C. *Mobilizing resources*

48. Promoting healthy lives, including good nutrition and control of infectious diseases, providing quality education, protecting children from abuse, exploitation, violence and armed conflict and combating HIV/AIDS are achievable goals and are clearly affordable for the global community.

49. The primary responsibility for the implementation of the Plan of Action and for ensuring an enabling environment for securing the well-being of children, in which the rights of each and every child are promoted and respected, rests with each individual country, recognizing that new and additional resources, both national and international, are required for this purpose.

50. Investments in children are extraordinarily productive if they are sustained over the medium to long term. Investing in children and respecting their rights lays the foundation for a just society, a strong economy, and a world free of poverty.

51. Implementation of the present Plan of Action will require the allocation of significant additional human, financial, and material resources, nationally and internationally, within the framework of an enabling international environment and enhanced international cooperation, including North-South and South-South cooperation, to contribute to economic and social development.

52. Accordingly, we resolve to pursue, among others, the following global targets and actions for mobilizing resources for children:

(a) Express our appreciation to the developed countries that have agreed to and have reached the target of 0.7 per cent of their gross national product (GNP) for overall official development assistance (ODA) and urge the developed countries that have not done so to strive to meet the yet to be attained internationally agreed target of 0.7 per cent of their gross national product for overall ODA as soon as possible. We take upon ourselves not to spare any efforts to reverse the declining trends of ODA and to meet expeditiously the targets of 0.15 per cent to 0.20 per cent of GNP as ODA to least developed countries, as agreed, taking into account the urgency and gravity of the special needs of children;

(b) Without further delay, implement the enhanced heavily indebted poor countries initiative (HIPC) and agree to cancel all bilateral official debts of heavily indebted poor countries as soon as possible, in return for their making demonstrable commitments to poverty eradication, and urge the use of debt service savings to finance poverty eradication programmes, in particular those related to children;

(c) Call for speedy and concerted action to address effectively the debt problems of least developed countries, low-income developing countries and middle-income developing countries in a comprehensive, equitable, development-oriented and durable way through various national and international measures designed to make their debt sustainable in the long term and thereby to improve their capacity to deal with issues relating to children, including, as appropriate, existing orderly mechanisms for debt reduction such as debt swaps for projects aimed at meeting the needs of children;

(d) Increase and improve access of products and services of developing countries to international markets through, inter alia, the negotiated reduction of tariff barriers and the elimination of non-tariff barriers, which unjustifiably hinder trade of developing countries, according to the multilateral trading system;

(e) Believing that increased trade is essential for the growth and development of LDCs, aim at improving preferential market access for LDCs by working towards the objective of duty-free and quota-free market access for all LDCs' products in the markets of developed countries;

(f) Mobilize new and substantial additional resources for social development, both at national and international level, to reduce disparities within and among countries, and ensure the effective and efficient use of existing resources. Further, ensure to the greatest possible extent, that social expenditures that benefit children are protected and prioritized during both short-term and long-term economic and financial crises;

(g) Explore new ways of generating public and private financial resources, inter alia, through the reduction of excessive military expenditures and the arms trade and investment in arms production and acquisition, including global military expenditures, taking into consideration national security requirements;

(h) Encourage donor and recipient countries, based on mutual agreement and commitment, to fully implement the 20/20 Initiative, in line with the Oslo and Hanoi Consensus documents, to ensure universal access to basic social services.

53. We will give priority attention to meeting the needs of the world's most vulnerable children in developing countries, in particular in least developed countries and sub-Saharan Africa.

54. We will also give special attention to the needs of children in Small Island Developing States, landlocked and transit developing countries and other developing countries as well as countries with economies in transition.

55. We will promote technical cooperation between countries in order to share positive experience and strategies in the implementation of the present Plan of Action.

56. Meeting our goals and aspirations for children merits new partnerships with civil society, including with non-governmental organizations and the private sector, and innovative arrangements for mobilizing additional resources, both private and public.

57. Bearing in mind that corporations must abide by national legislation, encourage corporate social responsibility so that it contributes to social development goals and the well-being of children, inter alia, by:

(1) Promoting increased corporate awareness of the interrelationship between social development and economic growth;

(2) Providing a legal, economic and social policy framework that is just and stable to support and stimulate private sector initiatives aimed at achieving these goals;

(3) Enhancing partnerships with business, trade unions and civil society at the national level in support of the goals of the Plan of Action. We urge the private sector to assess the impact of its policies and practices on children and to make the benefits of research and development in science, medical technology, health, food fortification, environmental protection, education and mass communication available to all children, particularly to those in greatest need.

58. We resolve to ensure greater policy coherence and better cooperation between the United Nations, its agencies, and the Bretton Woods institutions, as well as other multilateral bodies and civil society, with a view to achieving the goals of the present Plan of Action.

D. *FOLLOW-UP ACTIONS AND ASSESSMENT*

59. To facilitate the implementation of actions committed to in this document, we will develop or strengthen as a matter of urgency, if possible by the end of 2003 national and, where appropriate, regional action plans with a set of specific time-bound and measurable goals and targets based on this Plan of Action, taking into account the best interests of the

child, consistent with national laws, religious and ethical values and cultural backgrounds of its people and in conformity with all human rights and fundamental freedoms. We will therefore strengthen our national planning and ensure necessary coordination, implementation and resources. We will integrate the goals of this Plan of Action into our national government policies as well as national and subnational development programmes, poverty eradication strategies, multisectoral approaches and other relevant development plans, in cooperation with relevant civil society actors, including non-governmental organizations working for and with children, as well as children, in accordance with their age and maturity, and their families.

60. We will regularly monitor at the national level and, where appropriate, at the regional level and assess progress towards the goals and targets in this plan of action at national, regional and global levels. Accordingly, we will strengthen our national statistical capacity to collect, analyse and disaggregate data, including by sex, age and other relevant factors that may lead to disparities, and support a wide range of child-focused research. We will enhance international cooperation to support statistical capacity-building efforts and build community capacity for monitoring, assessment and planning.

61. We will conduct periodic reviews at national and subnational levels of progress in order to more effectively address obstacles and accelerate actions. At the regional level, such reviews will be used to share best practices, strengthen partnerships and accelerate progress. Therefore:

(a) We encourage States Parties to the Convention on the Rights of the Child to consider including in their reports to the Committee on the Rights of the Child information on measures taken and results achieved in the implementation of the present Plan of Action;

(b) As the world's lead agency for children, the United Nations Children's Fund is requested to continue to prepare and disseminate, in close collaboration with Governments, relevant funds, programmes and the specialized agencies of the United Nations system, and all other relevant actors, as appropriate, information on the progress made in the implementation of the present Declaration and Plan of Action. The governing bodies of the relevant specialized agencies are requested to ensure that, within their mandates, the fullest possible support is given by these agencies for the achievement of the goals outlined in the Plan of Action and to keep the General Assembly of the United Nations, through the Economic and Social Council, fully informed of progress to date and additional action required during the decade ahead using existing reporting frameworks and procedures;

(c) We request the Secretary-General to report regularly to the General Assembly on the progress made in implementing the present Plan of Action.

62. We hereby recommit ourselves to spare no effort in continuing with the creation of a world fit for children, building on the achievements of the past decade and guided by the principles of first call for

children. In solidarity with a broad range of partners, we will lead a global movement for children that creates an unstoppable momentum for change. We make this solemn pledge secure in the knowledge that, in giving high priority to the rights of children, to their survival and to their protection and development, we serve the best interests of all humanity and ensure the well-being of all children in all societies.

Bibliography

Alston, P & G Brennan (eds), *The United Nations Children's Convention and Australia*, HREOC/ANU/ACOSS, 1991.

Alston, P, S Parker & J Seymour (eus), *Children, Rights and the Law*, 1992, Oxford Uni. Press

Asche, A "The Best Interests Principle in Article 3(1) of the UN Convention on the Rights of the Child' in 1994 Congress Papers", *First World Congress on Family Law and Children's Rights*, Sydney.

Freeman, M, "The Best Interests of the Child? Is the Best Interests of the Child in the Best Interests of the Children?, *International Journal of Law*, Policy and the Family 360, 1997.

Harvey, J, U Dolgopol & S Castell-McGregor (eds), "Implementing the United Nations Convention on the Rights of the Child in Australia", *South Australian Children's Interest Burea*, 1994.

Krueger, A. and L. Mikael, *Education for growth: Why and for whom?* Working Paper Series. Cambridge, Massachusetts: National Bureau of Economic Research, 2000.

Kutty, B.M. and Ghazanfer Abbas, "Universal primary education", in *Child Workers in Asia*; 11(2&3), April-September 1995: pp. 10-16, 1995.

Lau, Lawrence J., et. al, "Education and economic growth: Some cross-sectional evidence from Brazil", in *Journal of Development Economics;* 41(1): pp. 45-70, 1993.

Lewin, Keith M., "The costs of secondary schooling in developing countries: Patterns and prospects", in *International Journal of Educational Development*; 16(4): pp. 367-378, 1996.

Lockheed, Marlaine E., Adriaan M. Verspoor and associates, *Improving primary education in developing countries*. Oxford: Oxford University Press, 1991.

Parker S, "The Best Interests of the Child - Principles and Problems", *International Journal of Law,* Policy and the Family, 1994.

Sandor, D, "How High - How Far? The Best Interests Principle in Family Law", No 19 Australian Children's Rights News, 1998.

Van G, Bueren, *The International Law on the Rights of the Child,* Martinus Nijhoff Publishers, 1995.

Index

(S.B.S)

Ok